The Uncompromising Diary of Sallie McNeill, 1858–1867

Number 109:
Centennial Series of the Association of Former Students,
Texas A&M University

The Uncompromising Diary of Sallie McNeill, 1858–1867

EDITED AND WITH AN INTRODUCTION BY

Ginny McNeill Raska

AND

Mary Lynne Gasaway Hill

Texas A&M University Press
College Station

Copyright © 2009 by Ginny McNeill Raska
and Mary Lynne Gasaway Hill
Manufactured in the United States of America
All rights reserved
Second printing, 2017

This paper meets the requirements of ANSI/NISO Z39.48-1992
(Permanence of Paper).
Binding materials have been chosen for durability.

Frontis: Pages of Sallie McNeill's diary, from the Levi
Jordan Plantation, Brazoria County, Texas.

Library of Congress Cataloging-in-Publication Data

McNeill, Sallie, 1840–1867.
The uncompromising diary of Sallie McNeill, 1858–1867 / edited and with an introduction by Ginny McNeill Raska and Mary Lynne Gasaway Hill. — 1st ed.
   p. cm. — (Centennial series of the Association of Former Students, Texas A&M University ; no. 109)
Includes bibliographical references and index.
ISBN-13: 978-1-60344-087-5(cloth:alk.paper)
ISBN-13: 978-1-62349-549-7 (pbk)
ISBN- 13: 978-1-62349-624-1 (ebook)
1. McNeill, Sallie, 1840–1867—Diaries. 2. Plantation life—Texas—Brazoria County. 3. Women—Texas—Brazoria County—Diaries. 4. Texas—History—Civil War, 1861–1865—Personal narratives, Confederate. 5. Baylor University—Alumni and alumnae—Diaries. 6. Brazoria County (Tex.)—Social life and customs—19th century. 7. Brazoria County (Tex.)—Biography. 8. United States—History—Civil War, 1861–1865—Personal narratives, Confederate. I. Raska, Ginny McNeill, 1952– II. Hill, Mary Lynne Gasaway, 1964– III. Title.
F392.B82M36 2009
973.7'82—dc22
2008024058

Dedicated to
Sarah Emily Raska,
who has grown up with Sallie,
her great-great-great aunt,
as another member of the family

Contents

List of Illustrations	ix
Preface	xi
Acknowledgments	xv
Introduction	1
Sallie's Family and Friends	18
Two Years Spent at Independence	23
Secluded and Remote from the Busy World	40
God Help Our Cause	89
No Concessions to Make	126
Epilogue	155
Appendix A:	
Baylor Classmates and Faculty	161
Appendix B:	
Letter to Sallie McNeill from Charlotte T. Nuckols	163
Notes	165
Bibliography	183
Index	187

Illustrations

1. Levi Jordan Plantation home — 12
2. Descendants of Levi Jordan and Sarah Stone Jordan — 19
3. Map of Southeast Texas and Brazoria County — 21
4. Emily Jordan McNeill — 24
5. Female Department, Baylor University at Independence — 30
6. Program of 1858 commencement exercises — 33
7. Diploma of Sallie McNeill — 43
8. Levi Jordan — 66
9. Carved shell cameo — 97
10. Page of Sallie's diary — 124

Preface

The diary of Sallie McNeill has been held by family members since she wrote it during the Civil War era. Little heed was paid to her work until Allen Andrew Platter quoted from it, nearly 100 years later, in his 1961 dissertation "The Educational, Social, and Economic Characteristics of the Plantation Culture of Brazoria County, Texas." During his research, Platter had the opportunity not only to peruse the diary, which family lore had ascribed to Sallie's sister, Annie, but also to interview a grandson of Sallie's brother Calvin, Levi Jordan McNeill Jr. During this oral history interview, the future family editor, Ginny McNeill Raska, a great-great-niece of Sallie, was listening as a child and had her first encounter with the diary. Over twenty years later, another grandson of Calvin, James Calvin McNeill III, sparked renewed interest in the diary and other family documents through research for his book *The McNeill's SR Ranch: 100 Years in Blanco Canyon*. This prompted Raska and other family members to begin reading and transcribing the diary.

Around the time that the diary transcription started, Dr. Kenneth Brown of the University of Houston had begun archaeological excavations of the land once occupied by the slave and tenant quarters at the plantation site on the Texas coast where Sallie had lived. Upon learning of the diary and the effort to transcribe it, he offered assistance, hoping to glean information about the plantation from a primary source. Raska, who had become the diary's family editor, read aloud the diary entries, recording them on tapes that were then transcribed by Dr. Brown's students. The transcripts were then corrected against the original numerous times. This comparative process between original and transcript has continued throughout the preparation of this edition. During the transcription process, Sallie's authorship became undeniable, and research on family history continued along with the archaeological excavations. One of Brown's graduate students, Mary Lynne Gasaway Hill, Ph.D., became interested in Sallie and the diary, using the diary as a starting point for her thesis "The Discipline of Social Corsets: Negotiation of the Gender Typification of the Southern Lady by Female Descendants of Levi and Sarah Stone Jordan." The continuing interest in the plantation history and the diary prompted Raska to begin planning this edition, and she invited Hill, then a professor at St. Mary's University in San Antonio, to join her. Raska focused her attention on researching information to annotate the diary, while Hill provided consultation on editorial decisions, and together they began preparing an introduction to provide historical context.

The actual survival of the diary is a surprising story. Sallie had no descendants to treasure it, and she wrote the last portion of it camped out at the beach, shortly before her death and a major hurricane. The diary eventually surfaced in the household of descendants of her brother Calvin, but he and his family experienced two devastating house fires in the years after Sallie's death. Despite these fires and various floods, as well as the adversities of heat and humidity, insects and vermin, the diary survived. While the diary sustained some damage over the years, it remains in remarkable condition, possibly due to storage in a lard can.

As a physical artifact, Sallie's diary consists of seven booklets with sewn bindings, written between 1858 and 1867. She completed each booklet, writing on both sides of the pages, before beginning the next one. Sallie modestly protested that her diary "will not deserve the appellation," possibly because of her failure to write regularly. She almost never wrote two days in a row, often writing only once or twice a month, while frequently commenting on the lapse of time since her last entry. At other times she was much more diligent, writing frequently in the first months of 1860 and in the last months of her life in 1867. Although Sallie's musings are recorded in various pieces, they form a contiguous whole, with most sections beginning almost immediately after the conclusion of the previous one.

The scarcity of everyday supplies in the South toward the end of the War and during Reconstruction resulted in her writing only a few entries during the last two years of the War, with a gap of about twenty months, before she steadily resumed her pen late in 1865. As the divisions between each piece seem to result from Sallie reaching the end of her paper supply, the editors have used events during her life to divide the diary into four sections: collegiate life at Baylor (May 1, 1858 to February 1, 1859); the antebellum years (February 2, 1859 to November 9, 1860); the Civil War years (November 12, 1860 to November 10, 1865); and Reconstruction (November 28, 1865 to September 28, 1867).

Though almost all of the booklets of the diary, which were rolled up tightly for storage, are curled, the condition of the various pieces differs considerably, creating several editing challenges. Some of the sections are relatively undamaged, but one section is missing much of the upper right hand corner. The earlier sections tend to be more easily legible than those written during the Civil War and Reconstruction. The quality of paper and ink declined dramatically after the War, with a few pages being so faded that the writing is nearly or completely indecipherable. Deciphering Sallie's penmanship is often rather difficult, as her letters were not always carefully or consistently formed, as if written rather hurriedly or carelessly. However, as she was writing this only for herself, she simply may not have taken much care with her hand-writing. Her writing equipment also affected legibility, as when her quill needed to be trimmed or when she used poorer quality paper and inks.

The greatest editing challenge came in handling the gaps where words were missing or illegible, especially as the appropriate editorial solution seemed to differ based upon the conditions of the various booklets. For the very few insertions needed in the sections in better condition, illegible or missing words were added in brackets if their meaning could be guessed. However, because the heavily damaged sections are sometimes missing several words in each line, bracketing every inserted word made the text too difficult to read. So, in those damaged sections, if the gist of her meaning can be discerned with the addition of a word or two, those are inserted without brackets. Elsewhere, when her meaning was unclear and could not be reliably discerned, ellipses were used to indicate where words have been deleted. In some cases, blanks have been used to indicate a missing word or name when the exact word could not be determined. Few other editorial changes were needed, as Sallie was a well-educated woman. She rarely revised her own writing, not even the essays she wrote for college assignments, but she had few errors in grammar, punctuation, or spelling. Also, appropriate usage for her day differs from that of today. Changes were not made in those areas unless meaning or readability was seriously affected. Sallie often underlined words for emphasis or to indicate foreign phrases, and her underlinings have been indicated by italics in this text.

Despite the various challenges of the text, the guiding principle in preparing this edition has been to remain as faithful as possible to the original while transforming what Sallie called her "disorderly book" into a readable record. The original physical divisions of the diary have been indicated within the chapters, as Sallie frequently made references to beginning or completing a new booklet. Sometimes, she recorded information near the final pages of a booklet out of chronological order, such as college essays, lists of quotations, correspondents, or college classmates. Most of that material has been moved to appendices or rearranged to follow a more logical order, with editorial notes to explain its original placement. Also, Sallie frequently did not provide a complete date for her entries. For uniformity, the complete date has been added in brackets before each entry. In a few cases, damage prevents a reading of the date, so the best estimate is provided. If scholars require more precise information, an exact transcription can be made available for more in-depth study.

Acknowledgments

Since I began working on this project over twenty years ago, many people have helped me in a variety of ways. First, I would especially like to thank my husband and daughter for their support, as well as their patience and willingness to adapt when I was busy with "The Diary." Secondly, I want to express my grateful appreciation to Mary Lynne Hill, who has guided, encouraged, and worked with me to bring this project to completion. I also want to thank my parents for fostering in me a love of family history and stories, and the many other relatives and friends who have provided encouragement and assistance throughout this process. Many others have provided help that was essential to the completion of this project: Ken Brown, for his invaluable assistance with transcription and his wealth of knowledge from research into the plantation history; my aunt, Sarah Kelso, for her research in family history and genealogy; my cousin, Keller Reese, for his detailed genealogy and family history records; my cousin, Cap McNeill, for his research and publication of the first book on our family's history; cousins Dorothy Cotton and Sarah Martin, for sharing their family information and starting our family on its journey to reconciliation; Carol McDavid, for support and all her efforts to collect and share information in libraries and on the internet; the board members of the Levi Jordan Plantation Historical Society, for their support and encouragement; Martha Freeman, for all the excellent research that she did and particularly for locating the family letters from Emily McNeill to Kate Jackson Bell; and Susan Solomon and Laura McCutchen for preserving those letters and other material and placing them in the Brazoria County Historical Museum. I would also like to thank our editors, Mary Lenn Dixon, for her patience with our slow pace and her continued interest, and Thom Lemmons for his helpfulness and dedication to our vision for this project. Also, I want to express our appreciation for the detailed work of our indexer, Joanne Sprott.

As a librarian and researcher, I must also thank all of my colleagues in the library world who have helped me so much in my research: the staff of the Brazoria County Library System, especially those in the libraries at Brazoria and Sweeny who have gotten me countless books through interlibrary loan; the staff at the Brazoria County Historical Museum for their great research collection and helpful guidance; the staffs at the Texas Collection at Baylor University; the Texas History Center at the Rosenberg library in Galveston; the Texas Baptist Historical Museum at Independence; the Harold B. Simpson History Center at Hill College; the George Memorial Library in Richmond; Sha Towers of Baylor University; and others who have helped along the way. I would also like to thank our state legislators for providing access through public and school libraries to research databases, which has allowed me access to a wealth of resources to do countless hours of research from home. Also, I want to express appreciation to all the generous people who have shared their research on the Internet, especially one whose postings of deed records from Edgefield County, South Carolina, led me to discover the ancestry of Levi Jordan, thereby fulfilling the life-long search of a beloved aunt. Having worked on this project for so many years, I am sure that I have forgotten to mention someone who has aided me in my research or given me moral support, so for all those who are unnamed due to my unfortunate memory lapses, please accept my heartfelt thanks and apologies for my forgetfulness.

GINNY MCNEILL RASKA

My first expression of gratitude is to my husband, Andrew J. Hill, who encouraged me to continue my studies by participating in an archaeological field school at the Levi Jordan Plantation in the summer of 1993. During this summer, I had the privilege of learning-through-doing archaeological fieldwork under the direction of Kenneth L. Brown, Ph.D., of the University of Houston, director of the project. I am grateful not only for what Dr. Brown taught me in the field with his keen eye, but also for introducing me to Ginny McNeill Raska and the diary of her ancestor, Sallie McNeill. I wish to thank Ginny for her invitation to collaborate with her on the production of this volume of Sallie's dairy. Her trust in my contribution to this task has honored me over the years, while her unflagging sense of humor has kept me faithful to it.

Along with Dr. Brown's work, the research of Carol McDavid, Ph.D., has proven invaluable for my understanding of plantation culture in Texas. I am grateful to her for her dedication to telling the complete Jordan plantation story—of those who lived in the Big House and those who lived in the Quarters—and for the friendship we have forged over the years. I am also grateful to Dorothy Cotton, as well as other female descendants of Levi and Sarah Stone Jordan, who assisted me with my own research on gender in the South. Finally, I wish to thank St. Mary's University for financial support for diary research through a faculty and development grant, as well as for research support provided by Caroline Byrd, Associate Director of the Blume Academic library.

MARY LYNNE GASAWAY HILL

The Uncompromising Diary
of Sallie McNeill,
1858–1867

Introduction

*"Am not remarkable for anything . . . possessed
of no accomplishments."*

Although Sallie McNeill described herself as "not remarkable for anything" her diary is indeed remarkable, both for its intriguing contents and for its very survival through the Civil War, Reconstruction, hurricanes, and house fires. Sallie began writing her diary in 1858 while she was enrolled in her final year at the Female Department of Baylor University in Independence, Texas. After her graduation, she returned to her family home, the Levi Jordan plantation in Brazoria County, Texas, where she continued to record her private thoughts as public events unfolded, propelling the Lone Star state into secession and the Civil War. Her diary concluded one month before her untimely death in 1867, when she boldly declared in her final entry that she had "no concessions to make" in a private family struggle in the aftermath of that momentous national conflict.

Writing during this eventful decade, Sallie's story offers an opportunity to view aspects of this crucial period from an often overlooked perspective. At the close of the twentieth century, Henry Louis Gates Jr. asserted that of those who created "nineteenth-century life, it is the inner lives of women, along with those of people of color, which remain largely *terra incognita*."[1] Until recently, these unknown inner lives had not been deemed worthy of serious attention because their artifacts tended to be remnants of everyday life. Traditionally, serious social and historical attention has focused on public events or figures, not the details of daily experience. However, we have grown increasingly aware of how essential these details of the daily lives of ordinary people are to our understanding of the culture of an era. We have also come to realize that we often better understand our own *terra firma* by exploring their *terra incognita*. Exploration of Sallie's diary, one of many artifacts from nineteenth-century life at the Levi Jordan Plantation, enhances our understanding of this unknown land.

Sallie's journal joins an esteemed collection of Civil War-era diaries written by female members of the Southern planter class. Some of the most well-known ones include *A Diary from Dixie* by Mary Boykin Chesnut; *Victorian Lady on the Texas Frontier* by Ann Raney Coleman; *A Slaveholder's Daughter* by Belle Kearney; *The Secret Eye: The Journal of Ella Gertrude Clanton Thomas;* and *A Rebel Wife in Texas: The Diary and Letters of Elizabeth Scott Neblett.* Each of these texts, as well as others more recently published, such as *Lucy Breckenridge of Grove Hill: The Journal of a Virginia Girl, 1862–1864,* and *A Maryland Bride in the Deep South: The Civil War Diary of Priscilla Bond,* offers us insight into the lives of those whose experiences were profoundly shaped by the Civil War. However, Sallie's writing provides a unique perspective to enhance our understanding of nineteenth-century women because of its blend of typical and atypical elements. She shows herself to be fairly typical of an antebellum Southern lady in her spiritual self-examinations and in her attitudes toward slavery and, ultimately, emancipation. Yet Sallie's work possesses characteristics that set it apart: her private focus in an era when diaries were often publicly shared, her college education in a place where educational opportunities were seriously limited, and her decision to remain single in a culture where marriage was expected. To contextualize this blend of elements, it is necessary to know more about the historical background of Sallie McNeill, her family, and where and how they came to make their home in the young state of Texas.

"Thither to the famed land of Texas"

In Sallie's words, her family "removed from Union Parish thither to the famed land of Texas" when she was about eight years old. Previously, her immediate family and her grandparents had been living on adjoining plantations in Union Parish, Louisiana, and Union County, Arkansas, since at least the time of her birth on February 13, 1840. Sallie was the oldest child of James C. McNeill and Emily Jordan McNeill, and her mother was the only child of Levi and Sarah Stone Jordan. The Jordan/McNeill clan also included three younger siblings of Sallie: Annie, born in 1842; Calvin, in 1844; and Charlie, in 1846. After the family settled in Brazoria County, three more children were born. Missie joined the family during the year of their arrival in 1848, followed by Mollie in 1852. The youngest child, Archie, was born in 1855, shortly after his father's untimely death in 1854. After her husband's death, Emily and her children continued to live at the plantation with her parents. Along with her own children, Emily also cared for others who came to live at the plantation, including Bob Stanger, who worked on the plantation for many years, becoming a dear friend to Sallie, as well as Kate Jackson, a child who was informally adopted by the family after the Civil War.

Emily's parents, Levi and Sarah Stone Jordan, were both born near the Savannah River, the border between South Carolina and Georgia. Sarah Stone was born February 3, 1793, in Edgefield County, South Carolina, to Jesse and Susannah

Lightfoot Stone. Levi Jordan was born later that same year on December 17 to Nathan and Rebekkah Wallace Jordan, who were also living in Edgefield County, South Carolina, by 1797.[2] The date of the marriage of Levi and Sarah is unknown, but Sarah's brother Abner Stone married Jordan's sister, Abigail, on January 9, 1817. Levi and Sarah may have married about the same time, as their daughter Emily was born on May 24, 1819, in Georgia where both families had property in Lincoln County. The Stone's first child was born in 1820 in Alabama, so the two families may have migrated from Georgia to Alabama soon after Emily Jordan's birth. By 1838, the Jordan family was in Dallas County, Alabama, where Emily married James C. McNeill on January 31, 1838.[3] McNeill, who was from North Carolina, was born April 21, 1809, to Archibald and Barbara Patterson McNeill. Abner and Abigail Jordan Stone stayed in Dallas County, Alabama, for the rest of their lives, but Levi and Sarah Jordan moved with their daughter and son-in-law to the border between Arkansas and Louisiana within the next two years. They remained there for about eight years before moving to Texas.

Although Sallie attributed their move to Texas to "a desire for change," the Jordan/McNeill family came at the beginning of a huge wave of settlers flooding into the state in search of new farmland. When Texas was annexed into the Union near the end of 1845, the estimated population was about 125,000. By 1850, the first United States Census of the state found 212,592 Texans, and the 1860 census recorded 604,215.[4] This tide of immigration almost quadrupled the population in fifteen years. Levi Jordan visited Texas in 1848, near the beginning of this dramatic population explosion. Looking for fertile land, he found the rich bottomlands of Brazoria County and reputedly wrote back to his family that they had worn out farms from Georgia to Arkansas, but he had finally "found a place that will wear us out."

Jordan found this promising property between the San Bernard River and Caney Creek, about fourteen miles inland from the Gulf of Mexico. He purchased 2221 acres, the western half of a league granted to Samuel M. Williams, a close business associate of Stephen F. Austin. Many of Austin's original 300 colonists had taken land grants in the area that became Brazoria County, settling along the fertile soil that bordered the Brazos and San Bernard rivers. Many of those who immigrated to Texas after annexation also settled in the eastern and coastal parts of the state along the various rivers where the rich alluvial soil was ripe for agricultural development.

Antebellum plantation owners were also dependent upon the rivers for transportation, as the railroad in Texas was still in its infancy. Although charters had been granted, no railways were operating when Jordan purchased the plantation. By the beginning of the Civil War only about 470 miles of rail track had been laid in the entire state.[5] Sallie took advantage of this new mode of transportation, making trips to Independence and Galveston, with stage and steamboat connections to complete her journeys. However, a closer mode of transportation was the San Bernard River, which was only about four miles east of the plantation. Jordan had built a schooner, the *Sarah Jordan,* in partnership with Caleb Letts, which was used in transporting goods on the river until 1863, when Robert and David G. Mills purchased the craft to use in running the blockade during the War.[6] Caney Creek, which was a few miles farther to the west of the plantation, was also a public waterway with paddle wheelers transporting goods into Matagorda Bay.[7] Jordan may have also used that avenue of transportation, as the rivers were sometimes blocked with rafts of logs or sandbars.

Although navigable streams were easier for transportation of goods, Brazoria County had begun developing a system of roads, which were usually thirty to sixty feet wide, including one from Brazoria to Caney Creek in 1838. By 1849, the county had been organized into twenty-one road precincts, with Sallie's father, James C. McNeill, appointed as overseer for Precinct 11. He was authorized to use his hands and those of Jordan, Elsey Harrison, and other planters to work the road which ran from the Brazoria County Courthouse to Craven's Ferry, past the Jordan/McNeill Plantation, ending at Harrison's on Cedar Lake at the Matagorda County Line. In 1851, Jordan succeeded his son-in-law in the position of Precinct 11 road overseer. The county also established public ferries across the San Bernard River, and in 1853 McNeill took over the operation of Cowan's Ferry west of Brazoria.[8]

This developing system of roads and ferries provided easier access to the nearby town of Brazoria, the closest center of commerce to the plantation. Established on the Brazos River in 1828 by John Austin, Brazoria was one of the major points of entry for immigration prior to independence in 1836.[9] By the time Sallie's family settled in the area, Brazoria was the county seat and an important trading center for this burgeoning agricultural area. In 1850 Brazoria County was ranked second in cash value of farms in Texas, but by 1860 it had moved to first. During this decade of population and agricultural growth, slavery also increased dramatically, with the slave population increasing from 27 percent of the total population in 1850 to 30 percent by 1860. The total slave population of the state grew by 214 percent over this decade, resulting in a 600 percent increase in cotton production.[10] Most Texas slaveholders had only a few slaves, with one-fourth of the slaveowners holding only one. However, fifty-four planters held one hundred or more slaves, and Jordan was numbered among them, owning 134 at the time of the 1860 census.[11] Like Jordan, many of these largest slave owners lived in Brazoria County where 72 percent of the population was enslaved in 1860.[12]

The plantation economy depended on these high concentrations of slave labor, especially for such labor-intensive crops as sugarcane. During the antebellum period Brazoria County produced about 75 percent of the total sugar production for the state, far outstripping the other Sugar Bowl counties of Matagorda, Wharton, and Fort Bend.[13] After McNeill died in 1854, Jordan continued to focus on sugar and cotton in the remaining antebellum years, producing 193 hogsheads of sugar and 77 bales of cotton in 1860. Along with sugar and cotton, Jordan grew food and forage crops. The census of that same year valued Jordan's real property at $69,200, which included a sugar mill, and personal property at $130,740. Jordan also lent money at interest, a common endeavor of wealthy plantation owners in Texas, as the state constitution prohibited the incorporation of banks.[14] He held loans of around $20,000 each year from 1858 to 1861,[15] and that economic endeavor combined with his productive plantation to make him among the wealthiest men in Texas, prior to the outbreak of hostilities.[16]

Although the War created hardships for everyone, Sallie and her family were not affected as dramatically as many others of this time period. Texas, being farther removed from the major theaters of the War, did not suffer as much as some of the other states. Despite its distance from the seat of war, Texas did suffer from a Union blockade and a persistent threat of invasion along the coast. Although the major port of Galveston was captured by Union forces in October of 1862, the Confederates recaptured it a few months later on New Year's Day, 1863. Few other military actions took place in the area, though Sallie catalogued a brief skirmish on the coast near her home in December of 1862.

Sallie also recorded friends and family who joined the Confederate forces. Bob Stanger was the first in her family circle to enlist, joining in December of 1861, and her brother Calvin soon followed in the spring of 1862. Charlie, being two years younger than Calvin, was not allowed to join as soon as he wanted, but participated in the skirmish Sallie described even before he officially joined the service. Bob and Calvin, and later Charlie, were all stationed nearby with Brown's Regiment of the 35th Texas Cavalry, and they managed to come home fairly often. On at least one occasion they were given a furlough to return home to help with sugar-making. While Calvin and Charlie emerged unharmed from the War, Bob was captured in a skirmish on Matagorda Island on December 29, 1863, and imprisoned in New Orleans. Although none of their family members were seriously injured or killed, they lost friends and neighbors.

The enlistments of family members created gaps in their home circle, but Jordan was past the age of enlistment and was able to continue running the plantation, providing food and financial stability for their family. Despite the War, Jordan was able to continue good production on the plantation, but the Confederate government required him and other producers to tithe their crops. In 1863, Jordan's tithe was levied on 9,000 bushels of corn worth $18,000, 30,000 pounds of fodder worth $900, 110 bales of cotton worth $27,500, 14,400 gallons of molasses worth $28,800, and 180 hogsheads of sugar worth $99,000. The Jordan/McNeill plantation was able to maintain these levels of production because, unlike the situation in some of the war-torn parts of the Confederacy, their slaves worked throughout the duration of the War.

However, when the War ended, and emancipation freed the slaves, Jordan and other plantation owners were forced to move to a new system of labor. Many of the freed people from the plantation stayed on as tenant farmers, but the economics of a new labor system and a new social order resulted in many changes. The War and emancipation dramatically affected the wealth of many plantation owners, particularly those in Brazoria County, which in 1860 had twenty-six residents with assets over $100,000. By 1870, only one individual was still able to maintain that level of wealth.[17] Although Jordan's wealth had declined to $53,000 by 1870, when Sallie began her diary in 1858, her grandfather was a very wealthy man.

The Audience of Sallie McNeill

"I never had a confidant; never told my inmost thoughts & feelings to anyone"

Jordan's wealth was the means by which he supported the education of his grandchildren. Although he had little or no formal schooling himself, he was an ardent proponent of learning, providing all of his grandchildren the opportunity to pursue a higher education. Although Sallie seems to be the only one to have received a diploma, all of the grandchildren who survived past childhood attended institutions of higher learning. Sallie's college experiences at Baylor are the apparent catalyst for her journal, as she begins her diary while suffering from a bout of homesickness. Throughout her life, she often resorts to her pen as an emotional outlet, using her diary as the confidant that she never had, expressing "her inmost thoughts & feelings" with the expectation that they would be kept confidential. While writing a diary was quite popular in the nineteenth century, her undertaking was atypical because she chose to write for herself alone.

Although determining the audience for women's diaries can be difficult, taken as a whole Sallie's diary must be classed as one written for a purely private audience. In *Inscribing the Daily,* Lynn Z. Bloom presents a series of criteria to determine whether a diary was written for a strictly private audience or was ultimately intended for a more public one. Of these criteria, which include purpose, scope, and style, form and structure, characterization, and contemporary value, Bloom states that the necessity of an "elaborate context is the critical difference between fully private and those private diaries that are public documents."[18] Throughout her diary, Sallie offers minimal contextual information about many of the most important people and events in her life. Through her pen, she does not cast herself or her family members as characters in her story or employ literary techniques to produce and edit a "good read," which are characteristics regularly found in diaries written for a public audience. On the contrary, she almost never edits any entries and often refers to family members and friends simply by a first initial with little or no detail about appearance or motivation.

While Sallie does sometimes provide a bit of context, she never makes any reference to a possible audience. Other diarists of the period often specifically address their children in the diary or mention how useful their record of events will be to future generations. Sallie, however, specifically states her expectation of privacy when she says, "I suppose I ought to be ashamed of all these complaints. However I only tell them here, confident that others would not appreciate, but probably ridicule my motives."[19] She also seems confident that her family will respect her privacy, evidenced by them allowing her to read a letter from a prospective suitor in a secluded spot,[20] and her lack of concern that prying eyes might read her very candid comments about her siblings. Though diarists of the period frequently read aloud from their journals to family and friends, Sallie never mentions sharing anything from her diary with others.

This choice of audience, the first atypical element of Sallie's journal which furthers our understanding of the inner lives of nineteenth-century Americans, contrasts sharply with the vast majority of published diaries from this era. Chesnut, Coleman, and Kearney composed with an eye toward publication, writing their reflections with a popular audience in mind. Clanton Thomas wrote as a Southern mother, with her children in mind, addressing comments, as Neblett did, directly to her children. Writing a journal for either a public or familial audience was the nineteenth-century norm for both female journal writers and for their male counterparts, who primarily wrote travelogues. By choosing such audiences, these diarists produced works which are retrospective, resembling more an autobiography or memoir as opposed to a diary, which is introspective, offering a private space of personal reflection.

As with these other genres, the choice of audience influenced what each of those diarists highlighted in their writing. By writing solely for herself, Sallie, however, was free from censoring her thoughts and ideas for her readers. This resulted in a journal that reflects a life in progress, not one constantly being checked by an eavesdropping audience. This lack of personal censorship is evident in her comments about her own physical and spiritual health, in her pointed remarks about family, friends, and neighbors, in her revelations of embarrassing incidents and, particularly, in her conflicting emotions regarding slavery.

Sallie's attitudes about slavery were ambivalent—rather typical among planter women. Although few spoke out against slavery, many recognized the hardships slaves endured, particularly those forced to migrate to the frontier, like the Jordan/McNeill slaves were. According to Cashin, a few of these women even recognized "some disturbing parallels in their own experiences as involuntary migrants. These women did not criticize the institution of slavery as a whole, but neither were they its unfeeling supporters."[21] Although slaves had no rights, Texas law required that they be treated with "humanity," forbidding owners to kill their bondsmen. Frederick Law Olmsted captured this ambivalence when he observed that whereas in the older parts of the South slavery was considered natural and hereditary, on the Texas frontier, "[t]here seemed to be the consciousness of a wrong relation and a determination to face conscience down, and continue it. . . ."[22]

Sallie revealed this ambivalence in her journal. Through her words, we know that she desired harsher laws that protected slaves from brutish masters; that Levi Jordan had kept a hospital on the property to address the health needs of the slaves; that Levi Jordan allowed slaves to marry; and that at least one of the slaves, Claiborne, seemed to have his own cabin. These factors indicate that perhaps the slaves on the Jordan plantation may have been treated with relative "humanity." However, Sallie also recounted an episode of a runaway slave who was hunted with dogs and whipped upon recapture. She is clearly shocked over the brutality of the slave's treatment, even though, simultaneously, she blamed the slave because he had attempted to escape. In another entry shortly following this one, Sallie confessed that she and her brother, Calvin, sometimes felt the desire to cry out against slavery, even though just a few months earlier she had asserted that the slaves were content with their lot.[23] Through these reflections, she made manifest Olmsted's observation about the desire of white Texans to deny their consciousness of the wrongness of slavery.

After emancipation, however, her attitudes toward the newly freed people grew harsher. She spoke of difficulties with the freedmen during the sugarcane grinding season, wishing that "the Yankees could have the insolent indolent Blacks in their midst!"[24] Her hostility even seemed to surpass that felt by the older generation, as she criticized her grandparents for not making the newly freed servants work harder. While this change in her attitude may have resulted from the difficulty of adjusting to a new paradigm, some of her anger might stem from the recognition that her own domestic responsibilities might increase.

Regardless of why her attitudes changed, by creating a space for personal introspection and contemplation of controversial topics such as slavery, Sallie was participating in the Romantic Movement in American literature. It was not until Romanticism took root that journals emerged as private, intimate spaces where a lady might engage in exploring her identity, or in "what the French call 'l'invention du moi.'"[25] In Sallie's work, we witness this exploration of identity poignantly through her self-critique, which is generally characterized by a persistent questioning of her faith and of her ability to contribute positively to her community. To engage in this self-examination, she often drew upon Scripture so that she might cultivate the emotional and intellectual self-control associated with being a good Christian and a true lady.

Throughout the South, in the aftermath of the Second Great Awakening, there was the widespread expectation that the perfect woman was also the perfect Christian.[26] Sallie wrestled with this expectation by actively developing her spiritual life from the time of her conversion experience until her death. She experienced her personal conversion at a revival she attended while at Baylor. She was escorted to this event by Mr. Horace Clark, Head of the Female Department of Baylor University, and his sister-in-law, Miss Mary Davis, Instructor of English Literature and Language at Baylor. For evangelical Protestants, such a conversion experience was a rite of passage for youth and young adults raised in the church.[27] For women like Sallie, this rite of passage also served as a type of "boundary marker by which 'good girls' could be separated from the rest, providing a renewed sense of self-affirmation."[28] Sallie's entries after her conversion reveal this sense of self-affirmation and her determination to continue to develop spiritually, particularly as she struggled to understand life beyond the Confederacy in the unknown of Reconstruction.

Sallie's wrestling with spiritual issues on a personal level reflects the private nature of her text, while also revealing some common ground with others of her time period. Letters and diaries of this period are often typically filled with Scripture quotations and concerns about living a righteous life. According to Anne Firor Scott, the most often quoted Scripture in women's diaries of this period is from Jeremiah 17:9, "The heart is deceitful above all things and desperately wicked."[29] Sallie follows this pattern, quoting or making reference to that self-castigating passage at least four times. She frequently expresses concern about her failure to accomplish any good and mentions her failings, such as traveling on the Sabbath. Yet, she also quotes scriptures of comfort and reassurance. She never seems to waver in her faith, even in the loss of her sisters and treasured friends, or in the difficulties of the War and the defeat of the Confederacy, often repeating the refrain, "He doeth all things well."

However, unlike many other diarists of this period, such as Lucy Breckenridge and Priscilla Bond, Sallie does not seem to have a strong identification with a particular religious denomination. While she was clearly a Protestant, claiming to have a "horror of Catholics and Catholicism,"[30] she does not identify herself as Baptist, even though the church she joined at Independence was Baptist. Sallie never identifies the denomination of her home church, making only a few references to particular denominations in the entire diary, whereas Lucy Breckenridge makes several denominational references in a single entry.[31] This lack of focus on denominational distinctions is possibly a reflection of the limited choices available to her on the frontier. According to the 1860 census, only twelve churches were operating in Brazoria County: one Baptist, one Roman Catholic, two Presbyterian, and eight Methodist.[32] This statistic mirrored the statewide dominance of Methodists, who had far more churches and adherents than the Baptists, who were a distant second, but an overwhelming majority of Texans of 1860 were not affiliated with any organized religion.[33] Sallie's lack of a strong denominational affiliation, however, was not any indication of a lack of religious commitment, as she regularly attended church, as well as privately recording her spiritual journey.

The Education of Sallie McNeill

"But I shall reluctantly bid adieu to my Alma Mater, and extend the parting hand with a sad heart to my much loved friends and schoolmates."

Along with her decision to write for herself as audience, Sallie's pursuit of her education also enhances our understanding of the *terra incognita* of the nineteenth century. Her entries offer us the rare opportunity to view antebellum college life from the perspective of a particular woman. She describes a range of universal collegiate experiences, from homesickness to unfinished homework, as well as individual experiences, from learning about religious diversity to the flowering of her own religious conversion. In a state which was still called in 1870, "the darkest field educationally in the United States,"[34] Sallie's educational experiences, from informal plantation school to Baylor University, marked her as unusual. In 1850, shortly after Sallie's family moved to Texas, only one child in every five or six was receiving any instruction at all, and there were only two institutions of higher learning with a total of 165 students. However, by 1860, the number of colleges had grown to twenty-five with 2,416 students, with the total number of antebellum graduates from Texas colleges being around 215.[35] When she entered Baylor, Sallie and her family were participating in the Southern educational trend of providing female students with a liberal arts education that was the equivalent of their male counterparts. Baylor's Female Department, led by Horace Clark, embraced these progressive ideas that he articulated in his 1856 commencement address. In this address, he supported "the intellectual equality of your sex with man" as a fact, rather than a theory, and stated that woman "is entitled, *equally with man,* to such mental culture as will discipline her mind, cultivate her taste and elevate her character."[36]

The Baylor Female Department grew under Clark's progressive leadership, requiring its students to take academic courses comparable to those offered in the Male Department, while continuing to offer the skills taught in finishing schools, such as music, art, and needlework lessons. Sallie studied geometry, the classics, Latin and French, but chose not to pursue any courses in the Music or Ornamental Departments. This seems to have been her own choice, as her sister, Annie, was enrolled in Music and Oriental Painting during her time of study.[37] According to Farnham, "Southern elites insisted on 'accomplished' daughters" in the social arts who also possessed a working knowledge of the literary canon as well as ancient and contemporary languages.[38] Such academic training was not viewed as contradictory to the gender conventions of plantation society because these young women, like Sallie, were not pursuing an education to enter the public world of men, but instead to be more sophisticated daughters, wives, and mothers in the domestic sphere of the plantation household.

Nevertheless, whether a student focused on academics or accomplishments, she had to participate in a public examination to complete her education. Northern schools required public exams although they did not permit female students to read their commencement compositions publicly, deeming it an inappropriate display for females. However, Southern schools, including Baylor, required their female students to participate fully in this commencement ritual. Farnham contrasts the differences between the two societies, with the North expecting "sober, cautious, and dignified behavior growing out of middle-class life-styles" while the South valued the charm and expression of the "belle, with her allusions to the wisdom of the ancients, references to classical antiquity, homage to home, and allegiance to the South."[39] Such allusions to wisdom and homage to home permeate the working draft of Sallie's commencement composition, "Footprints in the Sands of Time," which she recorded along with other compositions in her diary.

At Baylor these public examinations were festive annual events at which a Board of Visitors, consisting of fifteen persons for each department, conducted the examinations and reported to the Board of Trustees.[40] Although at many universities, anyone from the audience might question prospective graduates, only members of the Board of Visitors were permitted to question them at Baylor. However, despite the completion of these public exams and Clark's rigorous approach to female education, Baylor did not confer degrees on female graduates during the antebellum period, but issued only a diploma certifying the completion of the course of study, while the male graduates received bachelor's degrees.[41] Sallie's diploma, which survived, is pictured among the illustrations for this text.

While she was attending Baylor, a new main house was being constructed on the plantation. One of their neighbors, Mrs. Charlotte Nuckols, wrote to Sallie at Independence in August of 1857, telling her "The new house is almost done, it looks magnificent." As the original home was likely to have been quickly and crudely constructed upon their arrival in Texas, the new home was surely much nicer, although not nearly as magnificent as some of the other antebellum homes in the county. Jordan was always utilitarian rather than ostentatious, and the home was constructed fairly plainly with two rooms, both upstairs and downstairs, on either side of a central hall, which included a staircase. The chimneys were somewhat unusual, being built flush with the exterior wall, and they had fireplaces in both the upstairs and downstairs rooms. Sallie also describes a gallery and a piazza, which were common terms for porches. Although this house has survived, one of

1. Levi Jordan Plantation home, circa 1904. Courtesy Dorothy Cotton family collection.

only two antebellum homes still in Brazoria County, its porches have been lost. Restoration of the house is anticipated now that it is under the care of the Texas Historical Commission.

The letter from Mrs. Nuckols also expressed appreciation to Sallie for the Jordan and McNeill family allowing her daughter to attend school at the plantation free of charge, a school taught by Mrs. Durant, whom she describes as an excellent teacher. Sallie most likely also received her early instruction from such tutors on the plantation. Mrs. Durant's tenure was apparently not very lengthy, as Sallie records the dismissal of another apparent tutor, Mr. Neel, in May of 1858. Then, in February of 1860, Sallie records that "Mrs. Durant wishes to teach for us again, but Grandpa won't, & Mrs. Mims can't board her." Sallie is disappointed, for she wants "an accomplished teacher" for personal instruction in languages. However, Sallie, who has by that time returned from Baylor, is herself teaching the "petit school" on the plantation.

Sallie's attendance at Baylor appears to have paved the way for others from the area. She was the only student from southern Brazoria County listed in the *1857 Baylor Catalogue,* but soon her siblings, Calvin and Annie, joined her, as did their neighbors, David and Josephine (Jose) Mims, Frank, Manly, and Emma Rowe, as well as Mollie Reese and Pleasant McNeel. Because only members of the wealthiest families had the means to provide a university education for their daughters as well as their sons, female education was a status symbol for members of the planter class. Along with being a status symbol for the families, attending college was a marker of gentility for the Southern belles themselves. This mark of gentility often gave these young women a competitive edge in the marriage market, as collegiate life facilitated networking opportunities for courtship among planter-class children. The need for these opportunities had become more important with the evolution of marriage from the eighteenth-century norm of a property arrangement between the couple's parents to the nineteenth-century norm of a love-based arrangement between the couple.

This courtship networking strategy proved effective for several of Sallie's classmates who married influential Texans. Her classmate, Dora Pettus, married Edwin E. Hobby, who later became a state senator and judge for the Ninth Judicial District. Their son, William P. Hobby, served as governor of Texas from 1917 to 1921.[42] Mary Louisa McKellar, whom Sallie calls Puss, married William Smith Herndon, a state representative and delegate to many state and national conventions.[43] Sallie's dearest classmate, Rachael Barry, married Charles Stewart, who was admitted to the bar at age eighteen, served as district attorney of the Thirteenth Judicial District and city attorney for Houston before serving in the Texas Senate and in the United States House of Representatives.[44]

However, unlike her classmates, Sallie chose not to return the affections of any of her suitors during her collegiate years. She hoped to continue her education with a focus on literature and languages, particularly Latin and French, after she returned home following graduation. Such study was often difficult either because of the lack of books or the lack of an appropriate tutor. This frustrated her because the resources necessary to remedy the situation were controlled by her grandfather. In her frustration, Sallie revealed the tensions she experienced living as an adult, learned member of the upper class, with all of its attendant privileges, but who was nevertheless restricted in her life choices by the patriarchal order of the antebellum South. Throughout her diary, Sallie struggled to find her place within that order, particularly when she made the choice not to marry.

The Marriage Decision of Sallie McNeill

"Imagination cannot conceive of a worse state, than a loveless marriage."

Along with her educational and audience choices, Sallie's decisions and reflections concerning marriage offer atypical insights into the assumptions and mindsets of the mid-nineteenth century. Upon the completion of her studies at Baylor, Sallie, who celebrated her nineteenth birthday soon after graduation, returned home amid the swirl of societal expectations that she would soon marry. Although twenty-four was the average age of a Northern bride, the Southern average was four years younger than that; and women on the Southwestern frontier often married even younger than twenty, with many brides being only fourteen or fifteen.[45]

Regardless of whether a young woman was fourteen or twenty-four when she married, Southern females were expected to be financially dependent upon males. Initially, they were to be dependent upon their fathers, or in Sallie's case her grandfather, and then their husbands. This financial arrangement was rooted in the Southern adaptation of Separate Spheres ideology.[46] This ideology, which designated the public realms of civic virtue and commerce as the province of men, and the domestic realms of maternal nurturing and home economy as the province of women, permeated most of United States Anglo culture prior to the Civil War. As industrialization swept through the North, men left the home workspace for the sphere of the public one, while their wives, ideally, remained within the sphere of the home. Theoretically, at least, women developed some level of authority within the realm of the domestic corresponding to their husband's position within the realm of the public.

Although this ideology filled the literature that Southern women read, in the rural South of the planter class, the locus of production continued to be the home. Within this arrangement, the husband retained power over the entire operation. Wife, children, and slaves—what was often referred to as "the family, black and white"—lived under the patriarch's authority. The Southern lady, idealized as pure, pious, submissive to the will of God and man, did not attain her own sphere of authority per se; instead, she acquired a husband's protection from a harsh public sphere as well as from the threat of attack from slaves.[47] The ideology of separate spheres restricted women from the public sphere, a concept which Southern culture accepted, but unlike their Northern counterparts, women of the South were seldom given a similar level of authority within the private sphere as their sisters in the North enjoyed.

Within this ideological frame, a planter class woman had one major economic decision in her life: to marry or not to marry. Because the crowning achievement for women was dedication to husband and children, to be an old maid in the Old South was to occupy a lamented social position. To *choose* such a position was risky indeed. Sallie, however, *did* make this choice, indicating that marriage to one "unsuited" was a greater hazard than continued financial dependence on the family patriarch. Ironically, Sallie's decision not to marry is made possible only because her Grandfather Jordan permitted it.

In a culture in which a woman was initially defined by her family of birth and then by her husband and the family to which she gave birth, the choice of a spouse tended to have a substantial impact on a woman's identity. Sallie's dread of personal identity loss was rooted in trepidation of marrying the wrong person. Although clearly not opposed to marriage per se, Sallie contended that she could not conceive of a worse station in life than as a person trapped in a loveless marriage. She was consistently apprehensive that those entering a marriage be the right person for each other. She believed that not only would marriage to "one unsuited" risk misery for the couple in this life, but also that it would risk misery in the next life, as to marry the wrong person was a sin. The marriage of unsuited individuals risked the endangerment of each of their souls after their deaths. The challenges of being a "predestined celibate" as Sallie referred to herself, simply paled in relation to these other marital considerations for her. Unlike the stereotypical spinster pining for a suitor, any suitor, Sallie had an assortment of men interested in pursuing a relationship with her. Although she once copied a love letter from one of them into her diary, she confessed that her "beau ideal" had never presented himself to her, and rather than risk the sin or lower her standard to accept another in his place, she chose solitude.

Sallie's concern about the drawbacks of marriage was not uncommon among other young Southern women of this period. Lucy Breckenridge, though she had several suitors, said that "she hated the idea of marriage" quoting a passage that voiced her concerns, "The hour of marriage ends the female reign! And we give all we have to buy a chain."[48] Similarly, Lizzie Scott Neblett worried that "My identity, my legal existence will be swallowed up in my husband."[49] However, despite their concerns, both of these women chose to marry. They also exhibited the more stereotypical behavior of a Southern belle, flirting and making and breaking engagements. By contrast, Sallie seemed to have little interest in fashion and virtually no inclination to flirt or be coquettish. One of her gentleman friends warned her that she would have to "throw out some hints, that I am willing to take a husband"[50] if she wanted to get married.

Despite the teasing she sometimes endured from family members about her love life, the Jordan/McNeill family was ahead of its time in their support of Sallie's pre–Civil War choice of a single life. During the War, three out of four Confederate men served in either the Confederate Army or in a state militia. Of these men, nearly 30 percent, more than one of every four, perished.[51] In Texas, over 70,000 men took up arms against the Union; and, even though Lincoln's name was not even on the ballot in 1860, another 2,132 white Texans and forty-seven black Texans took up arms against the Confederacy. In a state whose white male population was only 92,145, according to the 1860 census, rare was the household which was not directly affected by the coming of the War.[52] In Brazoria County, 317 men (out of a population of 527 white males between the ages of fifteen and thirty-nine in the 1860 census)[53] enlisted in either the state militias or the Confederate forces between 1861 and 1863.[54] During this time, Sallie seems to record an increased number of marriages, as her friends and neighbors married before entering service or while on furlough. Despite these frequent marriages, Sallie either does not feel pressured to follow suit or does not yield to any pressure she may have felt.

As thousands of these marriageable young Southern men died in service, they took with them the chance of marriage for many young women. With the deaths of these soldiers, many families romanticized the single status of their daughters as a sacrifice to the Lost Cause. Rather than have daughters bear the stigma of the spinster, Southern families groomed the Cult of Sacrifice, crafting an acceptable social space for the single woman in postbellum Southern society. Such a path to the single life was a reaction to the social upheaval caused by the War. These families were making the best of the situation. However, Sallie's path to a single life was not such a reaction, but instead a bold act of self-definition performed before the Civil War had transformed her world.

Her bold act, however, was not without difficult repercussions. Sallie was aware that her decision placed her in an awkward social position. Through her refusal to marry, she entered a period in her life in which she was chronologically an adult, but in which she was not a socially recognized one. Also, even within her own household, her role was not fulfilling, seeming to lack a defining purpose. When she first returned from school, she was responsible for tutoring the children, but Dr. Stephen Rowe began teaching them in November of 1860.[55] While she apparently continued to have some instructional duties, she rarely mentioned schooling the children after the deaths of her youngest sisters, even though her youngest brother, Archie, would have been of an age to require instruction. Sewing occupied some of her time, but she often set it aside when frustrated. Her attempts at cooking are only mentioned a couple of times, but even those are not always well-received, as she comments that "Sometimes Grandma don't care to have us attempt cakemaking."[56] If Sallie had chosen to marry, she would have had a well-defined role with clear societal expectations, but her place in society effectively prohibited her from pursuing even a career as a teacher, and her place in the family left her with little responsibility and no decision-making authority. Although she is often critical of her mother's patient submission to her father's rule, Sallie also seems unable to break away from that gender norm, saying, "All my life I've been trammeled, by the wish and opinion of others—even of my neighbors, and the world, in general."[57]

While Sallie did manage to break away from the gender norm of marriage, Southern antebellum society did not offer many opportunities for unmarried women. If Sallie had lived in a more urban environment, she might have been able to participate in some of the women's benevolent, religious, or literary societies and find a greater sense of purpose and fulfillment and gain a sense of community. However, her rural location and choice of a single life added to her strong sense of isolation. Despite fairly regular visitors, some travel opportunities, and her correspondence, Sallie did not seem to have many close friends or even close relationships with her female relatives at home. Sometimes she even chose solitude over company. At the end of her life, while she stayed at the beach, she reflected on her situation almost as if in exile, making oblique references to not being wanted at home. Despite the difficulties engendered by her decision not to marry, she never expressed regret for her single lifestyle.

A Unique Combination of Artifacts to Meet Gates's Challenge

Throughout these years of calm and of upheaval, Sallie records her struggles to find a path for herself and a place in the new social order. Through its unusual blend of typical elements, such as her attitude toward slavery and her spiritual quest, combined with the atypical elements of her choice of audience, her pursuit of educational opportunities, and her challenging stance on marriage, Sallie's diary enhances our understanding of the *terra incognita* of the inner lives of mid-nineteenth-century women beyond that which other planter-class diarists have previously offered to us. Sallie's diary also contributes to the exploration of the nineteenth century in another unique way, as part of a larger anthropological project focused on the *terra incognita* of the slaves and tenants—of the people of color—of the Levi Jordan Plantation, a project described more fully in the epilogue. Her diary serves as a backdrop to the slave and tenant artifacts, which together provide a richer, fuller picture of the plantation culture of Texas and its transformation during Reconstruction. This fuller picture broadens our developing understanding of the era in which our nation made war upon itself, a moment in our national story which historian Shelby Foote called the "crossroads of our being." As physical representations of this crossroads, this rare combination of material from the Big House and the Quarters offers an unprecedented opportunity to tackle Gates's challenge: to explore the nineteenth century through the *terra incognita* of the inner lives of women and people of color.

Sallie's Family and Friends

*S*allie often refers to her family and friends by initials or nicknames. This list, though not comprehensive, may help with identifying and explaining the relationships of some of the most frequently mentioned people in her diary.

Family and Household

Levi Jordan (1793–1873) (Grandpa), her maternal grandfather
Sarah Stone Jordan (1793–1882) (Grandma), her maternal grandmother
James C. McNeill (1809–1854) (Pa), her father
Emily Jordan McNeill (1819–1885) (Ma), her mother
Annie Royal McNeill (1842–1877) (Mc, Annie, Sister A), her oldest sister
James Calvin McNeill (1844–1933) (Calvin or C.), her oldest brother
Charles Philip McNeill (1846–1926) (Charlie or Charley), her middle brother
Emily J. McNeill (1848–1861) (Missie), her middle sister
Mary Emily McNeill (1852–1861) (Mollie), her youngest sister
William Archibald Campbell McNeill (1854–1879) (Archie), her youngest brother
Barbara Ann Malloy Rainey (1831–?) (Cousin), her father's first cousin
Robert Stanger (1842–1881) (Bob), no relation, but lived with the family
Kate Jackson (1859–1955) (Kate), no blood relation, but informally adopted

Friends and Faculty at Baylor

A more comprehensive listing of the faculty and Sallie's graduating class can be found in the in the appendix.

Rufus Burleson (Mr. B.), President, Baylor University, head of Male Department

Descendants of Levi Jordan

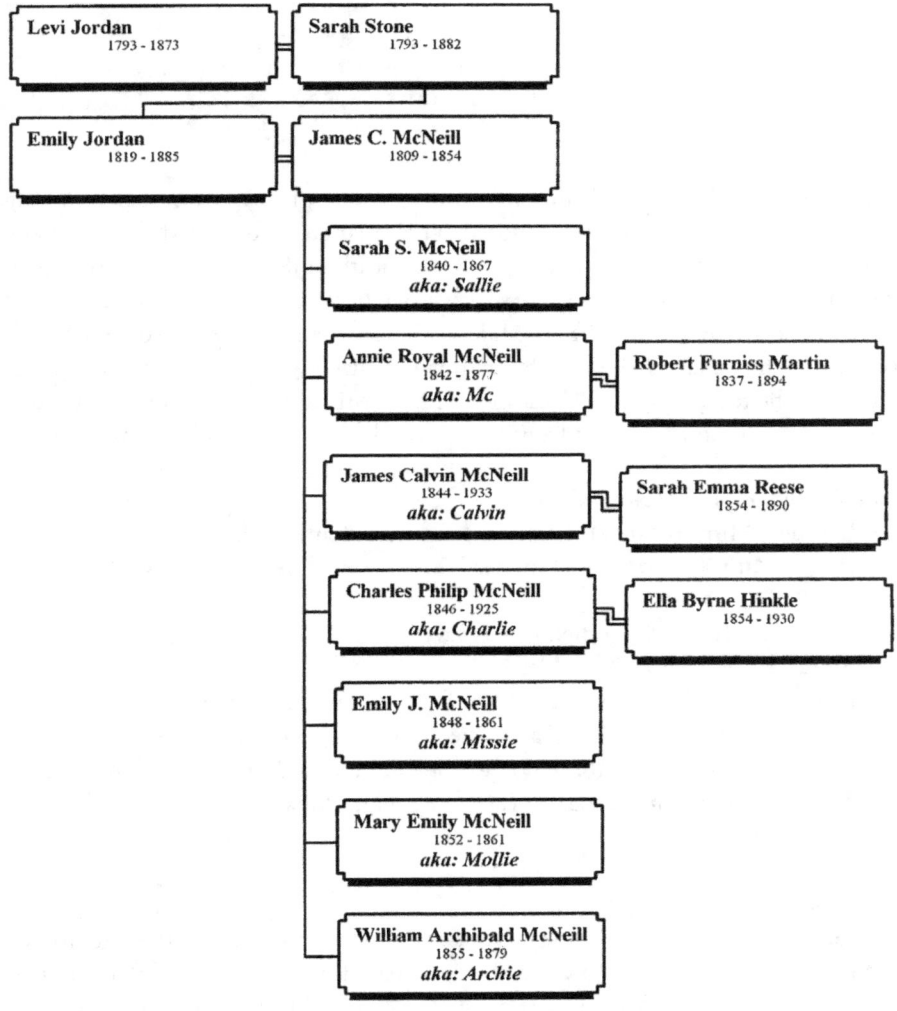

2. Descendants of Levi Jordan and Sarah Stone Jordan.

Horace Clark (Mr. C.), Principal, Female Department, Baylor University
Martha D. Clark (Mrs. C.), Horace Clark's wife, governess
Mary Russell Davis (Miss Mary), sister of Martha Clark, special friend of Sallie
Mary McKellar (Puss or Pussie), member of Sallie's graduating class and good friend

Mary T. Whiteside (M. T. W. or Mary W.), member of Sallie's graduating class

Neighbors

Mims Family
Joseph and Sarah Weekly Mims were early settlers of Texas, numbered among Stephen F. Austin's Old Three Hundred. Their plantation bordered the west bank of the San Bernard River. After Joseph Mims's death in 1844, his wife Sarah continued to operate the plantation quite successfully. In 1860, she was one of the largest slaveholders in Texas, and left an estate of 116 slaves and property worth $226,033 on her death in 1861.[1] Sallie and her family socialized with the Mims family regularly, and she took a trip to Galveston with Mrs. Mims. The two younger children, Jose and David, joined others from the McNeill family in attending Baylor.

Children of Joseph and Sarah Mims[2]
Lumbert Mims (b. 1822) (Mr. Lum) married Henrietta J. Norris in 1846.
Joseph Mims (b. 1826) (Joe) married Susana Caroline (Caddie) Nuckols in 1856.
Sam Mims (1832–1862) died in service to C.S.A.
Alexander Mims (b. 1835) (Mr. Alex)
Leonard (b. 1837) (Leo) married Sue F. (Fannie) Patton in 1861.
David Mims (1842–1862) (Davie) died in service to C.S.A.
Sarah Josephine Mims (b. 1844) (Joe or Jose) married Frank Rowe in 1862.
Two daughters, Ann Elizabeth (1836–1842) and Julia (1839–1844), died at an early age.

Rowe Family
The Shadrack Rowe family came to Texas around the same time as the Jordan/McNeill family, arriving by 1849 when they purchased 750 acres of land that was part of the Thomas B. Bell league, west of the San Bernard River. The family included Shadrack's wife, Sarah, and several children, some of whom were near the age of some of the McNeill children. Other children were already married, and Sallie refers to some of them by their married names. One of the daughters, Mrs. Henry Jones, lived in the Jordan household for a time. Three of the sons are known to have attended Baylor: Pobe, Frank, and Manly. Pobe and Frank married young ladies who had attended Baylor, as did Billie. After the war, Shadrack and Sarah sold their plantation to Sallie's brothers, Calvin and Charlie on April 10, 1866, and moved to Washington County, Texas.

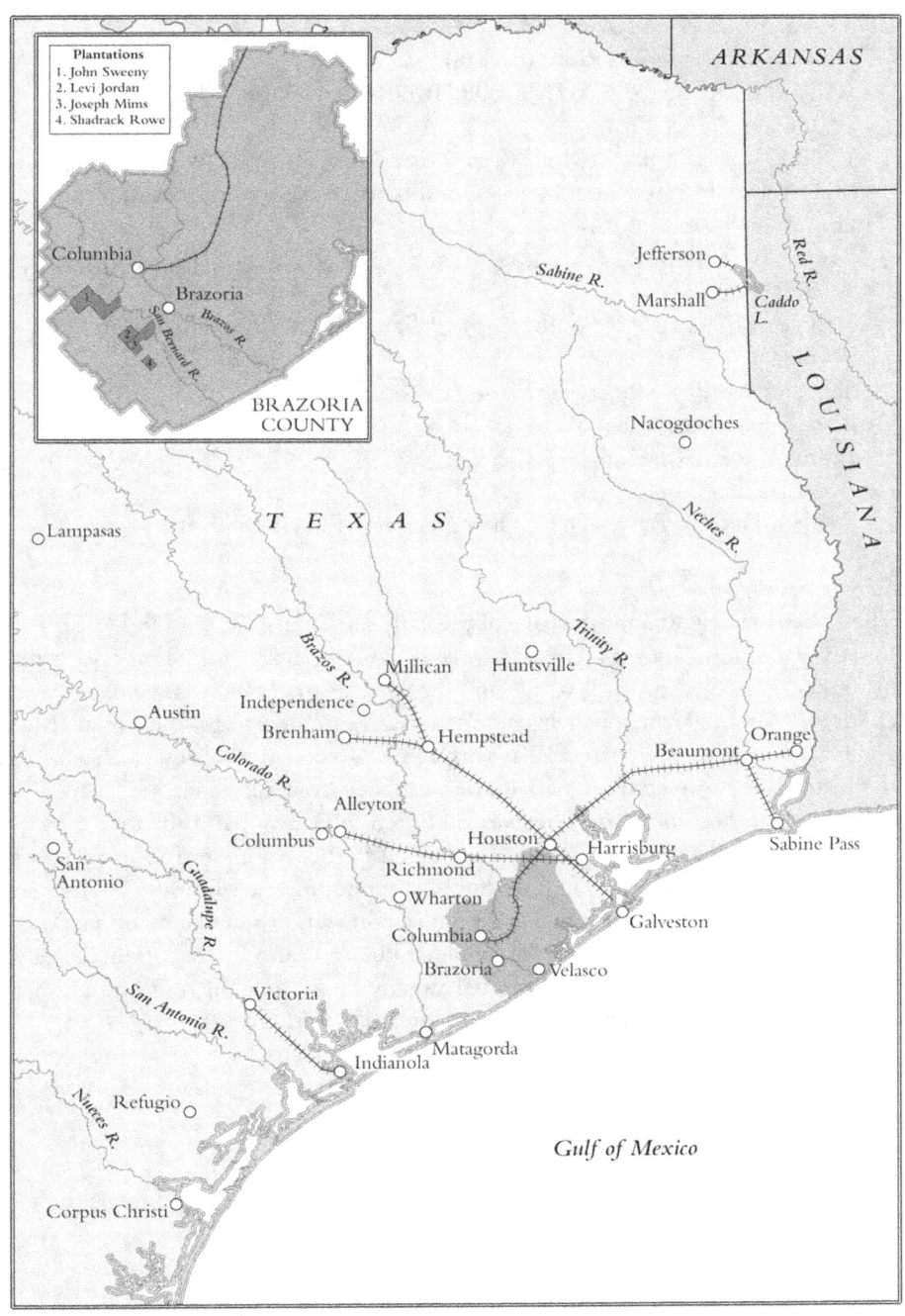

3. Map of Southeast Texas and Brazoria County. Courtesy Mapping Specialists.

Children of Shadrack and Sarah Rowe
>John Thomas Jefferson Rowe (b. 1828) married Josephine B. Hill in 1852.
>William H. Rowe (b. 1833) (Mr. Billie R.) married Martha Ellen Cooper in 1862.
>Virginia Rowe (b. 1834) (Mrs. Wilson) married William. B. Wilson in 1854.
>Mary Rowe (b. 1835) (Mrs. Henry Jones) married Henry B. Jones in 1856.
>Louisa A. Rowe (b. 1836)
>Benjamin Franklin Rowe (b. 1838) (Frank) married Sarah J. (Jose) Mims in 1862.
>Napoleon Bonaparte Rowe (b. 1840) (Pobe) married Virginia Cleveland in 1862
>Shadrack M. Rowe (b. 1842) (Manly)
>Rozella E. Rowe (b. 1844)
>Fanny A. Rowe (b. 1846)

Cousin of Shadrack Rowe
>Stephen Decatur Rowe (Dr. R.) first graduate of Baylor University

Sweeny Family

The Sweeny family was another one of the early settler families who lived near the Jordan plantation. Thomas Jefferson Sweeny came to Texas from Tennessee with his father, John Sweeny, in 1835. He and his wife, Diana Francis Haynie, had five children.[3] Although one of their daughters was near Sallie's age, the Jordan/McNeill family did not seem to socialize with the T. J. Sweeny family as much as with the Mims and Rowe families, perhaps because they lived a little farther away. The Sweeny home, according to Sallie, was about ten miles away, and she rode over to visit their older daughter, Elizabeth Ann, called Bettie. Another of John Sweeny's children is mentioned, his daughter Sophia. Sophia married Edward Holmes in 1838, and then after his death married John McGrew in 1851. Sallie mentions Mrs. McGrew a few times. The other surviving children of John Sweeny, John Sweeny Jr., Jordan Woodson Sweeny, and Samuel Sweeny were also living near one another in the Chance's Prairie area, which is now known as Old Ocean.

Two Years Spent at Independence

*S*allie begins her diary with a lament of homesickness written during her last year as a student in the female department of Baylor University in Independence. In addition to depicting antebellum college life in Texas, she describes her conversion experience when she joined the Independence Baptist Church. The Baylor entries conclude with a description of her commencement exercises in December of 1858, written after her return home to teach her younger siblings.

[05/01/1858, Saturday]

May 1st The rain is pattering on the roof, the clouds are dark and lowering, making all objects look gloomy, and causing my spirits to be depressed, so much are we affected by the things with which we are surrounded. Faint flashes of lightning are playing in the north, and the low muttering of thunder is heard at intervals. How sublime is the appearance of a thunder-storm, though there is danger in the forked-lightening, the knowledge of which generally prevents our admiration of this grand phenomena. On such a day as this, how unconsciously does the thoughts of the absent turn homeward. Memory recalls the loved ones, who are far away in the home of our childhood, and the thought rises, do they miss me at home? Much, much has been said and written on this one subject, nearest to the hearts of all, and yet can the theme ever be exhausted, or do we ever tire of hearing its praises sounded? Ah no, the dearest spot on earth, to me, is home sweet home, is the sentiment of every true heart. My Mother, what does that name recall to me? The Being whom most I love on earth, the dearest best of Ma's, how I long to see her this morning and I know full well, that she thinks hourly of her absent children, with the fondest solicitate for our welfare. Shall I ever be enabled to feel the debt of love

a. James C. McNeill, b. April 21, 1809, North Carolina, d. October 28, 1854, Brazoria Co., Texas (family records, tombstone in Cedar Lake Cemetery, Brazoria County, Texas).

b. May 9 fell on a Sunday, but the entry indicates that she wrote it on Saturday.

c. Mrs. Martha D. Clark, Governess of the Boarding Department[1]

d. Daniel 6:8b, also Daniel 6:12 and Esther 1:19

e. Miss Liane DeLassaulx, instructor of modern languages and of embroidery, *1859 Catalogue*, 8–9

and gratitude I owe my mother, alas, I fear not, how erring is frail human nature, when absent, I think I never could grieve Ma thoughtlessly again, and yet I often give her pain when with her. How bitter the sting of ingratitude in a child must be to a Mother. I can think without remorse of my conduct to Pa, when he was alive,[a] for I always loved and obeyed him, yet I feel I would love him more, if he were with us again, but never, no never can that be. But what would be my feelings if my Ma was taken from us, when I remember, the many acts of disobedience and unkindness that I have done, but I cannot bear to think of this. Oh, I want to go home; why did I ever leave it, why?

[05/09/1858][b]

May the 9th Rose early this morning, as Mrs. C.[c] says we must get up as soon Saturday as on any day of the week, but I don't think she wishes us to rise very early, but only so as to be ready for breakfast. However, the girls do not consider her laws like that of the Medes & Persians, which changeth not.[d] Mary Jackson[2] persists in clinging to her *downy* pillow. There, the first bell for breakfast is ringing, and Miss Morrill[3] dozing. We had a fine serenade from the brass-band last night, as everybody declares. But I could not think, there was any harmony in the discordant sounds so near us, I like its strains heard at a distance. After school yesterday, Miss De Lasseaux[e] proposed that a dialogue should be learned for the evening, which was very good, considering the short time for preparation. Fannie and Bettie acted as fashionably dressed ladies,[4] Miss Becca & Kate, while Lucy with her cap and knitting looked as venerable as a grandmother.[5] But Madge, the Irish servant, carried out her part to perfection. She was M. Whiteside,[6] and her broad, warm, [voice], would be uttered so naturally. Miss de Lasseaux was in Kate's room talking of some tableaux she intended to get up for next Friday, last night. She spoke of a procession of nuns, I remarked that I would not take part in that, as I was afraid of and had a perfect horror of Catholics and Catholicism. Here Kate & Lucy laughed and said it was a good joke, for Miss de Lasseaux was a Catholic. I opened my eyes in wild amazement, and rushed from the room amid their laughter. Although I had heard that she was a Catholic yet I had never

4. Emily Jordan McNeill. Courtesy Dorothy Cotton family collection.

heard her own it, I suppose I must apologize. I got a letter from Cousin M. A.[7] mailed only eleven days before. I will send my Ambrotype[f] to her as she seems anxious to have it. The likeness is good, but my dress not fashionable, and freckles are on my face, but I suppose that cannot be helped. Grandpa has returned from Galveston with a new relative, a Mr. Kelley. Ma says he is handsome and intelligent. I should like to see him, though he is only Dr. Jordan's nephew. Hardly any kin to us. Mr. Neel has been dismissed. The children free. Bon jour.

f. This photographic process was developed in the early 1850s and was less expensive than the daguerreotype

[05/22/1858]

May 22d Weeks have passed since I wrote in my Journal, something tells me, that I would be better for communing oftener with thee my irregular diary. Our tableaux party passed off pleasantly, Miss De L. asked me to be a nun and I consented, Puss[8] was the bride-nun and Lucy, Mother Abbess. The high priest Puss H acted admirably, while on each side of Em Alcorn[9] & dear Becca stood, by their other side as haut-boys. Annie Muckleroy, O. Gresham, and M. Wilson, G. Owen were arranged.[10] Rachel kneeled by my side, while Dearest Dora clasped her hands solemnly on the opposite side.[11] The Bride's dark curls were very beautiful. Mrs. Daffodil[g] was applauded, also her son Pete. The Count prosecuted his suit eagerly while George and Annie amused themselves at the expense of the rest of the party. The Witch was received with a shout, as also the Beaux. The bride and her Robber lover represented their characters to the life. But Mrs. Fitzgerald's[12] May scene was the most beautiful of all. Sister[h] in green was not as beautiful, as some of the others, her hair refused to curl. Green is my favorite color, as belonging to nature. M. Whiteside and myself seated ourselves, after the tableaux, soon Mr. O. Leland[14] took his seat just behind us, presently he was on the same seat. Mary proposed vamosing, and we retreated to a back seat. Mrs. Clark introduced Mr. J. Graves,[15] Senior to us, he conversed about an hour, and requested me to tell [him] the fictitious names of the Girls, but I could but refuse—leaving, he gave me (not gracefully) a common red rose—wrote a long letter to my dear mamma this [evening]. Would that I could be with her. Oh, how I long [for] home sometimes, especially when

g. Virginia de Forrest, a regular contributor of *Godey's Lady's Book,* wrote a series of humorous tales on the exploits of Mrs. Daffodil. "Mrs. Daffodil's Interview with a Count" appeared in the April 1858 issue and might have been the basis of this tableau. *Godey's Lady's Book* (1830–1880) was a popular periodical with a circulation of 150,000 in 1860.

h. Her sister, Annie Royal McNeill. She refers to her sister in various ways throughout the diary, calling her Sister A., A., Sister Mc, and Mc.[13]

I have deficient lessons. I do not like Geometry, and I can't learn it without [constant] application and this I am not willing to give. I [lack] all ambition. Mr. Rowe[16] monopolized _____ last night and J. Graves, Fannie. We visited [the Male College] last Tuesday, and heard & saw them exhibit . . . as Mr. B.[i] remarked. Last Sunday we were [disturbed by] someone trying to pull open the [door].

[05/29/1858]

May 29th Just returned from dinner. M. Whiteside complained that we had nothing to eat on Saturday. Have been trying to write an editorial piece for Le Mignonette, haven't half succeeded. M. won't help me at all. Lucy has an excellent piece for the Prairie Flower. Oh! such stormy and distressing scenes we have had this week, very different from last. Poor Mat.[18] is Suspended for a week, for What? Writing to that low fellow, as Mr. C.[j] calls, White Smith[19]. She confessed having written about ten, besides possessing his ambrotype and he hers. He refused to deliver up her letters and said he would not even before a can[n]on, right I think. Mattie talked of killing herself, even asked for Laudnum, I offered her Paregoric but she did not want that, I locked my Laudnum up, though I had not the most distant idea, that she would drink it.[k] She threatened to run off with White, and last night being missing, after Mr. C. had pronounced her sentence, Kate sent for her Brother.[20] She was found in the Music-room with Sue Rhem.[21] Lucy cried aloud and disturbed the whole house, as did Bettie. Bettie cried so much yesterday, that she seemed quite exhausted, and Mr. C. came in to see her, she called him Pa. Miss de Lasseaux says she is a piece of hypocrisy, poor Bettie did not have her sympathy as did Lucy. After keeping them in torturing Suspense, Mr. C. has finally excused them. Bettie [complained] yesterday that we all looked so happy, while she was [miserable]. Phelia[22] brought Fannie back from Mr. Burleson's, [she] owned that she wrote two letters to Thomas, but [denied] that they were love letters. But Bettie Carter [denied] writing any to C. Jenkins,[23] as Mr. C. proved. It [would] have been awful to expel or Suspend a Senior. _____ & Emeline are suspected of the same offense, as also _____ Gresham. The latter is very anxious to go home, while [others] are there already.

i. Rev. Rufus C. Burleson, President of the Male Department of Baylor University[17]

j. Horace Clark, Head of the Female Department of Baylor University

k. Laudanum, a mixture of alcohol and opium derivatives, was used as a painkiller and in many patent medicines of the day.

The girls never want to [write] again, I reckon. I have not heard [from] home this week, which is a source of much uneasiness to us. Sister Mc has written to Ma, but won't let me read it. Mr. C. did not give out letters Thursday. Fannie Oliphint,[24] wishes Miss Morrill to give her permission to visit Miss Maggie Robert, but She says nay. Parlor & Hall full of boys attracted by the reports of twenty suspended, I reckon. Mrs. C. has a new bonnet. Mr. C objected to the Bonnet trimming last Sunday and only let those go to church, who wore or tried to get Solid pink color.[1] Matt A.[25] & Lucy have a new bonnet with a skirt of the same. Lucy & Bettie Johnson[26] are Editress to the P. F. I am worried about the dedication piece, I wish I could write. Fannie Early[27] has been down this week, looks as natural as ever, says she and Phelia are going to Alabama soon. I don't believe Fannie will ever go to school as she intends. Well, I must write to Ma, how I want a letter.

1. The *1859 Baylor Catalogue* (27) specifies that young ladies should wear "Bonnets of white straw, plainly trimmed with pink ribbon of solid color, . . . no flowers or other ornaments allowed."

[06/05/1858]

June 5th Weather cool and pleasant, most of the girls going to town or abroad somewhere. I remember my poor Papa used to say gone abroad for going visiting. Emma M.'s[28] father came unexpectedly this morning, how delighted she is. S. Huckaby[29] burst into tears, on seeing them meet. Fannie, Dora & Mary are going out to Col. Powers, he came for them yesterday, but Mr. C. refused to let them go till this morning. I hear Fannie singing now. Rachel & Puss are intending to walk over to Dr. Robertson's,[30] while Mrs. C. has carried 9 or 10 girls (all with hats on) to town. Mary W. is going to Tula Clay.[31] Miss Morrill & DeLasseaux have gone to Mr. Gee's.[32] I am alone writing and it seems like old times when, I was so much alone last year. We all went to Prayer meeting last night. I did not hear much that was said towards the close, as a very large spider ran under my feet. I did not know but that it was a Tarantula. Mr. C. was sick last eve. [I pray that all] are well at home.

[08/06/1858]

August 6th Days have passed since last I wrote. My time is spent in doing nothing, and having no particular hour set apart for Journalizing, this must necessarily be very irregularly kept. All have gone visiting or to prayer-meeting (where I should be). Posy has just left me. I intended writing to my dear home to-night, but can't find any letter paper. I was greatly astonished to receive a letter from Miss Bettie Allen,[33] Chappell Hill, this evening. And displeased at its contents, I would not answer it if I did not think, she might construe my silence into a consent to her taken for granted assertions. However I will explain briefly to her the relation which exists between the gentlemen & myself and will make it cold enough to prevent her reply.

Here is her very familiar letter, and a precious one it is:

without date
My dear Friend Sallie—
I heard from you to-day, Sallie Foster received a letter from your sister. I recon (her spelling) you will think I have little to do to write to you, but I have written once or twice up there and I see now if you care anything for me. Oh! how! I wish that you was going to school here come next session, you can see a great deal more of pleasure here than you can see under Clark's eye. I have heard so much about you, you cannot guess who told me. It is one of your old sweethearts. God bless his soul, he is the sweetest being on earth, and you love him. I have heard about him going to see you in vacation. You shall not have him, please give me half of him. I see him pass by the window just now. He is as sweet a dear as ever. I went to church last night, and he was there. I cannot keep my eyes off him to save my life. I must close, give my love to all the girls, and tell them to write. I know you think I love him to Death, but I will have to give him to you for he belongs to you anyhow. It is nearly dark. Write soon.
Your friend, _____

[08/22/1858]
Aug 22d We, the Senior Class have just returned from the College, having attended this evening at an especial invitation. Some of the pieces were good, others contemptible, full of nonsense and love-sick speeches; And moreover they insulted us to our face, in a rhyme, calling us Mr. Clark's fair and happy cavalcade or yard. They all shouted and stomped,

but Mr. C. looked indignant, & I am sure those of us who possessed any pride, felt highly insulted. I never want to go again, never. If they cannot write about anything but abuse and ridicule, I hope Mr. C. will not patronize them at all. J. Daniel[34] spoke a sketch of the life of Houston, quite interesting. J. Thomas[35] had one on the evils of Intemperance.

[09/11/1858]

11 Sept. To-day is Dora's birthday, she intended to celebrate it by going to Washington, but has been disappointed. Annie's, Posey's and etc. hoops have come at last, been here ever since Thursday, without their knowledge. Received no letters from home to-day. Have not written my composition. Longing for Commencement day to arrive with my Mamma. Kate C. gone out to Mr. Gee on horseback. Miss Morrill failed to go on account of Miss De Lasseaux's wishes, she saying it would not be agreeable to have Miss M's company. Miss Mary is expected daily. Mrs. C. is moving into her new house. Mrs. Collins has a little babe, a son. Bet and Fan have gone to Mr. Daniels;[36] Ange[37] is mad about not getting letters. Mary Jackson has just finished arranging my hair. Been showing my examination dress to some of the girls, it is blue with flounces.

[09/25/1858]

Sept 25 Been sick for the last week in company with Ange, Rachel and a score of others. Missed all the merry-making, even the Lawyer's great party, their Examination and Graduation. I had fever Saturday night lasting till Monday noon. Sunday evening I while half asleep talked rather delirious, which alarming fact caused the Dr. to be sent for directly. He prescribed several times for me, such a pleasant way he has of speaking and so kind. Miss Morrill installed herself as chief nurse and well did she perform her part. Miss Mary, Hattie and Mrs. Clark, would visit us several times a day. Everybody is very kind to me. Mr. F. at the breakfast table said I looked as if I had been sick and that he was glad I was getting well. My pale face excites sympathy among all. Mr. Clark returned to-day from Gonzales. Bobbie's[38] foot is mashed. The girls all seem glad to see Mr. C, and he them. Got a letter from Ma Monday, Darling has been very sick,

5. Female Department, Baylor University at Independence. Sallie attended classes in this handsome building. Courtesy Texas Collection, Baylor University, Waco, Texas.

poor little fellow. I wished to be at home to get something to eat while sick. I went to school this morning, but have no recitations this evening. I have not commenced my composition yet. Miss Lizzy Scott has written to Ma and Missy, also Uncle A. wrote them.

[10/15/1858]

Oct. 15th The last time the La Mignonette is to be read, the last, the last, how sad to think of it. Mary T.W. has a valedictory in the paper. Only six weeks to the examination. Joyful news! But I shall reluctantly bid adieu to my Alma Mater, and extend the parting hand with a sad heart to my much loved friends and schoolmates. The memory of the two years spent at Independence will often recur to me when in my own home far away. Oh, I hope my Mamma will come for us. Sister A. and Rach are lamenting that they have to play this evening.

[10/22/1858]

Oct 22d Yesterday Mr. C. gave the valedictory to Fannie Rogers. He said all who did not like this decision could object, that he was a reasonable man, and his word could be recalled, no one opposed it then, but several are dissatisfied. Mary W. cannot but feel somewhat disappointed. There were only three claimants. Pussie had been here eight years, but had not attended regularly, nor is she as good a scholar as Fannie, who has been here for six years and noted for good scholarship and conduct. Mary has been connected with this school only about two years, but is the best scholar in school. If this honor had been bestowed on merit, she would have gained it, or if it had been left to the vote of the class. Mr. C. was not pleased at the compositions, though he said Bettie's was very good. All love Fannie, but she does not associate freely with the girls, and they think her proud and exclusive. Fannie says rather than be the object of envy to any she will resign; but Mr. C will not permit this, I am certain. He sent for me to-day in the French Class to give me ten dollars, but I wanted more, though I did not tell him so. I am expecting a letter from home but I fear it will not be the answer I wish. It has been two weeks to-morrow since I wrote home of the change that God in his infinite mercy has wrought in me in giving me an humble hope that He has forgiven my sins for the sake of the blessed Redeemer. Yet how unworthy am I to be a child of God. I have long since been convinced that I was a sinner and desired nothing so much as to be a Christian. But during our revival the spirit of God moved on my adamantine heart and caused me to feel how great a sinner I was. It seemed to me that black clouds were enveloping me, and God's frown was upon me. I thought it inconsistent with my duty to ask the prayers of the church, till I could feel the weight of my sins, but at length on Wednesday night I sought the anxious seat. Mrs. Davis encouraged me to press forward and not to turn back to the world. The next night Miss Mary walked with me to church, and I told her that my heart was so hard I could not feel as penitent as I thought I ought to. She told me she did not think I ought to determine the degree of sorrow I should feel, that God often ordered things in a way directly opposite to that which we expected. And that I must take hold of the promises of God by faith. And believe that through the merit of Jesus alone we can be saved. I again went forward that night, and Mr. C. said much the same to me. As soon as I began to view it in this light I felt greatly relieved, but was afraid to believe and thought that I had lost all my serious impressions. The next day I felt so different and happy, and that night I publicly professed my faith in Jesus. Not, however, without some doubts. I was very much afraid that I might be deceived. That my feelings were caused by excitement or some other cause. But I felt too that I would not abandon this faint hope for any consideration. Since then my mind has not been free from doubts and fears, but I still hope. I know that I have changed, perhaps it is not visible to others. I love to read my Bible, but not as well as I should, and my mind is confined to earthly instead of heavenly things. How wicked and deceitful is the human heart, how fervently should we pray for divine assistance and guidance! We held a small prayer meeting last Friday evening. Several of the girls behaved badly, how careless they seem to be of the salvation of their souls. Kate and Emeline were baptized on Sunday. Mary has not her own consent to join yet. I am waiting for permission from home. To-morrow is the convention day.[m]

m. The Baptist State Convention began on October 22, 1858, in Independence, Texas.

n. From "Self Examination" by Isaac Watts (1674–1748)

[02/01/1859—First entry written at home]

Febru 1st 1859 More than two months of my life has fled since last I wrote here, and "what have I done that's worth the doing"[n] in that time is the question that rises to my mind? I can hardly remember all the events that have occurred. First there was the preparation for Commencement day, filling all hearts with hopes and fears; then the appointed hour was postponed a week, much to our disappointment, and only to please the Faculty of the Male Department. Rach and others declared they would not study the last week; Mr. C. did not hear the Seniors recite either. Well, the long expected and anxiously looked for, yet dreaded day arrived, on the whole, our school acquitted themselves creditably, Mr. Kemble[39] (one of the board of Examiners) came with the expressed determination to tease & make us miss as he did the boys, especially in Latin. He succeeded in puzzling ____ and [all] afternoon wor-

BAYLOR UNIVERSITY.

APPENDIX.

COMMENCEMENT EXERCISES.
DECEMBER 23D, 1858.

11 *O'clock*, *A. M.*—ORATION, W. A. Mongtomery, Esq.,
THEME—Duties of Educated Woman.

2 *O'clock*, *P. M.*—PRAYER.
ESSAY.—Miss Mary Allcorn.
Is Genius compatible with Domestic Felicity.
ESSAY.—Miss Emeline Allcorn.
The Interest attached to the Tombs of Distinguished Persons.
MUSIC.

ESSAY.—Miss Sarah F. Chambers.
Human Pursuits.
ESSAY.—Miss Mary A. Eddins.
The Conqueror's Trophies.
MUSIC.

ESSAY.—Miss Catharine Clark,
Brevity of Human Life.
ESSAY.—Miss Rebecca S. Skilton.
The Hill of Science.
MUSIC.

ESSAY.—Miss Rachael Barry.
The Mission of Beauty.
ESSAY.—Miss Sally A. McNiel.
"Foot Prints on the Sands of Time."
MUSIC.

6. This portion of the Commencement Program lists Sallie and her commencement essay. A draft of her essay was recorded in her diary. Courtesy Texas Collection, Baylor University, Waco, Texas.

ried us with his simple questions. Becca missed, Rach & myself guessed through. He is very ungallant to Ladies. On Wednesday, just as we were starting for the M[ale] College, Ma came very unexpectedly from the wrong direction. I had looked for her in vain all the morning. I saw a carriage approaching but did not notice till I heard an exclamation from Mc a few yards in advance and her startled, "Why it's Ma" caused me to run forward and see grinning Ike, a glimpse of Ma, & Charley on the pony. I was so excited and glad, we turned back directly. "Here's my Ma" would be the short ceremony of introduction to everybody I met. Miss M. said it was so strange to see me "take on." Our Graduating day was the last, fourteen of us, all in different silks, with Mr. C. at the head, made our entrance Indian file in the Audience Hall and took our seats on the rostrum, we were received with much applause. The order in which Mr. C. arranged us was somewhat singular & noticeable. First Fannie R., M. T. Whiteside, Julia R., D. Pettus, Puss McKellar, Bettie Carter, myself, Rach Barry, Becca Skelton, Kate Clark, Sallie Chambers, Emeline Allcorn, Mary A., Mary Eddins. Mr. C's address was full of good advice and feeling. When I heard his parting words and felt that they were the last, my heart grew heavy, and tears unbidden, rolled down my cheeks. I could not help it, if it did make my eyes red. I wonder if Mr. C knows of the half the love we bear him. He kissed me on bidding him goodbye the morning we left, and I believe I prize its memory more than of any I ever received. We arrived at home and were gladly welcomed, and now to-day Sister A has again left us for Independence,[40] Ma accompanies her to Mrs. Mims.'[41] Josephine and Davey[42] will go with her. I have been teaching the children a month; Bob Stanger[43] will remain here. To-night seems lonesome. Mollie[o] is asleep, Missie[p] playing, the boys reading, & Grand Parents abed. We must soon follow their example as early to bed & early to rise, makes a man healthy, wealthy and wise. A few weeks before the Examination Fannie Rogers, C. Woodruff,[44] S. Rhem and myself were received into the Church and baptized, and I am so thankful that I did so since I find there is no Church here. I hope and pray, that I may not be a "cumberer of the ground" but may "bring forth fruit"[q] to the honor and glory of God. But without His help,

o. Sallie's sister, Mary Emily McNeill, b. 1852, d. June 1861

p. Sallie's sister, Emily J. McNeill, b. 1848, d. Dec. 1861

q. Parable of the barren fig tree, Luke 13:6ff KJV

how weak and sinful are we? O God, may I feel my dependence on Thee and ever look upward for Thy aid.

Essays Written at Baylor

The following essays were apparently written as compositions while Sallie was at Baylor. The first one bears the title of the essay that she delivered at her commencement exercises, but all of them were interspersed among entries written in October and November of 1859, apparently having been written in the back of a composition book that she had begun using as a diary.

FOOTPRINTS ON THE SANDS OF TIME
Sallie Mc

Oh Time! onward and evermore rolls thy untiring wheel. Nations arise and exist a few fleeting years, and then time is to them no more, but still continues to perform her ceaseless revolutions for the living. Who can reckon the beginning or end of time? Ere this world was created out of chaos, time may have existed, and when it too shall be no more, time perhaps will pursue her endless March. Years, months, weeks, days, hours, and minutes, pass swiftly away, hurrying man through life, till standing upon the shores of time, ready to launch his frail bark upon the ocean of eternity, he, looking back through the [span] of years upon his troubled life, feels that the fleeting moments of time can never be recalled. And what is Life? It is the brief period of man's probation on earth. It is the years allotted him to remain here to prepare for a future immortal life beyond this world of sin and sorrow. It is the threshold of eternity. And when man is stepping within its portals and son earth shall know him no more, how pleasing the hope that during this life he has left footprints on the sands of time, that no beating wave can efface. The good, and brave, the beautiful, have left traces on the sands of time, and their names "wrought out in marble with the nation's tears of deathless gratitude." Works of art crumble and moulder at the touch of time, but noble deeds and benefits conferred on mankind will never be veiled by time's dark shade of oblivion. The names of the great and good, though they lived and died ages ago, yet still are enshrined in our memory and the record of their virtues encourage others to follow in their footsteps. Will the names of Washington, La Fayette, Newton and Howard[r] ever perish or their memory fade from the minds of a grateful people? Man is not destined to live for himself alone, but to labor for his fellow-man. And the influence he exerts will either be for good or evil. Oh! what a fearful weight of responsibility rests on our conduct! Conquerors have risen and to gratify a vain ambition have caused the slaughter of thousands, even millions, of their fellow creatures. Their names are recorded on the pages of history, but the execrations of posterity are heaped upon their memory. They are the great but not the good of earth. Those only who have increased the happiness of the human race will live in the hearts of all till time shall be no more, and their footsteps will be indelibly stamped upon the shores of time. Not because of the wide-world fame that they have acquired, or of the glory attached to their names. But their names are revered as benefactors of mankind. Why need we repeat the oft-told tale of he of whom it was said that he was "first in peace, first in war, and first in the hearts of his countrymen." Our noble Washington needs no eulogy from my feeble pen. The deeds of the gallant Frenchman, who fought so nobly and shed his blood in our cause, are also well known to every true son of America. While the name of Howard, the philanthropist, who sacrificed his life in benefitting suffering humanity, lingers fresh in the memory of posterity.

. . . but still with each returning season steals silently and steadily on.

[This last phrase was on the page with the essay, but at the bottom and upside down.]

Spain

This country once high in rank and power with her sister state of Europe, is now reduced to a weak and small state. To her belongs the glory of aiding Columbus in his search for the New World. The enterprising spirit of a Cortez sailed from her shores to explore and subjugate her newly acquired provinces in a far distant world. Pizarro, the successful conqueror of the Peruvians, was also a spaniard. And in later times DeSoto, with a chosen band of followers, landed on

r. John Howard (1726–90), English philanthropist known for prison reform

the shores of America to establish his Government and religion, but sad was the fate of the leader and his gallant band. Spain has lost all her foreign possessions, Cuba alone remains to her. Her rulers are weak and powerless, while other nations are making rapid progress in the arts and sciences, and improving their condition, Spain alone remains unprofited and stationary. Like the Turk, she is decaying, how sad to behold her thus. The Spaniards are a proud race, they seem to have lost all hope of recovering their ancient glory and have sunk into despair. Poor degraded Spain, thy future destiny, time alone can reveal.

India

This country is situated in the southern part of Asia. The inhabitants, like all Asiatics are ignorant and indolent. Being far removed from civilization, they are still, for the most part, barbarians and heathens. The missionaries have, and are still, affecting much good in this benighted region. But many have fallen, most while endeavoring to teach the gospel to the poor heathens, either by the murderous hands of those whom they were seeking to save or by the influence of the climate of India, which is almost always fatal to Europeans. The British Government although possessing no rightful claims to India, yet has seized upon the native kings and deposed them from their thrones. Their professed design is to civilize the natives but in reality they are only exterminating them. Nor do they submit to such tyranny without a struggle. The natives are constantly rebelling and slaughtering all the whites who have the misfortune to fall into their hands. Thus India is the scene of war and cruelty. The pen would fail to disclose the extent of the atrocities committed there. India was for many years the scene of the labors of the great departed Judson,[s] near her coast in the bosom of the boundless ocean he sleeps. Amid the dense jungles of India are found Elephants, Tigers and other animals common to Tropical regions.

College Life

This period of life is never forgotten. During its continuance the characters of those, who are fitting themselves for

s. In 1812, Adoniram Judson and his wife Ann were among the first American missionaries to India. He died and was buried at sea in 1850.

[the] life battle with the world, are being formed. While the intellect is expanding the heart of the student is not allowed to remain uncultivated. More friends are listening to hear his praises in that distant home. And the laudable desire of pleasing the loved & absent ones incites the ambitious scholar to new efforts. Youthful companions share his toils and sympathy. The student has his cares and anxieties, but they are light in comparison to the trials of the man of the world.

The following sentences seem to be a part of this essay, but are separated from it, appearing on the last page of this section of the diary.

The years that have passed in college are never forgotten. Too often pupils are apt to imagine that this period of their life is dull and uninteresting, and long for the time when free from the restraints of school discipline they can leave the College and launch their untried bark on the ocean of life.

The Recluse

This unhappy being, becoming tired of the world & its heartless pomp & show, retires to some lone spot distant from the habitation of man to spend his days in solitude, without society save the songsters of the wilderness and the wild animals of the forest. There, in utter silence and loneliness he endeavors to forget the busy world from which he has voluntarily separated himself, with the resolution of never again mingling in its giddy throng. But does he fully succeed; can he still the voice of Nature, which prompts him to seek companionship with his fellow men? As society is natural to man, it is to be supposed that the hermit cannot without some violence to his feelings depart from the haunts of men, to a desert spot where he meets not a face of a human being, but time the healer of all sorrows consoles the lone being who misguided by religious zeal retires to a comfortless cell for devotional purposes. He vainly hopes to be free from sin in leading this self-sacrificing life, but alas, can mortal man be sinless? And is he filling the destiny, which his all-wise creator has appointed him? Man owes a duty to his fellow man. God has declared in his holy Book that "it is not good for man to be alone."

Below are phrases copied on the last page of the section of Baylor entries.

with the friends I love best! [appears in the upper margin]

Sweet vale of Avoca! how calm could I rest, In thy bosom of shade,[t] [copied 16 times.]

The visions of my youth are past, too bright, too beautiful to last.

t. From "The Meeting of the Waters" by Thomas Moore, a popular Irish poet (1779–1852)

Secluded and Remote from the Busy World

*S*allie begins her record of life on the plantation with this entry in February of 1859. Her new role is that of teacher, instructing her younger siblings. Her sister Annie returns to Baylor for the spring session in 1859 and will be joined by her brother Calvin in the fall of 1859. Sallie makes a few trips during this time period: visiting Wharton for a Baptist Association meeting, traveling to Galveston with their neighbor, Mrs. Mims, and returning to Independence with her mother for the Examination at Baylor. She also makes a number of visits to friends and relatives in the area and spends time reading voraciously and keeping up her correspondence with classmates and relatives. During this time, she writes often, sometimes several times a month, concluding this section in November of 1860.

[02/02/1859]

2d Febr. The morning passed off as usual, lessons indifferently known. Grandpa at the house all day, killing hogs. Boys rode over to Mrs. Mims' for Ma; Archie[a] glad to get home again. Mc & company reached Brazoria safe; if nothing happened they are at Daymonds[b] to-night. Ma brought home my watch, as Mr. L. Mims[1] has returned from Galveston. Grand Ma's present for me is a gold stone breast pin, cost nine dollars and quite pretty, but rather too fine for me. I suppose to-day is a specimen of what will be my regular routine of duties throughout the year. I hope I may be able to discharge them with some profit, both to others and myself. I don't know, but that I shall be quite tired of sameness, and long for excitement and change of place, though I have little inclination for visiting. I ought to be grateful for a happy home even if it is secluded and remote from the busy world, and too I will have less temptations to mingle with its giddy throng. tres bien.

a. Sallie's youngest brother, William Archibald Campbell McNeill, b. 4/25/1855, d. 5/19/1879

b. Town in western Brazoria County, now called Damon

[02/09/1859]

Mond. Febru. 9th Again days have past unrecorded here, but it seems as if I have nothing even now to write, worthy of being remembered. Sometimes, the misbehavior of the children almost discourages me, but I would be discontented, very, without something to do, or employ my time. I would tire of reading always, even if I was so fortunate as to have a great variety of books. To-day I have read Midsummer's Nights Dreams, though it is not the first time. Saturday mail, brought us welcome Harper[c] & papers; also a letter from Miss Morrill for myself, asking what I had done with the money she left with me at Independence to pay Mrs. Graves for making her dress, as that lady had written to her for the five dollars? This startling query, puzzled me not a little, for at first neither Ma or myself could remember having been entrusted with the money, but now since Ma has calculated the amount of her expenses at Independence, she finds that she must have had it, as she has too much. I can recollect receiving the gold, but in the hurry and confusion of the last day, forgot the occurrence altogether and probably it would never have been recalled to my mind, but for Miss M. I am very glad she asked an explanation, otherwise she might have considered the mistake intentional on my part. Mr. Davis[2] acknowledges the receipt of my draft, and informed me that Miss Mary[d] was visiting at San Antonio, I believe. Sister A. arrived there to-day at fartherest. Mr. W. Spencer[4] came over Friday bringing Grandpa a business letter, he invited me to visit his town, and etc. The same evening we all called on Mrs. S. Mims. Archie and myself took a short walk this evening. Bob failing to make his appearance from hunting at twilight. Charlie[e] proceeded to blow him up, with rapid success. I must conclude and read my nightly lessons in the book of [Life]. John L. Stephen's Travels in Greece, Turkey, Russia and Poland in two vols. 12mo muslin; also Travels in Egypt, Arabia Petraea, and the Holy Land, two volumes, twelve mo muslin.[5] Arabian Nights entertainments, Robinson Crusoe, Theodore Ernest, Life of Napoleon Bonaparte, Milton's Paradise Lost, Vicar of Wakefield.[f] Religious Experiences by Alexander.[g]

c. *Harper's New Monthly Magazine* began publication in 1850 and with slight name changes has continued publication to date. The magazine had a circulation of about 200,000 in 1860.

d. Miss Mary Davis, teacher at Baylor[3]

e. Sallie's brother, Charles Philip McNeill, b. 6/21/1846, d. 3/8/1926 (family records)

f. By British writer, Oliver Goldsmith, published in 1766

g. By Archibald Alexander,[6] *Thoughts on Religious Experience* was published in 1841.

[02/17/1859]

Febru 17th. Great excitement has prevailed here for the last two hours. Jacob's cabin caught fire at about eleven o'clock, when first discovered was in a light blaze. Grandpa & all ran, but could not extinguish the flames, which soon were communicated to the unoccupied Hospital. Calvin rescued old Lydia, who was chained to the chimney. The south wind was high and there was great danger of burning Claiborn's Cabin[7] & the cribs,[h] when all would have been lost. They stripped the old house, and poured water on it constantly. We ran about confused & half wild. Ma was so frightened, though there was no danger of losing life. We pulled down fences and kept it from reaching any combustible matter. I can see the smoking ruins now. How grateful we should feel that life was preserved, and let the stuff go without complaining. But poor negroes, they have lost their all of worldly possessions. Aunt Fannie and Milley[8] have nothing. Received a letter from Angie last mail and a valentine enclosing some strychnine for Grandma's dogs, from Brazoria I think. Ma sent Mc her five dollars. Read "Merchant of Venice" to-day. Calvin ran himself sick, he says I ran about the fire and gave more orders than Grandpa himself. The negroes came in haste from the field and Sugar House. All are tired with the unusual exertion. Missie cried till the flames subsided, poor, terrified child. This is the first accident of the kind that has happened to us in Texas. How thankful we ought to be for the continued mercies of God! Who ever watches over and shields us from harm. How easily can the work of years be consumed by the devouring flames; so is man's life, but a dream, brief and fleeting.

[02/28/1859]

Feb. 28 Two months of the year 1859 will soon have passed away, never to return, no never.—And how have those precious moments been spent, alas! I can scarcely tell. I cannot remember that I have learned much, if anything since my stay at home, though I am busy school days. But I, who have been of so little use during my life of nineteen years, cannot expect to accomplish a great deal in a few months. My birthday has passed, without being celebrated—the day before St. Valentine's is the anniversary of my advent into

h. Storage sheds for corn

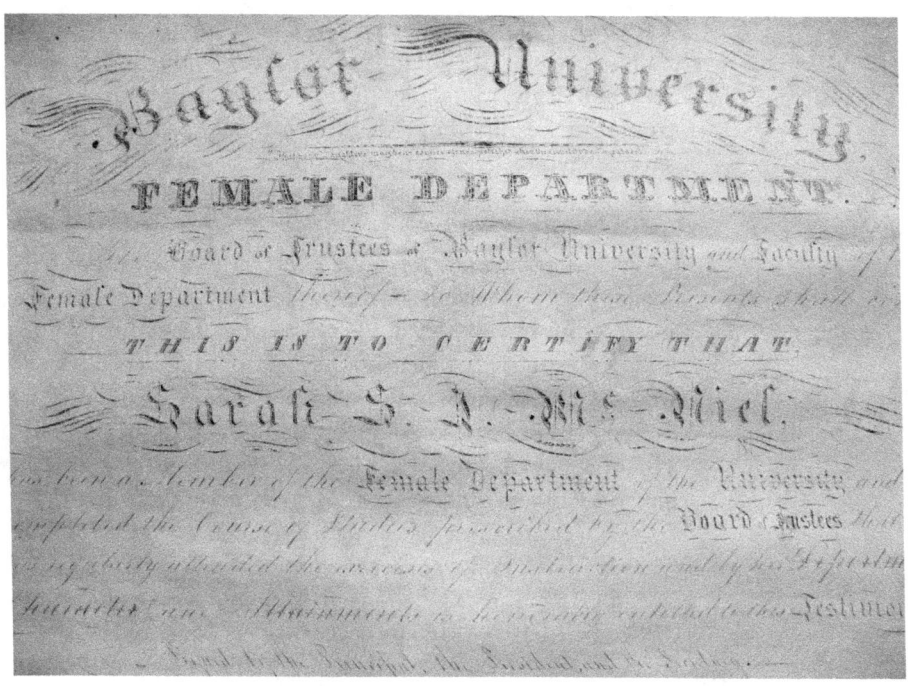

7. Diploma of Sallie McNeill. Author's personal collection.

life. How long it seems, and yet how short. Ah! I cannot realize that nearly a score of years have passed since first I saw the light, in the rough, log-cabin, away in the piney woods of wild Louisiana. There in happy ignorance the first eight years of my quiet childhood were spent. Then a desire for change, induced my Father & Grandfather to remove from Union Parish; and thither to the famed land of Texas, we came and made our home, amid the Bernard brakes, where for ten years we've lived, literally a home-life. Two years have I spent at Baylor University and now with a Diploma, testifying my education to be completed, I am again *a la maison,* quietly endeavoring to instruct my little school, composed of three boys and two girls. Whether my efforts will prove satisfactory to them or myself, the future alone will reveal. How little good have I done in the world. My friends do not say so, but I feel my deficiencies. Kept at school all my life, and treated as a child, with nothing but books to employ my thoughts, it is not strange that I should be indolent and idle.

I am a child still, dependent on others. I wonder if the future score of my life (If I should be permitted by our Creator to remain on this "mundane sphere" so long) will be as free from care. I cannot hope so, but trust that whether long or short, they may be a blessing to others as well as myself.

[03/31/1859]

March 31st Again after a long delay I resume my pen to sketch hastily the events of the last few weeks. All of little interest, but serve to break the monotony of a country life for a few hours. Mrs. Henry Jones[9] is stopping here a few weeks, while her husband is making preparations to clear the Bernard of rafts, so as to communicate with the railroad. Their baby is a source of amusement to us, and tolerably pretty. Grandma accompanied Mary to her father's Tuesday. Have not heard from Sister A. for three weeks, and then Grandpa Fitzgerald was supposed to be dying, and others were ill. Ange R. & C. Woodruff wrote me then and M.T.W this week. I have written to Becca S., Puss McK and, S. Huckaby. I have experienced some trouble in governing my unruly brothers in school lately. I dislike to have Grandpa punish them and Ma can't, or won't. Isaac,[10] who had the misfortune to break his leg two weeks ago, while loading the schooner, has suffered great pain and is complaining now. Bob went to Brazoria this week, for the filly Elfleda, who swam across the river. I hear Bettie B. has written home for a silk dress, etc. Mrs. W. Wilson[11] is recovering from her misfortune. For more than two months she has been unable to walk. Charley killed his first deer the other morning. He was highly elated. Grandpa covered his face with blood in honor of the occasion I suppose. All the corn is planted to-day. Mr. Dance[12] and Casey[13] were to dinner here. Dewberry are turning. How tired and dissatisfied I am sometimes with this quiet life, And yet I would not change it I believe. I would like to go away from home for a short while. I am afraid I shall grow quite rustic in taste and appearance. But my chief desire is to avoid evil and to do good, though I often and continually fail. I hope to become better by the grace of my Heavenly Father! I am conscious of my deficiencies in many things. Vale, Vale.[i]

---

i. Latin for "farewell."

[06/21/1859]

    June 31st Three months have "dragged their slow length along"[j] since I last confided my random thoughts and the few passing events to the silent pages of my book; which does not merit the appellation of Journal. These days have been spent pretty much as their predecessors. In trying to accomplish some good; and often failing. But I must learn to be patient; and endeavor to improve the Present without so much regard for the Future, whose mysteries cannot be revealed to mortals. I do not certainly idle away my time, as formerly. Yet I cannot feel that mere sewing, which is only mechanical and easily performed, should occupy the greater portion of the day. All our faculties are given to us to be cultivated, undoubtedly. I have long been considered lazy and deservedly. Who would not obtain such an appellation when sitting contentedly for hours with folded hands idly dreaming. The Home Magazine[k] has been added to our Periodicals. Consisting principally of light reading however. With the help of a Dictionary, I have read some fifty pages of "Vie de Washington." The progress of my petit school is not very flattering to me, and less to others. Sister A. will be *a la maison* Sunday, nothing preventing. Mr. Evans has been gone for negroes two months; after drawing Grandpa's $10,000 he has suddenly disappeared from the horizon of our limited vision. Doubts are being entertained of his honesty, in the minds of not a few.[14] My correspondents have wholly neglected me for months. I wanted to attend Commencement this week but did not wish to go alone. I may never go. But I don't like to think this unpleasant thought, probably. We have had rain this week, which has long been wanted. Within this month, General has gone "the way of all the earth." Adaline and Phebe have been, also, very ill. Fayette was a general favorite with us, but Death is inexorable, snatching his victims at will. He doeth all things well.

j. From "Essay on Criticism," part II, 1.357, by Alexander Pope (1688–1744)

k. *Arthur's Home Magazine* (1852–98). Elsewhere she refers to it as *Arthur's*.

[07/28/1859]

    July 28th Another interval of time has elapsed, ere I again assume my pen, to record nothing worth recounting. Life, with us, is the same as of old, with the addition of Sister A. to our home circle. Lately we have had some lady visitors.

Cousin B. A. Rainey[15] came up for a few days, the first time in a year and half. Jimmie[16] is quite a pretty child, but badly spoiled. We've written for Ange to come and go to the Gulf shore on a short pleasure excursion. The children are rushing in here frightened at the mischievous pranks of the boys. Grandma is crying to order and I'll retire. Vale

[08/03/1859]

Aug 3d All this week have I indulged in a bad humor. And the cause—I hardly know. The noisy children irritate, but do not anger me. If school-keeping is productive of such bad feeling, I had better throw up my "commission" and resign. Perhaps the better course is to reform my own temper. Though I always imagine I possess little spirit, yet it is difficult at times to keep in check. And what could I do with a furious and ungovernable temper! I am discontented with myself and consequently must be ill at ease. I wish I could leave home awhile. I am so tired here. I & Charlie rode out this evening and found a cane broken; it was sweeter, than we supposed it could be, and argues well for the coming crop. I am trying to write to Rach, but am sadly out of heart. And then I must answer Becca—And offer my sympathy to poor, dear Mary, who has lost her mother. All my correspondents are forsaking me, and I will soon have nothing left but the memory of *auld lang syne* far away at our old Alma Mater. *Eh bien,* such is nature and human fallibility, and I must submit, patiently.

[09/01/1859]

Sept. 1st Alone again.—Sister A. & Brother Calvin departed for school this *matin*. I feel so low and depressed, but time will bring forgetfulness. I have no actual sorrow like bereaved Mrs. Wilson, who has lost her Willie this week. I went to the burial with Ma & G. W.[17] who has been visiting us for the last two weeks; he returned home yesterday. He is changed somewhat, but not much. I wish to go to the Association in Wharton[1] if possible. But old folks forget they were once young, and are too often inclined to detain young person at home. Well I ought to be contented, though I cannot always feel so. I believe I am a restless being, and

---

1. The county seat of nearby Wharton County, on the east bank of the Colorado River, approximately forty-five miles from Brazoria

must have inherited the propensity for rambling from the McNeill's. I soon tire of company, especially the nonsensical talk of most young men. It is a poor compliment to my sex (weak though they too often are) to suppose they can be only amused by flattery and sentiment. If I could only get new books occasionally, I would be happy while reading. But I must not be selfish. Life promises little of worldly pleasure for me. If I only was good, I could not help being happy. But I am such a sinful creature. There will always be troubles and trials here, and I must endeavor to exercise patience, knowing that the end is not in this world. My faith is very weak sometimes. Oh if I could ever lift my spirit above the perishing things of this world! What endless praise is due to our Father in Heaven for his mercies and love!

[10/15/1859]

Oct. 15th, 1859 Autumn is upon us again, though there are few visible traces of his presence here, in our Southern clime. The verdure of field and forest is still bright & fresh. Old Boreas has begun his warning blast, which will soon drive us to the cheerful fireside. All seasons are to me much the same. Yet I am not sorry to greet drear winter in stead of the enervating heat of Summer. Enough of such thoughts—I did go to Wharton at last. Mrs. Adams took me in her Buggy and Mr. W. Rowe & Mrs. Wilson had the Barouche. I cannot say that I was not somewhat disappointed at my visit. Leo Mims[18] accompanied us. The Association[m] lasted several days and was then protracted in Town. We heard excellent sermons, I regret that I did not profit more by them. I go from home so seldom that my attention was so distracted half the time, that I could not listen as I should have done. Four persons joined the church, among whom were two of our neighbors, W. and M. Rowe.[19] I met several of the Brethren of the Convention of last year. And too I met D. Pettus for a few moments in church. She gave me to understand that she would leave town, directly after dinner, though I learned subsequently that she remained till sundown. I could not but feel, that she cared little for my company, or she would have either called on, or sent for me. Though she expressed her sorrow that she could not stay

m. The Colorado Baptist Association meeting was held in Wharton beginning on Friday, September 16, 1859.

longer, and urged me to visit her in Richmond. I saw all my friends in W. but Mr. Weekly. The river was so high, crossing was difficult. Some of them promise to come down in two weeks when Mr. Stribling[20] will hold a meeting here and baptize the boys. My books have not come yet. Grandpa will commence making sugar Monday. Wharton is a small poor place, worse than Brazoria.[21] I staid with Mrs. Veazy[22] and Mrs. Sol Thomas.[23]

Sallie ends the first section of her diary here and begins the second portion with the new year, recording the following quotations on the back page of this section before beginning her journal entries.

[01/01–07/1860]

Jan. 1. Stand upon the edge of this world, ready to take wing,—having your feet on earth, your eyes and heart in heaven—Wesley.

Jan. 2:—As in a letter, if the paper is small, and we have much to write, we write closer, so let us learn to economize and improve the [remain]ing moments of life.—Jay.

Jan. 3. Let us esteem the creature only as it comes from God, or brings us some report of his love.—Baxter.

Jan. 7th.—There are no fragments so precious as those of time, and none are so heedlessly lost by people who cannot make a moment, and yet can waste years—Montgomery.

[01/05/1860]

Brazoria, Texas, Jan. 5th 1860

Thurs. Once more the New Year, has opened its portals to Earth's living. And again we set forward on the journey of Life, with various hopes & aims. Yet all seeking the same goal. All aspire to be happy. And though again and again doomed to disappointment, few despair till death ends their earthly career. But blessed is the hope of felicity beyond the grave, to those, who do the will of Our Heavenly Father. This precious Faith alone gives strength to endure the ills of life. If one could always attain this blessed assurance, of the love and forgiveness of God, undimmed by doubts & sins, there would be small cause for discontent and wretchedness. Alas! human frailty too often grieves away the Holy Spirit,[n] for It will not always strive with man.[o]

n. Ephesians 4:30a KJV

o. Genesis 6:3a KJV

[01/07/1860]

Saturday 7th.—One week of 1860 almost gone. And I've done nothing but read and hear a few recitations of Charlie's & Missie's. Am pleased with the "Lay of the Last Minstrel."[p] Though I believe I like everything Scotch, because Scotland is the land of my Fathers. Slightly sketched "Lalla Rook"[q] this week; M. T. W.'s[r] favorite poem. Ah! Mary, how unjust to forget the friend of "Auld lang Syne." Sometimes tempted to make a third effort to obtain her correspondence. But pride opposes. I can't believe both my letters miscarried. Of all my fourteen or rather thirteen classmates,[s] she was one of two most beloved. Yet she never showed the same preference for me, and now my affectionate letters are unanswered. Time is said to heal all sorrows, but I am not going to forget her neglect. Not that I intend to "nurse my wrath to keep it warm,"[t] no I cherish no feelings but of regret. In the new & responsible relation, she is said to be about, to assume, my hopes & wishes are for her happiness.

Dr. S. Rowe[25] came down this week with his Cousin. He brings the news of Fannie Oliphant's marriage to J. Arnold. Somewhat sudden to me, as College-love rarely proves serious. They are young, but F. is pretty and amiable & J. is worthy of her love.

Other rumored engagements are afloat, but all are not worthy of credence. I half-wish Sister A. had returned. She will gain little good & maybe harm by continuing. Calvin appears to maintain his character well. Methodist preaching to-morrow, by the new minister. The Rev. Dr. Worthington passed yesterday. He has been, shame to say, drunk at Mat.[u] for weeks. He is traveling from La.

[01/09/1860]

Mond. 9th.—Did not attend Church yesterday, expected Ma & Grandma to go. Mr. Rowes returned with Grandpa & Charlie. They say we have a poor preacher. Read, "Abbots way to do Good"[v] & this morning Moore's "Loves of the Angels."[w] It seems to me almost a profanation, for a poet to attempt such writings. I have seen but little of Milton yet. Am undecided about going to Galv.[x] It is very uncertain, that Mrs. Mims will go at all. Have letters to answer.

p. A narrative poem published in 1805 by Scottish writer Sir Walter Scott (1771–1832)

q. "Lalla Rookh," a narrative poem published in 1817 by the Irish Romantic poet Thomas Moore (1779–1852)

r. Mary T. Whiteside of Retreat in Navarro County[24]

s. There were fourteen in the graduating class of 1858 of the Female Department of Baylor University, including the diarist.

t. From "Tam O'Shanter" (1791) by Scottish poet Robert Burns (1759–96).

u. Matagorda, until 1894 county seat of Matagorda County, which borders Brazoria County

v. *The Way to do Good* (1836) by Jacob Abbott (1803–79)

w. *Loves of the Angels* (1823) by Thomas Moore (1779–1852)

x. Galveston

y. Beginning with its first edition in 1857, the *Texas Almanac* included some accusations against Sam Houston concerning his conduct at the Battle of San Jacinto and during the Revolution.[26]

z. A veteran of the Battle of San Jacinto, Eli Mercer settled in what is now Wharton County in 1829.[27]

aa. Baptized

bb. Houston ran for governor in 1857 while a lame-duck senator. He was defeated, but ran again in 1859 and was elected.[29]

cc. Her sister, Annie, who was attending Baylor at Independence

[01/11/1860]

Wed. 11th.—Sewed all yesterday, making myself a gingham dress. No letters last night, only Mollie's "Pilgrim." Read "Texas Almanac" this morning. The different accounts, concerning the battle of San Jacinto, and the revolution of 1836, given by Houston & Sherman, are enough to confuse anyone.[y] Sherman however has the best proof, for I believe Mr. Mercer's[z] account true. He is a strict member of the Baptist church, I heard him exhort several times at Wharton last summer. Gen. Houston has also been immersed,[aa] and though I know little of his private character at present, I have heard him acknowledge his past transgressions. He was admitted in the Church at Independence.[28] He is very sarcastic & egotistical in his political speeches. He declared he would not accept any office after his defeat as a candidate for Governor, yet he is now filling that office.[bb] Mrs. Houston[30] is a strong minded woman I think, not very good-looking. Her eldest son[31] is dissipated but the girls are possessed of good abilities.

[01/16/1860]

Mon. 16th—Dr. Rowe has just called on his way home. Ma sent Mc[cc] a pair of shoes. He intends to come again next summer, he says, as the weather was so inclement, he failed to see much of our neighborhood. Mrs. Rice, Mr. Harrison & Mrs. (Gelet) Stanley and son, were here yesterday. Quite an excitement was produced among the Blacks, by the marriage of Jane and Bos, Saturday-night. The Bride appeared pleased and the Groom elated. How easily they are made happy in their simplicity. Bob had a letter from Calvin, last mail, by the new carrier A. Parks.[32] Must write letters to-day, to Cousin M. A., Mc & J. Mims.

[01/20/1860]

Frid. 20th.—The merchant (pedler) Mr. Zemonsky, who was here a few weeks ago, came again last night. Persuaded Ma to get herself a Lava breastpin. Grandma got a cameo set for Sister A. & some studs for Calvin & myself of him before. Mr. & Mrs. Jones traded some, Mr. J. purchased a gold watch & chain for $90 while mine is smaller & yet cost

$135. My only purchase this morning was a roll of hairpins. Got Peterson's Magazine[dd] Tuesday, like it as well as Arthur's I believe. Read Vicar of Wakefield. Much as this work is praised, I can't think Dr. Primrose & family were so wonderfully wise, at least mother & daughter were often foolish. Sophia I like best, & the Dr. Hastily examined Scott's Rokeby, Marmion, & Lady of the Lake. Am not a judge or critic in regard to the merits of the poems. Glanced at Milton's Comus.[ee] I always run over a work to catch the substance of the story before I can settle down to patient reading. Read Ovid's Metamorphoses with much pleasure; most of the stories were familiar to me. Of course I haven't touched a needle this week. Mrs. Harrison[33] just sent to borrow some paper. Bob carried his gun to Columbia[ff] yesterday, having bursted her. Ma visited Mrs. H. Mims[35] one evening, the day the two Organ-grinders came along; I had never seen one before, poor music however.

dd. A popular ladies' magazine. *Peterson's Magazine* began publication under that name in 1853.

ee. "Comus (A Maske Presented at Ludlow Castle)" (1634) by John Milton (1608–74)

ff. Nearby town, now known as West Columbia.[34]

[01/23/1860]
Mon. 23d I snatch the remaining few rays of sunlight to jot down—nothing. For all my endeavors end in nothing. It is useless to form resolves. Spent Saturday in Ma's room sewing on a new calico dress, brown, and spoiling a pot of Sugar-candy. Evening and Sunday morning perusing the Febr. no. of Peterson. A late letter from Calvin. He says he & Davie has a bet on hand concerning a report, that I will be married before Summer, all to tease him likely. To-day sewed & read Addison's Campaign,[gg] etc., felt somewhat indignant on account of the severe criticisms on many of his writings, just though, perhaps. Threatened to tie Missie, to force her to obey & sent her from the breakfast table to pare her nails. Bob commences plowing to-day for the first time. Haven't seen Archie up stairs since morning & haven't been down myself, only to meals, go now.

gg. Joseph Addison (1672–1719) became famous for his poem "Campaign" (1704), but is better known for his essays in the *Tatler* and *Spectator*.

[01/26/1860]
Thurs, 26th Sewed to-day. The children get on smoothly now they haven't much to do, only recite two Latin-lessons and read, spell & define. Arithmetic of course is kept up. Mrs. Jones has been down to her father's[36] this week: her

hh. Probably Kenner's Prairie in Matagorda County, where the Rainey family lived

Cousin Mary has arrived from Ga. Heard Cousin has a new daughter.[37] Want to go down to the Prairie[hh] about Spring.

[02/02/1860]
Thurs. 2d. Feb.

Saturday evening Mrs. H. came just as I was basting the finishing seam of my dress. She remained till the next afternoon. Mrs. Adams & Mrs. Wilson appeared Sunday. Mrs. W. on her way to Wharton. I went with Mrs. A. Monday to Caddie's[38] & Mrs. Mims's. Little Mary is pretty, and the baby good, is called Columbia. I held her in the Buggy going over to her Grandma's.[39] Saw Leonard & Mother. He in his brown hunting suit. Mr. Rowe stopped yesterday noon. The stage was smashed Monday morning and Genie being sick Mrs. W. is still at Mrs. Gimerson's. I conclude Wharton is a miserable place.[40] Mr. Sol. Thomas is hopelessly ill Mr. Wil. says. He & Gerald[41] have rented Mr. Weekley's place while the old man has gone to Gonzales. It seems in their case, that trouble never comes singly. Two Arthur's Sat. mail, & a letter from P. McKellar[42] & Mc, Ma one from Calvin & Mc last Tues., also, Harper and my first letter from Cousin Barbara McNeill. She has returned home from N. C. to find her Brother James married & so mean & unnatural as to refuse her a support. All her means is in his power. She will have recourse to law, but will hardly succeed, as he is an accomplished rogue. Neither is her other brother Archibald much account, though good to her she says; taking her at his expense to N. C. & has now returned there to remain. I am ashamed to acknowledge such relatives. Aunt Betsy[43] is said to have been a strong minded woman. But I am always inclined to think, that the parents of dishonest, dissipated men are to blame for their conduct. This is the case generally. Grandpa McNeill's son John was not strictly honest to his relatives,[44] though upright in his dealings with others. He seemed to be envious of the prosperity of his brothers. Cheated & caused Pa an expensive lawsuit. He lived at Grandpa's & taught Ma for years. Grandma talks of the Dr. yet. He died ten years ago in Ala. leaving no children. And now little Jim as he was called revives the memory of his misdeeds. Cousin B. says her mother left all the property to J. & her father gave a larger portion to his sons than daughters. She has two married sisters. I earnestly hope that she will recover her rights.

[02/03/1860]

Frid. 3d. Sewed on Missie's embroidery this morning, must finish Miss Mary's letter this evening. Jane is making Archie green plaid breeches, and Ma a ruffled shirt. Mr. Coruthers has just called in time to get his dinner. I wonder how he lives! I pity his wife and four children. Cad asked me of S. Copeland? I only know she has married a Mr. Dorsin, Capt. Duncan's overseer.[45] All my home schoolmates[ii] are married but one, and I suppose she is impatiently waiting a chance. Heard of the death of Tippie Fuller,[46] a graduate of Baylor. She was a stately, beautiful, intelligent girl, a resident of Houston. Saw her twice at our Examinations. H. Clark[47] was or is in Houston. Mr. C. is getting up a Library by buying contributions on the girls' pocket money. Mc sent for her's. I am anxious to go up in the Summer.

ii. Sallie must be referring here to girls she went to school with at home, before going to Baylor. Nothing is known about what sort of school she might have attended— very likely just lessons taught by a school teacher in someone's home, possibly her own.

[02/06/1860]

Mond. 6th Sat. & Sunday gloomy, wet weather, not any hard showers, which have been needed so long. Bob and negroes exposed to the cold and rain, till nine o'clock Sat. night, boating shells; gone again this morning. Grandpa praises Bob's industry at plowing—. Cut off my pink mohair skirt Sat. want to finish it this week. Read Happy Home again Sunday, it contains many useful hints about governing children. Recommended its perusal to Mrs. Jones & Ma. A new letter from Calvin to Ma & Bob. And a Male Catalogue to myself from D. Mims. He has moved out of C.'s room. Embroidering for Miss to-day and trying on waist of new dress, must write to C. in company with Ma and Charlie, who has been given the evening for the purpose. Vale.

[02/07/1860]

Tuesd. 7th Missie detained to finish a sum in Reduction, is crying and whining instead of ciphering. She needs a real whipping, but I don't like to hurt her, bad as she is. With all my boasted philosophy, children try and worry me beyond patient endurance. They can't anger but irritate me & I don't always remember not to speak harshly.

[02/09/1860]

Thurs. 9th. Roused at daybreak, by Uncle Ambrose hurrying up-stairs for medicine for the black mare, Jane Weekly; who was found to be very sick with the colic. At one time fears were entertained for her life. However she is considerably better now. Clarence MacGreal brought a letter from his *pere*,[48] asking the loan of $5,000. Grandpa refused, because he intends to use all his means, for purchasing negroes. Though he has as many already as he can attend to.[49] Mrs. Mims came up last evening. Mrs. Durant wishes to teach for us again,[50] but Grandpa won't, & Mrs. Mims can't board her. I want an accomplished teacher, so I can take some lessons in languages etc,. Clarence says old Mr. Durant condescended to visit & kneel to his divorced wife, lately, trying to gain her good graces again but she knows his wiles by experience. All accompanied Mrs. M. to the Sugar House on her return home. I climbed up on the filled Hhd.[jj] leaving the print of my foot upon the tops. Ma has headache to-day. Bob brought up some fine oysters. Charley & Miss are in the dumps because they have not finished their lessons. Archie wet himself in the duck-hole, thereby deserving the thrashing, that he did not get from his doting Ma.

jj. Abbreviation for hogshead, the large barrels or casks in which sugar and molasses were stored[51]

[02/13/1860]

Mon. 13th. My birthday. I suppose I have lived all of twenty years. Yet I can't realize it. I wonder is this is the same feeling with every one. Only one year out of school and still am twenty. Well, I must bid adieu to childhood and my teens and take womanhood, with as good a grace as is possible under the circumstances. Youth is slipping away rapidly, and I haven't spent it profitably. I don't expect much of the so called pleasure of this world, and so will try not to be disappointed with my lot, whatever betides. Life! what is it? How often do I ask myself the question! But none can know, but by experience. What right have I to complain who have so many undeserved privileges? I would be sorry to feel that I should never be better in heart, than at present. "Life is real, life is earnest" & the grave is not its goal'![kk] Hope beckons us onward through this "vale of tears"! And with the blessed hope of a mansion in Heaven, we must be content & should be happy.

kk. From "A Psalm of Life" (1839) by Henry Wadsworth Longfellow (1807–82)[52]

[02/15/1860]

Wed. 15. Mrs. Rowe, Mrs. Adams, Mr. W. Rowe & his Cousin John, who is visiting him, came up to-day. The cousin is a gay, good looking young man. Mr. Hinkle[53] escorted two strange gentlemen to Mr. Rowe's and finding the widow gone followed her here. I knew Dr. Walsh as soon as he stepped inside the gate and pulled Mrs. Adams to the window to see "*our Dr.*" as we called him. We met him at Mrs. Maynards[54] on our way to Wharton last Summer, when he doctored Genie, who was sick. Leo. Mims, laughed at me for reading, when I knew he was trying to converse with me. But I did not feel called upon to entertain a stranger, when I prefered my paper. He is tall, awkward, fair skin, jet black hair, and not to my liking. Mr. Hinkle and B. Bridges stayed all night there not long ago, and he told them he was coming down to see me. So Mr. H. was so officious as to bring him over. The widower Mr. White accompanied him to look at Mrs. Adams.[ll] They all have been trying to plague me all day, and in fact I was confused a little at first, to find he was goose enough to come. But now I shall joke Mrs. A. when I see her about her strange beaux. Well the gents haven't had any conversation with us after their long ride; for Grandpa took them all out on the Gallery. We only saw them at table. They are verdant certain.—Mrs. Mims & I are going to start for Galveston Sat.

ll. Mrs. Adams was already twice a widow; see the note concerning her husbands in the entry for 4/09/1860.

[02/17/1860]

Friday. 17 Rode over to Mrs. Mims' yesterday evening, to arrange the particulars of our visit to the Island City.[55] She has concluded to go on the cars, and will not start till Monday. Caddie & babies were there. She was making herself a white Swiss with square-neck and closed sleeves. I objected to the cut of the sleeves, but she considers herself too old to make them open. The boys were trying a corn-planter. Charley dismounted on the road to gather some violets, the first of the season. Ma had a long letter from Calvin last night. He is sorry to say he spit in the face of a boy who called him a liar. Manly R. backed him. Was awakened this morning by Ma's mournful exclamation, "poor old Troup is dead." The children arose & hurriedly dressed, lamenting his sad end. In accordance with Calvin's request, they have placed him on a bier, and with Charley's assistance the little negroes have borne him to his last resting place, where they are busily engaged digging his grave. Missie accompanied the procession ringing a bell. And Ma in Grandpa's great-coat, as it is drizzling. I hear Grandpa pacing the Piazza,[mm] thinking doubtless of the loss of his faithful companion in many a hunt. Poor fellow, he was always loved & respected by all. Green be his memory.

Mrs. Jones sent me up a Southern College Magazine from Florence, Ala. where I was surprised to find M. T. W.'s old composition on Hungary, with her old fictitious name of "Lallah Rookh"[nn] dated from Retreat, Tex. So Mary is turning authoress. Success to her efforts. How forcibly did the sight of that old name bring back old-times! And Mary has forgotten me—no, such a being as she never forgets, there must be some other reason.

Grandma gave Mrs. Jones a brilliantine[oo] dress to-day, it is brown & yellow. I hear the report of a gun, fired in honor of the memory of poor old Troup I guess. How often has he sprang delighted at that sound which he is now deaf to, for the first time. No more will he chase the nimble deer, or scent his presence from afar. There goes another gun. And grandma's laugh in derision. Honor to whom it is due.

[02/18/1860]
Sat. 18 Slapped Missie for playing instead of dressing this morning. Am making her read the "Tempest" as a punishment. But in reality it is a pleasant task. Read all of Addison's books but one. Am delighted with his excellent sense and true piety. No wonder Mr. Clark recommended its perusal to youth. His views of life are in exact accordance with my own. His sound judgment is not controlled by imagination.—Have half doz. letters to answer but must defer it till my return. Charlie has gone to Columbia for his gun. Mr. P. McNeel[56] is going to give a large dancing party on the 29th. Must go to Mrs. Mims to-morrow, am sorry because it is the Sabbath. Wish I could keep it better. Sal

[02/27/1860]
Mon. 27. Went with Ma & Archie to Mrs. Mims' Sunday evening. Left for the depot before sunrise Monday,

---

mm. Porch or veranda

nn. From the poem by the same title. The phrase is Persian for "tulip-cheeked one."

oo. Glossy fabric of cotton and worsted or cotton and mohair

reached the Bridge before ten o'clock. The cars arrived about twelve. I could hardly realize, that this was my first sight of the "iron horse," because I have read and heard of the cars so often, that everything seemed natural. Stopped at the junction[57] to wait for the Harrisburgh train, in order to meet the steamboat. Here saw a forest of pine trees. Arrived in Harrisburgh a few minutes before the boat. Left our shawls in the station house to look at the boat and forgot them. Took tea on board the Diana, a splendid steamboat. Were at Galveston next morning before day. The wind was so high that it blew me a few steps down the street on leaving the hack at the Tremont Hotel. Mrs. Mims caught me or I don't know where I should have blown. It was laughable as well as ridiculous. Mr. Dargan called on us, and after dinner we went shopping in his store. Helped Mrs. Mims select some things. Bought a bonnet for myself of white braid & one for Ma & Grandma. Would have purchased more things needful but Grandpa was unwilling to trust me I suppose. Found Roseburgh's the cheapest establishment. Mr. Dargan was very polite, would have me go to the theatre one night to see the "Flying Dutchman"[pp] acted. The play scarcely realized my expectations. Don't care to go again. Had a long walk in search of Miss Lizzie Scott and too bad to find that we were deceived; she was not in town. Had my ambrotype taken, think it flattered some. Stayed in town two days and a half. Firemen paraded the streets and gave a ball at the Tremont on the 22d. Saw some of the ugliest dresses and ladies. Stood on the Porch with some of the Boarders and watched the dancing through a large window. An absurd sight. Left the "Island City" on the cars about one o'clock Thursday.[58] Reached Houston before night. Was taken in a splendid omnibus to such a poor looking hotel, was provoked to have to stay at this Fannin house at first, but soon learned it was as respectable as any other. Four young ladies belong to the house, very intelligent. Heard F. Rogers lives seven miles in the country. And that T. Fuller was not dead.[qq] R. Coffee & husband, were at the old Capitol but I didn't care to hunt them up. Took the cars for home at 7 o'clock. Mrs. A. Winston & children were aboard.[59] The cars continued through to Columbia, but the carriage came to Oyster Creek for us. Found Mrs. Durant at the bridge going to Galveston alone,

pp. English play (1826) by Edward Fitzball

qq. Sallie had recorded in the entry of 2/03/1860 that she heard of T. Fuller's death.

about her lawsuit. Surprised home folks by my unlooked for appearance Friday evening. Mr. A. Mims came over with me. Thus ends my first visit to Galveston. A letter from Jose[60] & Rachel awaiting me. R. confesses that her brother was my unknown correspondent. Thinks M. T. W.[61] will marry a Mr. Ashford. Sis Coleman[62] will soon be a bride. Saw Mary's aunt, Mrs. Terry, on the cars.

[02/28/1860]

Tues. 28. A cloudy, rainy day. Part of the cane field has been burnt off, exposing the black, rich soil instead of the golden brown carpeting it has presented so long. The carpenters are roofing the new shop before the door. Grandpa never dreams of sacrificing use for beauty. A great many sick negroes lately. Look pale myself, more so than usual, have a cold; expect to be a confirmed invalid before I am thirty. Such will be the consequence of my sedentary life, yet haven't the energy to change it.—Have a new "Peterson." Not particularly interesting. Wrote to Angie & Sister Mc.

[02/29/1860]

Wed. 29 Worked on Missie's embroidery nearly all the forenoon, have been reading Addison's last & sixth book, concerning his criticisms of the "Paradise Lost." His paper on wedlock coincides with my views on the subject. Pity he didn't take the advice he gave. Since he shortened his life by perpetrating matrimony, according to the accounts of his contemporaries.—Think, I have read some of that Mr. Ashford's letters to Mary T. called friendly, but only a pretense. He was in Tenn. and had long ceased the correspondence. No, I remember another correspondent, John Riley. Well, I can't distinguish names or facts now. She has neglected Rachel lately. I wonder if happiness renders everyone deaf to the claims of friendship. Must answer Puss. All, nearly all, have forgotten each other in one year—oh! human nature, how fallible & weak.———

[03/01/1860]

Thurs. March 1st. Have tried to finish Becca's[63] long-commenced letter to-day. And Cousin B. A. McNeill's. Poor Coz, what trouble she has in that Bro. Little Jim, as he is called, always bore a bad character. Enough to humble anyone's pride to have such kin.—Missie exhibiting her amiable temper about an obstinate sum and Charlie his love for teazing. Mrs. Jones, Ma & myself swung yesterday eve with the children, nearly blistered our hands. Such good exercise & how lazy we are! Walked down the road with Missie, found it mudie. A scold from Ma for damp feet. Negroes clearing a potato patch, below the Turnip fence. Dislike the idea of being surrounded by clearings.[rr] Want the woods near if I do rarely visit them. Read Dr. Gunn's praise of white mustard seed for a variety of diseases.[ss] Have tried it with little benefit heretofore. Think I will follow his directions awhile. Bitter made me sick the other night. Do wish my Mama had physiced me when it would have been of some use. Nobody thinks anything is the matter so long as you can eat your allowance and seem well. I am habitually constipated, always was, but I get worse all the time and don't know when it will stop. Am of little account now, what would I be as an invalid? Examined some definitions, like to hunt out derivatives of a word.

rr. Jordan was more interested in the productivity of cleared land and had increased his improved acreage from 350 to 600 acres from 1850 to 1860.

ss. John C. Gunn was the author of a popular home medical guide.[64]

[03/02/1860]
Fr. 2d. Wrote a rambling sort of letter to Puss Mc. Have several others to answer. Mail will come to-morrow, hope for something pleasant. Spring is here in the bursting leaves and flowering violets. Mr. Jones has gone again to see Dr. Brown about the money due him for three negroes. Tried to keep some oranges for Coz but couldn't. Heard Gerald W. was engaged to a very pretty girl, a Miss T. his mother opposed the match. Would like to hear from Mr. Thomas, who was very ill at last accounts.

[03/06/1860]
Tues. 6. Read Moor and sewed Sat. on Aunt Fannie's dress. Received a letter from Calvin with his ambrotype for Ma, great rejoicing over it. Got two magazines and Sunday Mrs. H. sent Harper's Weekly and some borrowed books with a note abusing me for staying so closely at home, and proposing that I should furnish a carriage and herself the horses for a visit to Mat.[tt] during the Episcopal convention to be held there next month. Mrs. B. and C. with J. Wal-

tt. Matagorda

derman[65] were there visiting her Tues. Would like to see Julia. Mr. W. Rowe came Sun. eve; gave us an account of the McNeel party. His father & mother and a great many old folks were in attendance at the dancing, in fact it was a regular ball. I think, that it is just as bad to dance as to go there to look on, but opinions differ. And I fear to give expression to mine lest I wound some one's feelings.—Such places and crowds, give me pain instead of pleasure. I like good company too, but solitude better I believe. But I wish I could live in a city awhile or see more of the world, than here. I am not learned, I feel keenly my deficiencies away from home, though here literary subjects are entirely put aside. I must keep all my thoughts to myself. This is one great reason, why I stay so much *a la maison*. I must have a strong incentive to overcome my natural indolence and want of energy. Most girls do not fancy a quiet, home-body like myself. Eh bien! The end is not yet of all this. I must only depend on myself for content, knowing that Earth affords no sure resting-place; soon we shall go hence, our places filled with a new generation, and our very names forgotten—such is outward life. I can never be miserable, if I do right; but I feel so sinful often. Looking back through the past year; have I progressed in the path of wisdom, is my heart any purer, have my duties been faithfully discharged? I fear that a truthful answer to these self-questionings will be expressed in the negative. And yet my chief aim is to be good as I should try to become. It appears to me, that I was better in almost every sense when I left school, than at present. Instead of advancing, growing worse, when will it stop? I long sometimes to become a thoughtless school-girl again, dreaming pleasantly of life's realities; though told & believing them delusive. "Distance lends enchantment to the view."[uu] and experience is a severe teacher, but youth (fools) will learn in no other.— But away with sad repinings. And take up the cross of life courageously, submissive to the will to Him, who doeth all things well.[vv]

[03/07/1860]
    Wed. 7. Grandpa & Mr. Evans started for Gal. by daylight; going in the carriage. Mr. Jones left Mond. Mrs.

uu. From "Pleasures of Hope" (1799), pt. 1, line 7, by Thomas Campbell, (1777–1844)

vv. Mark 7:37b KJV

J. had been crying and grieving ever since, as if she should never see him again. She would have gone with him if he had consented soon enough, taking Arthur herself. Says she cares more for him, than her child. Well! I cannot judge of her feelings never having experienced them, but I think I would not waste so much devotion. She dotes on his beauty. His features are regular but I cannot think him handsome. There is a nameless something, and I reckon that must appear in one, to strike me as noble; mere beauty of features I affect to despise, not because of envy either. I am an admirer of intellect & goodness. I trust no one of loose principles. I always endeavor to act aright, and will not be persuaded to evil. But I suppose it is very easy for me to follow the dictates of reason, who have so few temptations to commit wrong. I did not think it exactly right to attend the Theatre in Gal. I refused at first, but knew once would not hurt me, and that Mr. & Mrs. M. would be displeased at my persistence. I was in a manner obliged to go. If I had felt that it was positively wrong to be there, I should have resisted all persuasions, as I did about the ball. But I am afraid all this sounds like the "Pharisee's" boast.[ww] If I do not transgress all the commandments, it is because the fear of God helps me to resist. My heart is very sinful.—Have been trying to explain "the means of Grace" to C. & M. who are all interest. They cannot grasp all the ideas presented. I used to believe that morality was all that God required. Teach us Heavenly Father, the error of our ways!

ww. Luke 18:9–14 KJV

[03/08/1860]
Thur. 8. Breakfasted alone with Missie this morning, every one else having finished before we descended the stairs. This tardiness is quite common with us. Grandpa has got tired of noticing it. There ought to be a reform. Charlie has gone for Ma, who has spent the day with Archie at Mrs. Mims. Missie has been vomiting, looks pale, an enormous eater. Mrs. Jones is braiding a little pink gingham dress. I have just finished embroidering the pantalets laid off for Missie to work. Am re-reading Stephens travels in Greece & Russia. Poor fellow! His wanderings have terminated in death.—Wrote to Rachel Barry.

[03/09/1860]

Friday. Charlie in a fret about composition writing, Missie having finished hers. Her first attempt at storywriting; pretty good. Was sick last evening.

[03/14/1860]

Tue. 14. Did not attend church Sunday; felt unequal to the task of riding six miles horseback along a thorny road, in danger of being torn off. Am so weak and spiritless, as if under the enervating influence of Summer. Hardly know what is the matter, can't complain of being reall ill. Mr. & Mrs. Gibson & Mr. Bowie & J. Walderman passed going to church. Expected them to call on their return, but they did not, though Ma met them in the road. Mrs. Gibson wishes me to go down to Matagorda also Mrs. Harrison kindly proposes for me to accompany her. But I am indifferent as usual & Ma & all opposed to the plan, want me to teach the children. I don't think it strange at all.—Mr. W. Rowe brought his sister a letter & some things, from Mr. Jones, last evening. And Grandpa came with Mr. Nelson and another man; bringing our shawls, left at Harrisburg, sent by Mr. Dargan. Ma had three letters from Sister A. & one from Calvin Sat. Poor Acy Chandler is dead of Pneumonia. Mc sent Miss de Lassaulx's photograph, very like. Saw Emma's & Frank Rowe's too. Mr. Rowe handed me a minute of the convention held at Waco.[xx]

xx. Probably the Baptist State Convention held in Waco from October 22–26, 1859.

[03/16/1860]

Thurs. 16. Heavy showers of rain have deluged the parched earth all day. Much to farmer's delight, as it has been wanted long. Poor little colt, not a week old, took the brunt of the storm, but is now sheltered.

[03/21/1860]

Mond. 21. Mrs. Jones went home Sunday, when her Brother came for her. Arthur was sick Frid. She had letters from Mr. J. on the eve of starting for St. Louis. Mr. L. Winston[66] will give a party Thursday. Hear Mrs. B. Sweny has returned from Ten. There is to be a Quarterly meeting in Chance's Prairie[67] and Brazoria soon. Would like to go to one or both. Leo. Mims called Sat. on his way over Caney.[68] Calvin writes he hears A. Mims is here frequently, and Mc says __ Cleavland, told that it was reported by Calvin, that I would be married shortly. Pshaw! what do I care for such rumors? Somebody would care here, if I were coquetish at all. But, if I know my own heart, my *beau ideal* has never presented himself for my inspection. According to novelists opinions, I should have felt the grand passion long ago. And since I haven't the conclusion is, that I am, as I have always been called, a predestined celibate. *Eh bien!* I am free to act much as I like with my self. But when one marries, their identity is generally lost even. "Love, honor, serve, & obey" is the motto of life. I don't say that I would not marry for any consideration; but that I never will give myself to one, whom I cannot not Love as well as Respect. Imagination cannot conceive of a worse state, than a loveless marriage. A certain gentlemen advised me, that my sentiments in regard to this matter, would change in a few years. But they are reasonable and bid fair to last, since I am not at all anxious on the subject. I look forward to a lonely life with no apprehension, since if "*God*" wills it is all for the best. And if my earthly destiny is otherwise ordered I shall certainly know it, without troubling myself. I never claimed a sweetheart. It seems immodest to me, to do so even if I had any such desire. Marriage is far preferable in some respects, than a single life, though the risk is greater. It is a life-long mistake, as well as sin to marry one unsuited. I am higher, than I merit, but I will not lower my standard. And with the help of my Heavenly Father will endeavor not to render myself or another miserable, through ignorance.

[03/23/1860]
Wed. 23. No letters yesterday, but Peterson's magazine came. Mrs. Chinn,[69] Bowie and son passed on their way to Galv. Leo. Mims called going over to sit up with Mr. Harrison, who is ill. Grandpa with Archie went to see him to-day. Leo. accompanied Maj. B. and Miss W. to Mat. Monday. Commenced embroidering a pair of pantaletts, for Mollie, perhaps. Finished the "Spectator" yesterday. Semper eadem.[yy]

yy. May be translated as "forever the same."

[03/24/1860]
Thu. 24. All day have been stitching, and thinking over the same old thoughts. *Wished* here to call forth new reflec-

tions. Pen refuses to perform its usual office, worn out like myself. Perdon! perdon!

[03/28/1860]
Mond. 28.—Been embroidering for the past few days. Went a mile on the river road to meet the new carriage of Grandma's Saturday. It is a rock-a-way,[zz] not a fine finish. Grandpa says it is not the one he chose. Capt. Letts[70] is loading now. Walked the same way yesterday and found the knife Archie lost the other day. Ma, Mollie & Archie went to Mr. Rowe's yesterday to see Mrs. Jones who is sick. Mrs. H sent borrowed books home yesterday, says she is lonesome, begging books.

[03/29/1860]
Tues. 29. Leo. Mims came this morning from Mr. Sweeney's.[71] I did not know he was here till near dinner time. He staid all the evening. It seems to do me some good to have him or most anybody to talk to, once in a while. W. Rowe is so quiet, I can't be at my ease with him. Leo. says he saw Miss B. Sweeney & several other young ladies at the Quarterly meeting. Miss Bettie manoeuvered so as to get him to bet a diamond ring, that she would not be married in two years. Matrimony was the principal topic of conversation as usual. Though I don't think he had anything new on the subject. Advises me to quit teaching and go about more offering to escort me. I returned my acknowledgements for the intended kindness, but declined troubling him, he persisting that it would be a pleasure. Says I will never get married if I don't throw out some hints, that I am willing to take a husband. I reply, that I am indifferent altogether, & am content to be an old maid, and wish I could get a dog for a pet. He returned that I would certainly be thought one, if I peted cats and dogs, but said he could get me a dog. Wanted me to go with him to Mr. W's party if invited. Tell him I am opposed to dancing on account of the motives, that impel one to get them up or attend them. Remarks with evident pleasure that Sister A. will frequent such assemblies on her return, and will consider herself marriageable. He thought Miss Emma would marry if she could. I imagine that Miss S. will not suit me from his remarks concerning her. Would

zz. A light, four-wheeled carriage with open sides, named for Rockaway, N.J.

like to see her however. Wrote to Calvin yesterday asking the name of his informant in regard to my intentions concerning matrimony? Mr. Burleson sent me his complements & an invitation to the Ex. Grandpa not well this evening, laughed some at Leo. After he had gone, when Ma shewed some calculations in regard to money matters, said that he was not going to break if we didn't do it. Ma replied we won't, & I was silent for he is not reasonable on the subject, Said jestingly he wished I would marry & leave. Don't though only when angry. Long for something better than the Present or Future promises. Contentment.

[03/30/1860]
Wed. Worked all the morning and re-read part of Stephen's travels on the Nile. Offered Grandpa, Alexander's "Religious Experiences" Sunday. He asked last night if I had read it, & pronounced it a splendid work, though he thinks some of the accounts of the feelings of others are heightened by imagination. Says the experience contained in the 9th chapter accords with his own. Julius came to-day for the letters brought by the mail carrier. Mrs. Adams asked the loan of our magazines. I like to get any reading matter so well myself, that I do not hesitate to oblige others, when possible. I think it is somewhat hard, that I cannot have many books or society either. Grandpa says I may have all I need, but he has no idea of allowing that I do *need* many. Sometimes I know I too easily submit to deprivations & Ma always. But anything for Peace. And he is sure to get angry and say hard things. I don't like to disturb & irritate his feelings, when he is so old, I reasoned with him once and we were both so excited I am afraid I wasn't as respectful as I should have been. I never intend to contend about extravagance with him again, though I cannot altogether abide by his decisions. I am no longer a child to be governed by his rigid and old fashioned notions and he cannot expect me to be as compliant as Ma is.

[04/02/1860]
Mon. April 2d. Went to the Quarterly-meeting in Brazoria Sat., made a few purchases. Grandma dined with Mrs. McKinney,[72] & I at Mrs. McMaster's.[73] Was introduced to

8. Levi Jordan. Courtesy Dorothy Cotton family collection.

Miss Addie Watts. Found Mrs. Mc, Miss Fuller & Purcell very pleasant. Miss Purcell intends returning permanently to Europe in a few weeks. On Sunday Ma & I attended Church. Mr. Mc would have us stop. He seemed to think so much of my Pa years ago. Called on Mrs. Banton[74] returning home, found Mrs. L Mims, the children & Leo. there. They were at church & Mrs. M though sitting opposite, did not recognize either of us, very amusing as well as strange. We had silk veils over our faces, was the reason I presume. Mr. W. Spencer[75] again spoke of sending me that beaux, offered to bet, that I would like him. Wouldn't give his name. Had a letter from Richmond Sat. signed Jas. Walsh. He begged an answer by return mail, but I am not going to hurry. Ma gave me his letter with a meaning smile, remarking that Grand Pa had been "examining it suspiciously." And you also, I was ready to reply. I took it very coolly, and after laying aside my wrappings stood at the window and read it once composedly. Then placing it in my trunk descended to Grandma's room, where I was plied with questions, but made no confessions. Have only thought of it twice or thrice since. The Dr. "entreats me to accept and give a partial & due consideration to the few lines, which he has taken liberty to send me.—

"Such a cold method of addressing you as letter writing, I would in no wise resort to, had circumstances given me an opportunity of verbally addressing you. I am unfortunately yet, so much of a stranger to you, that I feel restricted in expressing my sentiments concerning you lest you might condemn me as a sycophant; suffice it to say that I could almost adore you; but your piety, your disposition, your congeniality, in a word, your loveliness makes you to me an object of the greatest consideration.—Esteeming you as I do, will you, Miss Sarah, confer on me the favor of corresponding to you.—Whether or not please let me know by return of mail.—I took the liberty of calling at your home, & as I afterwards heard, that it was believed by some persons in your neighborhood *expressly* on you. I take the opportunity to say they are mistaken. It is very true I would be more than happy to see you at any time, but believe me, if my call had been expressly on you it would have been by your permission, for I would have asked you for the privilege.

"Before closing, let me again entreat you, by the ardor & sincerity with which I admire you & which encourages me to manifest my feelings, to give my request due consideration. Could you, but for a moment, imagine the exaltation of spirit & Mind and the exquisite pleasure it would afford me to get an affirmative answer to my request, I believe you would readily comply to it. I shall await your answer, Miss

Sarah with anxiety, believing it will make me either very happy or exceedingly miserable.

"I have the honor to remain your humble servant & sincere admirer,"

. . . .

Have taken the trouble to copy this flattery! I believe him to be honest in his feelings, but romantic and *very* susceptible as one could infer from his extravagant ideas of my *loveliness*. I could almost believe he is ridiculing me. No one ever paid me such compliments before! I cannot conceive how he learned so much of my character in a half-hours conversation. I am not the one to fall in love at first sight. But nonsense! The affair isn't worth talking about. It seems my fate, to be admired by those whom I treat with cold indifference & as strangers.

[04/03/1860]

Tuesd. 3d. Grandpa brought me a letter from P. McKellar to-day. She complains of receiving love-letters from ignoramuses and asks if she must answer them. I hold that all gentlemen are entitled to a reply. S. Kavanaugh[76] has a little daughter. S. Huckleby[77] tells her P. Harris[78] is betrothed to Liz Eddins.[79] I am glad of it. He is one of my quondam admirers & there is a prospect of being rid of his attentions. I respect him very much but have a feeling amounting to disgust when thinking of myself in regard to him.—Finished Mollie's pantaletts. Wrote to Sister A. in answer to hers of Sat. Said she thought the news of my marrying to "good to be true." I told her in response she would be glad to have me at home, commonplace as I am. She need not fear me as a *rival* we were "too different for that." Poor Angie[80] has gone home a confirmed invalid. Jose, E. Rowe[81] & Florence D.[82] were intending to join the church.

[04/05/1860]

Thu. 5th. Exceedingly warm to-day & yesterday. All of us proceeded down the new-road to burn the brush-piles on each side of the road, last evening; Grandma saying, to "prevent their harboring snakes." Got a burnt dress & bonnet for my pains. The corn is being re-plowed. Charlie stamping and abusing Davies' sums. Expect to go with Grandma, down to Mr. Rainey's to-morrow, accompanied by Uncle Ambrose & Bettie. Have answered the Dr.'s letter, declining the intended (offer) honor of his correspondence.

[04/09/1860]
April 9. Returned from the Prairie to Mr. Rowes Saturday. Called a few minutes on Miss N. R. Cousins were very glad to see us, and Phebe's eyes sparkled with delight, while Jimmie looked on in wonder. The baby is called Emily, in honor of Ma. Went to church Sunday, very few out. Mrs. Adams[83] has put up her tombstones over her two husbands. Mr. A.[84] has inscribed a sentence of the Sacred Book, "He sleeps in Jesus"[aaa] while Mr. B.'s[85] is "To live is Christ, to die is gain."[bbb]

aaa. I Thessalonians 4:14 KJV

bbb. Phillipians 1:21 KJV

[04/10/1860]
Apr. 10. A letter from Mc, saying Calvin has been ill.[86] Dr. Rowe pronounced the attack Pneumonia. Poor little boy it is bad to be sick, absent from home. He had every attention of course. Davie & the Mr. Rowes[87] stayed with him. And Mc & Miss Mary[88] went to see him. She says he is up now. And that Mrs. Smith told her "old Rowe" could talk about nobody but Sis. Remarks that she hates him. Went to a concert lately. They are going to have a grand May-party, says she don't care about it, because it will be troublesome. Complains of being fleshy, and wants to see us all. Tell's Ma to make me write her a composition.—Mr. C. Bell[89] called to-day with a paper for signers and subscriptions to raise $6,000 to get four lawyers to abolish the Railroad-tax. Grandpa subscribed $200 but authorized Mr. B to add more if necessary. Ma is looking so poor and sallow, complains but little as usual.

[04/16/1860]
Mond. 16. Last week spent as its predecessors. Work and read little. Want something new, but I suppose I can reread my old books, it will not do to get in the habit of complaining & become discontented. The children are trying lately. And I sometimes feel altogether out of sorts. Well life consists of many things, and I would not mind unpleasant feelings sometimes, if I did not think they forebode indis-

position. Any condition is almost preferable to ill-health.—
Mrs. H. came over Sunday, looks ill. Mr. & Mrs. Jones
are here preparing to visit Miss. in a week. He came last
Wed.—Calvin writes he has recovered from his late attack of
Pneumonia.

[04/20/1860]
Frid. 20. All of us have been helping Mrs. J. sew. I
tried-on her traveling gingham, it is too large for me and
shorter, than on her. Capt. Letts is here, bringing Sister's Piano.[90] And Mr. Suttles, the state engineer, endeavoring to sell
Grandpa the low tract of land lying between us, & the river.
He asks $5 which G. will not give. Two new colts have lately
appeared. Want to give them pretty names. We ridicule Bob's
because it has a white face. Both are bays. The carpenters are
putting-up a carriage-house opposite the dwelling. I objected
to the situation, but of course convenience must decide the
question here.—A long letter from Sister A. Mr. W. R.[91]
called Tues. bringing our mail-matter. Have a new Peterson.

[04/23/1860]
Mond. 23. Finished a letter to Puss commenced Friday.
Stopped to see the Piano. It is of Rosewood, handsome,
Chicerings[ccc] make, three of the keys are out of tune. Mr.
J, Grandma & myself went fishing Sat. eve leaving Archie
screaming to go. The boys came towards night and leaving
the flat I went with them in the skiff, farther down the river,
but failed to catch anything except two crabs. Two men were
fishing also, caught one red-fish and croaker.—Yesterday was
a rainy day, preventing Mrs. J. from visiting home. A negro
passed going for Dr. Chinn[92] for Mr. W. Rowe. She[93] has
gone to-day leaving Arthur.

[05/02/1860]
May 2d. Wed. I suppose Mrs. J. has reached her des-
tination ere this. Her father's family are recovering. Rode
over to see Mrs. H. Mond. eve, she has been quite ill for a
week. Miss Hawkins[94] was at Mrs. Bowie's,[95] she & Miss
Duncan[96] are on the eve of departure for the North. Mr. B's
sons go along to N. C. to College. Wish I could travel, but
haven't any one to go with me, even if I could gain the con-

ccc. Pianos made by Chickering & Sons of Boston were widely known as quality instruments and were advertised for sale in the *Galveston News* in 1860.

sent of all. Ma needs change very much. But no-one realizes the necessity, much as her recovery is desired. We sent for Dr. Fitchs Six Lectures on Consumption;[97] much of it, or all is new to me.—Miss M. wants me to come up a week before Commencement, but I can't. Poor Grandma Fitzgerald[98] is dead! Ange better.

[05/07/1860]

Mond. As we were all gathered in the piazza yester-eve, talking & reading and eating walnuts, a horse, or rather mulemare appeared trotting up to the gate and threw himself from the saddle familiarly. Bob advanced to the gate & I disappeared in the Parlor to peep at the new-comer from behind the curtains. He greeted Bob cordially, and as he turned his face towards us a moment I thought it must be Gerald W.[99] but noticing his slight form I knew this was a wrong guess. He approached with his hat over his face, but before he reached the steps we were all exclaiming "Manly Rowe" My first question was an eager inquiry for the health of all, thinking he was the bearer of bad tidings. It soon came out that he grew too anxious to stay, hearing of his Brothers' & Mother's illness and not receiving letters. Calvin writes for my ambrotype.—Mr. Weekly has lost four negroes, two of his most valuable hands. I am sorry for their misfortunes.— Sat. Grandma would have me go with her, to see Mrs. Bowie & Chinn, though Mr. Billie R.[100] was here, looking very badly from his recent illness. I suppose I ought not to have left him here, but our arrangements were made & I did not see him next morning: he & Charlie were hunting. I ran in a few minutes to leave some pickles & magazines for Mrs. H. Found her worse, Mr. H. was keeping off the flies; she talked very weak. Had a very pleasant visit. Mrs. B. was alone; she showed Grandma her sewing-machine, a nice piece of furniture, useful as well as ornamental. She talked so pathetically of the death of her little Anna, who was burned about Christmas. Insisted on Sister & myself coming to stay awhile with her in Mata.[ddd] also Mrs. Chinn, the Dr. volunteering to come up for me. Of course I wouldn't allow him to be at that trouble. Mrs. C. is very lively, played several pieces for us. "Gentle Annie,"[eee] and the Dr's favorite, "Sweet were my dreams of thee."[fff] Says they are coming over, now we have

ddd. Matagorda

eee. By Stephen Foster (1826–64), first published in 1856

fff. Published in 1847 by lyricist L. H. Naghel and composer Charles Goff

returned their many visits. Mrs. C. insisted on my taking the works of the talented but fragile "Mis Davidsons."[101] What sweet characters those sisters were, and how spontaneously their thoughts flowed into rhyme. I was surprised at Margaret's criticism on Mrs. Herman's works. It coincides with my opinion, suggested to me by the universal one perhaps.— Rach keeps a long silence. Wrote out Ma's case & sent it to Dr. Fitch V. Z. for consultation. She objected, but I was determined to try his profession.

[05/10/1860]

Thurs. Had no breakfast to-day and consequently feel wrong; am trying to starve in order to cure myself, small prospect of success. Made me a new calico. Children vexatious, worse than usual. Grandparents gone to see Mr. and Mrs. H. Mr. Millican[102] came to breakfast. Did not go down.

[05/14/1860]

Mond. 14. Sick folks within, bright sunshine without! Charlie complained of sore throat Thurs. eve when Manly & brother were here, he on his return to In.[ggg] Next day he had fever, and it still continues. Ma thinks he has the gastric fever. Dr. S. will be here soon. He talked strangely in his sleep last night. Ma would sit up. I remained awake and up two or three hours and have taken a nap since breakfast, my head feeling giddy in consequence. I burnt Charlie trying to cup him. Missie has a sick stomach this morning. I & the little girls went to church yesterday. The text was "Behold the Lamb of God, which taketh away the sin of the world."[hhh] Mrs. Norris[103] was out, for the first time in years; she didn't recognize me. Mr. Rathburn[104] says he overhead Dr. Cochran[105] ask B. Churchill, "what young lady was that in green, looking so sanctified?" and the reply was, "That's Miss Mc." Mr. Rowe gave me a letter, he received from Calvin. Ma has one of the same date.

[05/17/1860]

Thurs. 17. Charlie convalescent. Ma has a boil & stye, the effect of both making her feverish. Grandma is at Mrs. M's to see Sallie, who is very ill. A letter from Annie Mc, a long one, talking of the approaching Ex.[iii] I ought to answer

ggg. Independence, where he was a student at Baylor

hhh. John 1:29 KJV

iii. Examination

some letters and receive others. No news of Uncle Archie yet. Hope he is well.—Mr. H. called to-day. Mrs. H is not improving, is notwithstanding anxious to remove to Mat., he has bought a place there. Mrs. & Miss Gibson called late Tues. eve, all alone. Played a little for us. Not pretty I think, though some *do*. Mrs. G. seems to be a good, kind woman. Both insisted on us visiting them in Town; but Grandpa said "that's out of the question." Mary & Brother went by this morning some where. I am writing with a quill, Grandpa made for Mollie. I like them much better than steel ones, though the mark is too heavy. Tried to make some linen collars. Have a new Peterson. "Arnold's" Plot thickens. The "Burnhams" have ended in a marriage as usual.—Mr. R. caught a Mexican lurking about the premises last night, on returning from a fire-hunt.[jjj] Called Grandpa out & scared the fellow considerably. He acknowledging he came to trade with Negroes.[kkk]

[05/21/1860]

Mond. 21st. Little S. Mims[106] died Thurs. Her parents did not think her very ill, till too late for the Dr. to relieve. Grandma, children & I went to the River to the Burial. Poor Parents we pity them! Sallie was the smartest & one of the best of their children. A companion and help to her mother!—On returning from this solemn scene Bob handed me a letter—long expected from Rachel. The Dr. & Mr. R. were here, so I did not attempt to read it, till the gents had retired from the table. Then I broke the seal, little expecting its unwelcome contents. It was a fitting time to receive her sad & saddening letter! I sympathised with her for the sad loss of her only Parent; but I half forgot my pity, when she told me this was an invitation to her wedding. Yes, she wrote very quietly, almost sadly about this change. And the time is so soon, the announcement came like a shock.

"I see you open your eyes in astonishment, but nevertheless if nothing prevents the 5th of June will find me a married lady; And who is Rache going to marry? Not Wes as you may suppose: but Mr. Charles Stewart. You never heard his name before did you? I know you thought that I would marry Wes, but my love for Wes, was a child's love, this is different. Mr. S. is a lawyer, about 6 ft 6 inch high,

jjj. A hunt where the participants use torches or fire to shine the eyes of animals in order to spot and shoot them in the dark.

kkk. Unauthorized trading with slaves was a criminal offense in Texas (Campbell, *Empire for Slavery,* 102).

fair skin, light hair, & rather (of) a commanding appearance. How do you like him? Of course I think, that he is all that is noble & good. He is 24 years old & I am the first lady he ever visited or shewed any attention whatever, indeed, he has almost gained for himself, the reputation of a woman-hater. He is very grim-looking, distant & modest. Isn't it strange that I should be the first to attract the attention of such a man when there are so many pretty nice young ladies to be found? I see nothing attractive in me. It seems so strange to me Sallie that I am almost afraid something will happen yet to prevent it. Sallie I want you to come if possible. You are the only one of my schoolmates, that I have mentioned it to, & the only one I intend to. I don't want you to say anything about it except to your Mother until it is all over with, then you can tell every body you knew it before. I shall look for you Sallie & if you can't possibly come please write as soon as you receive this. We speak now of going to Galveston to see his parents immediately afterwards. This is all Sallie, that I have to write. Be sure to direct your letter to Rachel Barry, for something may interpose.

—I answered her, considering it almost a final farewell. I always thought she would marry early, but hope she is suitably matched. "Farewell & if forever still forever fare thee well"!lll

lll. "Fare Thee Well" (1816) by George Noel Gordon, Lord Byron (1788–1824)

[05/28/1860]

Mond 28th. Went to see Mrs. H. Friday-eve. Found her little better. To-day she starts for Mata.—Charlie was a little sick again Sat.—Mr. R. came up then, and went bee-taking with Bob at night. Leo. M. came Sund, though he knew I could not go to Chancey's Prairie to church (on account of obstructions in the road) as I wished. A. M. called in the evening.—The schooner is taking the last produce.

[05/31/1860]

Frid. The last day of pleasant May, is going out steadily; bearing on its floating hours our moments of idleness and of work. As for mine, I am dissatisfied with them as usual. Have been sewing considerably lately, getting ready for our In. trip. Grandpa says we had better take the cars and I am pleased with this arrangement. He does not oppose my going at all. Says jestingly, I don't intend to return & he'll be glad to be rid of me." Ma's very unwell, and frets and troubles about the children's learning. Have reached the limits of my disorderly book—suddenly, a type of life often

[no date] Five months since I first attempted to tell a few of my thoughts and actions to the silent pages of this—my irregularly kept book. Minutes, hours, days, and weeks of the various months will return no more. 'Tis saddening to think of my Past, very often. And have none, no bright hopes for the future. Few of the so called pleasures of the world delight me! I do not anticipate much from my long expected visit to my auld Alma Mater. Oh! that I knew myself, that I could do & feel just right always. I feel that I could do better in different circumstances. What is wanting? Alas! I do not know—all vain.

Sallie concludes the second portion of her diary and begins the third segment about the end of May. She seems a bit confused about the dates, as she mentions the last day of May, but records the weekday as Friday, which would have been June 1. This third section is the only one with a heading, written in the top margin.

[This] book intended for a Diary, but will not deserve the appellation

[5/31/1860]

May 31st, 1860. This, the last, last day of May commence recording here a few thoughts, and fewer transactions of my imperfect Life. I never had a confidant; never told my inmost thoughts & feelings to anyone. They have never found utterance—perhaps, are not worth it, and even if I could find words, would shrink from writing them here. It matters little however. I am only "Sis" at home, "Miss Sarah" around the neighborhood and "Sallie" at Independence. Am not remarkable for anything, least of all for personal beauty. Have what is called a good education; possessed of no accomplishments. And am generally considered a plain, matter-of-fact young lady, already looked for an old maid; that despised title, to so many. It is well this lot in Life does not disturb my equanimity. I am hard to please, almost exacting in my estimate of the qualifications of a *husband*: so never expect to find my ideal. I believe I am different in some things from most girls. Few were brought up as I have been, but each have an individuality of their own. But, here I remember with all my self-examinations I do not know myself. The heart is deceitful—very. I must look to a higher Power to guide my weak steps aright. May I always possess the consciousness of having discharged my duty, then I need not fear the consequences of an act of mine!

[6/5/1860]

June 5, 1860. To-day is Rachael's wedding. How I wish to be there for the next few hours. If I only could just see her & her strange lover![107] Sober reason convinces me, that wild wishes are vain. Probably we'll never meet again on the shores of this Earth. I had hoped to see her at the Examination soon; but this unpleasant marriage has broken up, suddenly, all my arrangements. Some of "our class" will be there, I do not expect all or half of the "fourteen." Few are dear to my heart and memory as Rach, the bright & endlessly merry one, who with myself & "Becca"[108] guessed through "Cicero": She who of all the "girls" came most often to "our room." May the best *quid* of life be ever yours Rachael, friend of "*auld* lang syne!"—And there is another still, to whom memory clings. Though months—a year, has intervened since last she wrote. I suppose it is folly to think of those, who by their silence ignore my existence even. Yet I cannot forget. The Past will recur. *Eh bien!* It cannot harm me.—Mrs. S. Mims came yesterday. She is glad of the arrangements for returning on the cars from Independence. Mr. Rowe was here Sat. just returned from a Beach-party. We are going to get up one, on the return of the long absent, possibly. This week our Quarterly meeting.—I am so tired [of] doing nothing, I am almost sick or will be, I anticipate—only the unenvied life of a confirmed invalid. A just reward for laziness. Sewing much tires me, and it is too hot, to write here, worse out-doors, and then the dust's a foot thick, enough to suffocate one. My pen scratches—adios.

[6/14/1860]

Thurs. 14. One week hence, we (viz., Mr. W. Rowe, Leo Mims, Rivers Erwin, W. Taylor perhaps, Mrs. Adams, Ma & myself), a goodly company, set out for the classic seat of

Baylor University. Preparations are being completed. But Ma
has many misgivings. Archie has been drooping for several
weeks & she would not for any consideration leave him
unwell. Charlie too is not perfectly well. While she, herself
is really worse than either; with a complexion sallow, almost
green. Grandparent imagines the trip will benefit her. She
will undoubtedly enjoy the novelty if well. Have a short
letter from Miss Mary,[109] begging earnestly, for me to come
at least a week, before the Ex. or stay after it awhile: promising to find me an escort home. It is strange, She takes so
much interest in such a poor body as I! I would like nothing
better, than to have her come home with us, could I hope
to make the stay a pleasant one, but home is isolated. We
have had a two-days-meeting, though the presiding elder
did not appear, will be here next month. Mrs. Buckingham,
the preacher's wife came over. I asked her to visit us, as did
Mrs. Winston afterward, when she decided to accompany
Mrs. W without the slightest apology or excuse to me. I am
not over sensitive or touchy, yet I couldn't help thinking her
manner cool and strange. I am not the head of the house, of
course, still I was the only one acquainted and my invitation
at least deserved some notice. I presented Ma Sund. She said
to her, she would call some time.—Miss M. Gibson was
there Sund. I did not recognize her till we were leaving, and
then she was in a conser with the Bates.[110] She bowed as I
entered the carriage, catching my gaze. E. Norris[111] came,
dressed in a *floral* organdie & Miss M. Bennett[112] spoke to
me for the first time in several years; she rarely attends. Mr.
Rainey came here from church with Mr. R. going to B.[mmm]   mmm. Brazoria
on the next morn. Cousin wasn't very well. She expects to
be here on our return.—Mr. Shepherd is here, looking more
like an invalid than ever, leaning on a staff; going away for
the Summer.—Drouth prevails all about, never so dry at
this time of the year before in old folks experience. Cistern
almost empty. The yellow tasseled corn still looks fresh &
verdant. Farmers anticipate short crops. "Sallie don't sit up so
late" comes Ma's warning & I obey. Vale!

[6/20/1860]
    Wed. 20th. To-morrow is the appointed day. Yesterday
both Ma & I were so worried about our work. We put off

the evil-day as long as possible & consequently are hurried. I sewed and ripped my beige-sleeves nearly all day, without success. Ma tried to help, but she has less patience than I. And then my indifference provokes her. She told Grandpa my answer to every inquiry as how I would have the work cut, was "I don't know." Truly I know little about such things and don't want to know, for then I should have to do it. Finally, I threw down the sleeves in disgust if not despair and betook myself to the cushions and magazine. Miss V. Townsend's good advice soon restored my lost equanimity. Ma declaring, I was just like Pa: I would prefer being like him, to all or any others; she ought to be aware of this fact. Grandpa tells me, to invite Miss Mary home, he "would like to have her come."—E. Norris, her mother & brother came Mond. bringing some dresses for us to take Mary Reese.[113] Emma is a real nice girl; performs creditably on the piano, has only had lessons two months. Loaned her the "Vicar of Wakefield and Rasselas:"[nnn] she promising me one of Scott's novels. Must return her visit on my return. Says she endures her lonely life, living only in hopes of a better one. To-morrow we leave before this hour. May "joy go with us & peace behind us!" Vale. Sallie McNeill

nnn. *The History of Rasselas, Prince of Abissina* (1759), a novella by Samuel Johnson (1709–84)

[7/2/1860]

July Mond. 2d. "Home again, from a foreign shore."[ooo] One week has sped rapidly away, a very pleasant one too to me, though I have been and am still anxious for Ma's health. But to begin at the begining, though I can't remember much less [tell] of the events, and sayings & feelings of the past few days of our visit to Baylor.—We reached Columbia in good time for the cars, meeting Leo M. there. Had lunch with us, and procured a bath for our dusty faces as well as coffee & ice-water at the eating-house. How unpleasantly dusty traveling in carriages, just now! I have almost ruined my new "Sabbath bonnet" (as B. Carter called it) not wishing to be troubled with a box. It was Ma's and Leo's first trip on the cars and we all enjoyed it; but M soon became sea-sick. Ice cream & water helped her some. We reached Houston in time to shop, getting Calvin's suit. Stopped at the "Old Capitol." Embarked next morning in a crowded car, the greater portion bound for Independence. Fearing but we should not

ooo. From the song "Home Again" (1850).

succeed in getting seats in the stage from Navasota, we reluctantly concluded to go as far as Brazos-city, there taking stage for Brenham. This stage was also crowded and together with the dust, heat, and heavy roads, Ma was almost overcome. A half hours stay for dinner at Chappell Hill refreshed us considerably. We were obliged to remain in B. till eleven o'clock; then B. Carter[114] joined us from LaGrange. She appeared delighted to see me. Kept the whole stage awake, with her rattle-brained talk. About four o'clock approached our old Alma Mater, recognizing the buildings in the faint moonlight with unbounded delight. Sprang hurriedly out at the gate and hastened to the door of the old boarding house, and knocked for admittance. Ginnie Barnes knowing my voice opened quickly. I soon found my way in the dark to Annie's room. All had just returned from the party & were sound asleep. On awakening them M. Reese & Jose both called my name and then such a confusion in the dark. Mrs. Fitz[115] sent up candles soon. But we could not quiet down. Ma fell asleep through weariness. Before breakfast Miss Hattie[116] came up to see us & Mamie ran almost breathless, crying to see me, also Florence. I proceeded up to Mr. Clarks after breakfast, greeted rapturously by all. My reception should flatter my vanity if anything would. None were received with so much gladness. Miss Mary took entire possession of me letting me go out to dinner and tea a few times, though she grumbled at the necessity and brought me back every night. We had one good long talk Sat. while she was putting the Reading-room in order & I assisting a little.

[7/12/1860]

Thurs. 12th. It has taken me so long to quiet down & become rested, since my unwonted journey, that I have neglected to write. I can't possibly give the details of my visit. I never witnessed an examination conducted so well.[117] I seemed carried back through two years, to my own classes & exercises. I wanted to stay longer, oh! so much Miss M.[118] urged & others, even Mr. C.[119] said he would find me an escort if I would consent to remain. But Ma would not consent & I was not willing to leave her in such poor health. They tried to exact a promise that I would return with Brother & remain till after the Convention. Alas! I am not free and do all I can, find it impossible to please all. Here I must stay; but I will not allow myself a repining thought. I can be content thank Heaven!—Cousin spent a week with us. C., A. & myself took them home, remaining two days. Visited the Beach for a few hours, delighted with the unusual prospect; gathered shells at the risk of burning our complexions. It is such a pleasant place. The cool breeze is exhilarating. Mr. Rainey lives five miles only, across an open Prairie.[120] Calvin called on Hi, who was delighted to meet him. He sent Charlie the "Scalp-hunter," which he is now reading industriously. I read it last night, while Ma scolded & threatened desiring me to go to bed. I as usual not listening or heeding until the end of the Chapter was reached. I suppose I was & am "disobedient," not regarding her wishes; though I like & generally do as I please about reading. Seeing & knowing this, it appears right to me that she should not insist on my obedience. I rarely think of the act as disobedient, though it is really. Ah bien! I am not & never will be faultless here! I am afraid I don't try hard to correct this one.—Jose, Cadie & Sam came home with us from Church Sund. All our late representatives were there, greeting each other joyously. I think their conduct, slightly astonished the "natives." Leo M.[121] & F. Rowe[122] & Calvin did not reach Navasota on our return in time to take the cars with us, being behind with the baggage. This delay was a great disappointment to us as well as them. We came down Sat. while they were obliged to remain in Houston Sund., reaching here Mond. Still we had a merry party, with the Richmond and Sandy-Point students. Rivers Erwin, the two Mr. McNeels & Mr. Herndon contributed not a little to our party. Mr. E. says, "he had a glorious time." The trip will long be remembered.—

[7/22/1860]

22d. Tues.[ppp]—Lazy am I not! But I haven't been able to fall back in my old routine. We have had company. Mollie R. and Emma N. came up, when we persuaded M. to stay the next day, as we were expecting the Rowes, who came to see Jose & from thence here with Davie. We begged to have them remain over night, when we had quite a concert. Mr. Chase[123] performing on the Piano and Mr. Clevland on the

ppp. July 22, 1860, fell on Sunday, not Tuesday, but the date is very clearly written as "22d. Tues."

Flute. Dr. Rowe was here also. D. *almost* disgraced himself with his noise & pranks; fussed with M. Reese, even pulled each others hair, till Mr. Chase interfered. Next day went home with Mollie taking Dave & Oscar C. along. M. devoted herself exclusively to the entertainment of O. C. How she can & does flirt! The boys have been here several days hunting; went up to Old Ocean on a camp-hunt.—Last-eve Mr. Holmes, a music-teacher from Columbia stopped; seemed delighted with Mr. C's musical performances. He sings well, but does not excel in execution. We remained up till twelve o'clock, when V. Rowe would go home. Tomorrow we are to visit Mr. Rowe's Place: expect Jose here tonight. Charlie must go for Mollie,—Had a long letter from Puss McKellar, rather a foolish one talking principally about her beaux and dresses. Eh bien! I want news of Rach.— O. Chase praises Calvin much.

[7/31/1860]
Tues. 31st. How the days, uncomfortable as they are, disappear! And how little good I accomplish. I almost feel with Oscar, that "there is more evil than good in the world." I begged him on parting not to put me on the worst side. We and Jose met Mollie and nearly all of our Independence party (Mr. Herndon included) at Mr. Rowe's; remaining over night. I had several pleasant *talks*. When Mr. C. delivered the above opinion, I was in much too good a humor, to agree with him then. But now—(Alas for poor mortals!) I am dissatisfied, sad at heart; and the cause I scarcely know. Only last night, I lay looking out of my window so quietly contented, watching the peaceful moonlight shadowing field & fence; thinking its subdued silvery light was a type of rest, and should be of our lives; if it only could be possible! We are changeful. Life is composed of alternate Storm & sunshine, of light and shadow. And happy are those who can through all its vicissitudes, possess their souls in peace.— Yesterday the children vexed me beyond measure. Punishment produced no effect. I almost despair of doing any good. "I look before and after, and pine for what is not."[qqq] Mr. O.C. accuses me of being suspicious & severe. Says "I jump to conclusions, etc.," I suppose to pay me for detecting him in acting out a story, when he pretended he killed

qqq. From "To a Skylark" by Percy Bysshe Shelley (1812)

rrr. From "To a Louse" by Robert Burns (1786)

the deer. 'If we could only see ourselves, as others see us.'rrr I wish I knew myself. I've been charged with inconsistency. In conversation, when animated I forget and say foolish things no doubt; it is so seldom I can have company. If this is so it is well I'm secluded.

[8/3/1860]
Frid. 3d. Aug. A few more weeks and Brother Calvin, must again leave us to repair to the classic-halls of Baylor University. Sad as this parting is, it must be endured. If he will only do himself justice, we will fear no danger. Rode out this morning; old Doc trotted so rough Archie cried to be taken onto Bill. Called on Mrs. M. last eve with Calvin.—Grandpa sadly out of humor.—

[8/10/1860]
Frid. 10th. Fine rains this week, almost too late to benefit the crops much. Mond. was election-day; the time appointed for a general rising of Negroes against the Whites. Urged on by Abolitionists they burnt towns & houses in the northern portion of the State.sss Patrols & vigilance committees are being appointed. There is little danger apprehended.—Made myself a dress, nothing else lately. 'Lie on the bed all day Ma says'; but I haven't anything to do in reality. Nobody writes me now-a-days. The children are incorrigible. Subdued Missie yesterday once. Bob, a careless fellow, has lost part of a borrowed book.

sss. Unexplained fires in North Texas in July of 1860 led to rumors that abolitionists were fomenting slave rebellions.[124]

[8/14/1860]
Tues. 14. Attended Church Sunday. Found a fallen tree across the road; fortunately succeeded in making a way around it. Indignant, that Charlie did not return to tell us about the obstacle, since he started long before us. I am sadly afraid he is too selfish to care about others. The Rowes & Mr. O.C. came this far yesterday morning, intending to go on to Wharton, but just as they were making a start, Mrs. Veasey drove up. So, they all returned home again. Mrs. V. met with quite an adventure; rather a painful one though. Being overtaken on the road by night, with her four small children and Negro driver & woman; she sent the man up to a house at a distance from the road for aid. Some time

elapsed, yet the negro did not return. She called him repeatedly, her fears becoming excited momentarily. Remembering the report of Negroes rebellion, she at length became so alarmed, that she left her children in the carriage and hid herself in the woods, thinking the little ones would be safe till she was found. The driver, who had lost the way for awhile, on regaining the carriage, searched & shouted for his Mistress; but in vain, as she in her terror ran from the sound of his voice. Finally he proceeded to Mr. Dance's, when the whole neighborhood were aroused for a search. The driver was suspicioned of murdering his Mistress. Mrs. V. was deaf to all calls till daybreak, when she ventured to approach a house and distinguishing a white person, discovered herself, to the joy of all.—She could not speak of her terrible fright without laughter & tears.—Mr. Chase & P. McNeel[125] came yesterday evening, have now gone to Mr. R's. P is a nice pleasant little fellow.—

[8/26/1860]
26th Mond.[ttt] Raining still, had constant showers last week. *We* had a pleasant gathering at Mrs. Mims' not many days ago. Though I committed a very childish and unusual act, for a grown woman, regardful of proprieties. Mr. C. McGreal[126] had promised to send me a Newfoundland pup, at my request. I knew he was coming to Mrs. M's, but did not dream of seeing the dog. Well! when Leo saw him bringing it in his hand, he called out to me, reading or talking busily, "here's your dog!" Without thinking, and not knowing he was already at the door, I sprang up and went into the Hall, saying I must see it. There stood C. in the door, holding the Pup and laughing. I was embarrassed and really don't know whether I bade him good-day or not. I asked if that was my dog, and went back to my seat, without ceremony. Everybody laughed loudly, and I too, though my face flushed. Afterward I thanked him for his kindness, and proposed he should bestow a name on the Pup. He declined at first, but finally called him 'Bernardo.' C. intended coming home with us, but A.[127] & Leo M. told him we were all amusing ourselves at his expense, for the degrading act, of bringing a dog from town; to use A's expression he was 'so bewildered,' that he concluded to return home. I did not

ttt. Again she seems to be confused about the date. August 26, 1860, fell on Sunday, not Monday. The next entry is also dated incorrectly, but is consistent with this mistake.

know of this, till several days afterward, when Mr. A. was here. I was surprised to hear of this original idea. And told him I did not believe they were all laughing on this account, but at my surprise and confusion. And that I meant to explain to Mr. McGreal the first opportunity. I declare I ought to have been indignant at his suppositions. He remarked he would like to 'accommodate me,' but he could not do that. I make great allowances for Mr. M's I think that if he ever alludes to the circumstance again, I will tell him he might consider it an honor to be permitted to bring me a dog. He told Mc[128] 'she sang better than she played,' much to her silent surprise, at his unasked candor.

    Dr. R. and T.C. have at last departed for I. The Dr. wishes to return here and secure a practice, and will probably teach our children. O.C. left yesterday morning intending to start to Tues. He is popular with all, though Miss E. Norris charged him with an attempt to insult her by flattering her musical capacity. He is so innocent & simple-hearted.—The days go over me, in idleness and often weariness. I read some, haven't finished Josephus yet, furnished me by the kindness of Mr. W. R. My self-examinations are disheartening. Instead of growing better daily, it seems to me I'm worse than ever. I'm cross and impatient of trifles, with some folks. I don't know why, but Ma can stir up fretfulness in me so quick. And the same word or act from another would scarcely be noticed. We disagree on almost every subject. I just know, I care as much or more for her, than the other children do. I can't understand myself. If I could only keep still, but that 'little member'[uuu] is so unruly. I say hard things of neighbors too, though true, which had better be left unsaid. If I go on, in this way, where will the evil stop? My teachers always have a good influence over me; this is also unaccountable. If I could only see them sometimes. But here is my lot; God knows best. I'm troubled to think of Jose's fickleness. Leo. says she will dance, and she told Mc she intended to withdraw from the Church. Poor, misguided child; I can't hope to change her. I intend to lend her the 'Path of Life,' and talk to her on the subject, the first chance. I don't know but she will consider me officious and intrusive. I told her Miss Mary had recommended her to my oversight. It is often wrong to admit unformed character into the Church,

uuu. Her tongue—reference to James 3:5–8 KJV

but we are short-sighted and can't know the certainty always. Our *Father* alone can keep us; to Him we look for aid! Adios.

[8/30/1860]

Frid. 30th.[vvv] After a four miles canter, towards the Lake, Mc, Archie & myself, return to our breakfast, with sharpened appetites. Mc tried Mr. Rathbone's[www] pony; well-pleased with his paces. Capt. Spencer[129] called yesterday. I'm a little afraid of him, and dislike his character. I like to have the good will of all; and knowing his partiality for our family 'on account of' Pa's memory, I came down. He shook my hand cordially and remarked, "how like her mother and father too." Praised, the appearance of my brothers: "They don't look like fools" etc. Said he didn't care so much for Grandpa, as he had for my father, (in Grandpa's presence). He also asked for Annie, but she would not come down. Poor old man, he abandoned his wife & children, twenty years ago in La., and came off to Texas, where all runaways then, and often now, find a refuge! Brother C. goes next week,[xxx] Alas! for the necessity!

[9/7/1860]

Frid. 7th. He is gone; since Tuesd. with M. Rowe.[130] We all wanted M. to go, not only for his own sake, but to care for Calvin. They hated to say good-bye. C. got on his horse to keep off kisses. He intends returning Christmas. This morn all of Ma's hopeful progeny, mounted to ride to the River before Sunrise. Charlie and Archie were perched upon a very fast-trotting donkey. We went there soberly enough. But upon our return started in to a gallop, forgetting Missies & Mollies inexperience. Billie Barlow wanted to go ahead with them, in spite of cries and admonitory jerks from the irritated & frightened Missie. I had to square Old Doc across the road to stop him. How Miss did quarrel! Dreamed last night of meeting M. T. W.[131] Thought she was in [a] consumption. Reproached her for not writing me this long while.—Answered Angie last week, Rach & Puss also.

[9/17/1860]

Mond. 17th. Sund. week went to church, thence, Ma wished to go to Mr. Rowes, returned in the eve, bringing

vvv. August 30, 1860, fell on Thursday, not Friday, and is consistent with the mistake on the previous entry.

www. Apparent misspelling of D. C. Rathburn, age twenty-six, overseer, in household of Levi Jordan (1860 census, Brazoria County)

xxx. To attend classes at Baylor. According to the *1859 Catalogue of the Male Department* (37), they were to begin on Monday, September 3, 1860.

Emma to stay awhile. Mr. Buckingham will not preach for us again, am sorry not to have any minister. Mond. we rode over to Mrs. Mims' before breakfast, intending to surprise Joe. Stayed an hour or two, Joe returning with us. Next day I proposed visiting Miss Sweeny; and we went, though it was nearly ten miles. Found Miss Bettie, a fine, dashing looking girl, spirited very; and Mrs. S. very pleasant. Had a fast ride home and so jolted we did not care about trying the experiment again soon. Emma has been sick ever since. Her Ma is staying with her. She is slowly mending. We were going to make several other visits, if she had kept well. Had a good letter as usual from Miss Mary, said she hoped Calvin would call on them. He says he believes F. has given him the 'slipper.' He boards with Mr. Cleveland; complains of Blues.

[9/28/1860]
28th. Sat. Emma went home. A. & C. visited the Norris'es & Bells. I wouldn't [leave] Em alone; D. M. stopped here with Hit Williams one day this week. He is very tall & slender. Cares little for Ladies I think; quite self-satisfied and conceited; good-looking. A. said she wasn't coming down to see them, but telling D. secretly; at my suggestion he sent for her; so she came then. Last week Coruthers sold Grandpa eight mules, and yesterday Col. Hawkins[132] called to look at them, suspicioning two of his mules were stolen by C. None of these were his, but Lum M. has one. He will prove the theft and in all [probability] C. will be doomed to the Penetentiary for years. He [came] to oversee here. Is a man of little or no principle. An inveterate liar, and now a convicted Rogue. He is a disgrace to his family, but will be little loss to them I hope.

[10/5/1860]
Frid. 5th. Mr. Coruthers, has returned and says he can prove, that he bought the mules. Attributes the slanderous reports to envy.—Calvin writes, that Dr. R. is on his way down.—Last Sat. Ma, Mc, Charlie & myself, drove to Mr. Bennets. Met E. & F. Rowe there by appointment. Like Maggie much. She is a quiet, low-voiced, gentle girl, apparently. & Handsome. Mr. L. Bennett[133] is quite a lover

of the Poets; pointed out to me several favorite passages. It was a pleasant visit.—Mr. Evans returned several weeks ago. Accompanied by a dozen negroes. Grandpa will take ten or eleven, one a woman, half-indian, bought for Mrs. Adams. Mr. E. has a little indian, so bright and interesting, called 'Promise,'[134] appropriately. He visited our relatives in N. C. Cousin Barbra sent her ambrotype. Uncle W. wished to come out with him, but Aunt and Cousins objected. Speaks in praise of all; says Coz James is tall and handsome.—Dr. Rowe has come. He will commence teaching the 1st of Nov. Calvin came down to Brenham with him, to get winter clothing.—

[10/23/1860]

Tuesd. 23d. Nothing to do.—Ma asked just now if idleness brought me happiness? I replied, "that is an unnecessary question to me even." So betook myself to my room and pen. A poor occupation this. I'm lazy. I know I am. But, alas! I have *so* little incitement to do anything! I believe it is useless to expect, or look forward to a better outward Life. Sometimes, not always, this one is a trial. Nobody understands this feeling, or appear to. Eh Bien! Why should I not bear these crosses, which after all are comparatively light ones. Mc is satisfied to feel free from restraint. I am grateful for my many unmerited blessings, and [try] to be content. I rarely complain, but feel good-for-nothing. . . . I can't understand all that is within me. I feel, I know I could be so much, and do so much better in different circumstances. What these should be are not definite to my mind. I am tired of this stagnant, hermit Life! And still could not endure a fashionable one. I know & see nothing here, but through the friendly medium of books and I can't even have enough of these. I've read carefully 'Paradise Lost' lately and intend to become better acquainted with Milton. Some of his vivid pictures almost frighten one, as those of Chaos and Hades.—I suppose I ought to be ashamed of all these complaints. However I only tell them here, confident that others would not appreciate, but probably ridicule my motives. The end is not yet, and I must be submissive to Him who doeth all things well. I do so little good. I look around and ask myself, what can I do? I never find the answer. If I only had energy to rouse up and see, poor, weak creature that I am. My talent is sadly rusting I am afraid.

[10/30/1860]

Mond. 30th_. Oh! I have read 'Beulah'![yyy] I enjoyed it immensely. Mr. W. R. gave us the opportunity!—Mr. & Mrs. Jones have returned, glad to get back.—Puss McK. is going to be married![136] Well! What need I care? I never like my friends to marry. I hardly know the cause.—S. Pier[137] wrote me a long letter!—

[11/9/1860]

Frid. 9th. Went with Grandma to see Cousin! Returned to find Dr. R. here. Missed seeing the Gibsons Monday, who spent the day here. Must answer letters! Have been reperusing 'Tales of my Landlord.'[zzz]

yyy. A novel by Augusta Jane Evans (1835–1909)[135]

zzz. Sir Walter Scott published several of his works under this title, which came out in three series, from 1816 through 1819.

God Help Our Cause

*T*his section stretches from November 1860 to November 1865, beginning with Sallie's remarks about the election of Abraham Lincoln and concluding with her comments about the defeat of the Southern cause. She writes regularly for the first couple of years, but blames a shortage of paper for her failure to write during the later years of the War. Although Sallie chronicles some of the events of the War and the deaths of soldiers from their circle of friends, she focuses on everyday life on the plantation, which seems to continue pretty much as usual. Her grandfather, being too old to be drafted, continues to run the plantation, and Calvin and Bob are even given furloughs to come home and help with the sugar-making. Later, Bob is taken prisoner in one of the few skirmishes on Texas soil, but the family's greatest tragedy during this time is the loss of Sallie's two youngest sisters.

[11/12/1860]

Mond. 12th. Stirring news! Lincoln is elected doubtless![a] But then will be bloody struggles, ere he reaches Washington! [South Carolina][1] in arms; others will follow her example. Meetings were held in Brazoria & Columbia to call volunteers.[2] The "Lone Star" is floating *all alone* over both places. Cousin Barbara writes she is "tired of the excitement." Oh! I am just beginning to realize the possibility of a civil war, with all its *horrors!* God forbid, that our glorious Union should be dissolved! Or if a separation is inevitable, would that it could be effected peacefully. Oh! it is heart-sickening to dwell on the possibilities of the Future. Our worst foes are in our midst. Negro insurrections will be constant and bloody, under the guidance of Abolitionists.[3] I have always pshawed & hooted at the idea of Disunion. But I can no longer close my eyes to stubborn facts. It is terrible the thought of fighting against one's own, for we are one people. I earnestly hope the North, will not as a body, hold to Black

[a.] November 6, 1860, was Presidential Election Day.

Republican principles. Southerners will not allow interference with their peculiar institutions! We can hope!

[11/26/1860]

Nov. 26. Mond.—Returned from a pleasant visit Sat. to Mr. R's to find a pleasant letter from 'Dear Miss Mary' awaiting me. Our political troubles are increasing! Oh! for a 'Geo Washington' to rule through the coming storms. I am not a fire-eater. I am not reconciled to *Disunion*. What folly—what infatuation possess's those Northern ignoramuses!—If they were with me, at the window, and could notice the respectful low, and pleasant "good morng Mam" from a little darkey passing with his donkey-cart; perhaps they would be obliged to judge him at least content with his lot. Or beholding the pleased faces and generous display of ivory, on yesterday as the 'niggers' received new shoes, hats, & handkerchiefs, etc., one would be compelled to think them satisfied . . . As a little child is delighted with a new toy so were they pleased with the shining buckles of their hats and gay colors of their handkerchiefs. Fanatics forget "Where ignorance is bliss, 'tis folly to be wise."[b] They are not capable of much advancement. Are inferior as a race; and need the guidance of Whites. Some Masters are cruel—very. Stronger protective laws are necessary for such. But it is needless to moralize on the subject. The end will come.

[11/30/1860]

Nov. 30th. Frid. Miss Townsend[c] is concluding her last story "Come & Go," thus moralizes—" So, the lights and the shadows have come and gone over my life as the days "come and go," with their swift, noiseless feet over our lives, as the shuttles "come and go" through the looms of human life, weaving that great, mysterious pattern which God's eyes shall behold to all eternity—as the years "come and go," dropping gifts and graves all along their paths, and speaking to all human hearts, that old, sublime lesson their lips have proclaimed unchanging amid all the changes through which they walk the earth—that old teaching of the Royal Israelite, "Fear God and keep his commandments, for this is the whole duty of man."[d]—We can have no more Northern magazines till the impending political crisis is past. I

b. From "On a Distant Prospect of Eton College" (1742) by Thomas Gray (1716–71)

c. Virginia Frances Townsend (1836–1920) was an associate editor of *Arthur's Home Magazine* and a writer of many stories and several books, some for children.

d. Ecclesiastes 12:13b KJV

shall,—all the children will miss the pleasant stories, with an instructive moral to each and the life-like engravings, as well as patterns, embroideries, etc., so useful to country folks. We have few of the so-called pleasures of life, at best. Perhaps, I ought not to think or say so, we have more than our desserts. Have much to be thankful for.

[12/13/1860]
Thurs. 13th. The last ten days have been given to visitors & visiting. M. Reese & J. Mims have been with us most of the time. A party consisting of ourselves, the Rowes' & Mims went to the beach, Sat. There were about twenty of us. And all had a nice quiet time, rambling on the smooth shore, gathering the bright-hued and curiously formed shells, and listening to the roar of the mighty waters. Lounging on a large well-polished tree, thrown up by the ever active billows, I thought of the words of Byron "Roll on thou deep and dark blue ocean, roll!"[e] and felt I too could love the ocean. What a delightful spot to dream in, with the white surf breaking at your feet! One is insensibly carried far away from the realities of the present. We remained several hours, and after lunch was over, unanimously agreed to retrace our steps homeward, reaching Mr. R's before dark. Sund. morn we came home, finding Mrs. Banton here. Two Sabbaths in succession opened upon us, away from home. I dislike visiting on this day. Once I could not avoid it. Mond. Mr. Millican was here before breakfast, to see Mrs. B. we divined immediately. Trying to tease her, I scribbled some nonsense, not expecting him to see it. However, she showed it. I was considerably plagued, as he is almost a stranger to me. And remarked he must excuse, what was not intended for him. Here is some of it. "Christopher the second came on a voyage of discovery. The Land of Beulah, I hope he'll find it (her)! To whom are we indebted for the honor of this visit? Appoint a committee of investigation! Mrs. Banton one." He, answering said "the visit was not intended for any one."[4]—A short letter from Rachel, still in raptures about her husband and housekeeping! One from Miss Mary several weeks since. Pobe Rowe & D. Mims have gone to I.[f] Pobe will stay there till Manly returns from home. They kindly carried a mule for Calvin to come home on. Grandpa, intent

e. From "Childe Harold's Pilgrimage," (1818), canto IV, st. 178, by George Noel Gordon, Lord Byron (1788–1824).

f. Independence (and also in entry for 12/26/1860).

on catching his runaways, gave Mr. Jones and Evans the best horses and saddles, much to our dissatisfaction leaving only an old saddle, that C. would not deign to ride, . . . one must be sent for him. Ma never opposes Grandpa's wishes. She is only making trouble for herself, I tell her, for we are not as content & submissive as she is to all his notions. And next morning Mr. Jones did not go, I was glad of it, though it was provoking to see C's horse standing at the gate, instead of traveling to her master.

[12/26/1860]

Dec. 26th. Christmas is again with us. Ushered in, on our part, by firing guns, trees, logs, etc. The customary egg-nog was duly served. Of course, the Turkey and cakes were not forgotten. We are enlivened by the witticisms of Mr. W. Jones, who is here visiting his Brother. Manly R. came up last evening, he is lonesome at home; his sister & Brother are in Wharton. Calvin is hunting nearly all the time. We complain, he might as well have remained at I. for all we see of him. Mc grumbles about 'dull Christmas.' Ordered the horses for a ride or visit & now refuses to go. Yesterday was sunshiny; to-day gloomy under a canopy of leaden-clouds. Expected Joe M. and Leo over to accompany me to Mr. Rowe's. Suppose they have scarcely returned from the 'Ball.' I hope Joe did not attend. Looked at the Negroes' dancing; thought they seemed strangely in earnest. Cousin is not well enough to be here. Mr. Rainey ('Foul-weather,' says W. J.) came. I have a letter from Angie. Must try to answer Puss' rhapsodies, and Rach's. I am afraid all in these troublous times, do not wish 'peace and good-will to men,'[g] but trust there are many who welcome with joyful thanksgiving this anniversary of our *Savior's birth*. 'Glory to God in the highest'[h] for His "unspeakable gift."[i]

g. Luke 2:14 KJV

h. Luke 2:14 KJV

i. II Corinthians 9:15 KJV

[01/07/1861]

Jan. 7th 1861. Lowland, Brazoria Co., Texas.

Mond.—Another year has gone, nevermore to return. Its joys & sorrows live only in our Memory. Its changes may not be perceptible to the outward eye, but we feel changed, in some degree. If our changes only, could be for the better; we would not regret the passage of Time, so much! Alas! for me!

I am weak, oh so weak! Instead of being, better, stronger, for the past year's experience, I gain little or nothing; sometimes think I'm worse, if somewhat wiser. "Wisdom's ways, are ways of pleasantness & all her path's are of peace!"[j] If I could walk in *her ways,* all would be well with me. I despair of ever being wise (even in my own conceit). Lately I have several causes of disquiet. My conscience blames me, I suppose, and yet I don't know the nature of its accusations. I'm sorry for the disappointment of one, whom I esteem. Still I have never intentionally deceived anyone. I cannot be long cold & reserved even when pride whispers of wrong received at the hands of one. I would do violence to my (own) feelings not to treat with politeness, those persons who honor us, with visits in my own home. I wish everybody could see, have nicer perceptions of real truth. I can feel, instinctively whether I'm the object of the good or bad-feelings, of others. I laugh & talk with those for whom I have little or no respect. Thrown in contact with such characters' daily, I can do no less. And yet they ought to be aware of the estimation in which they are held. In the country one cannot be exclusive, without incurring (the) hatred. My friendly nature cannot brook pride & ceremony. There's my proud Bro! (Poor fellow, he is gone back to school) Wraps the icy mantle of reserve closely about his dumpy little figure & looks & acts the man & only sixteen! I like to see him proud, however. Little cares he for the opinions of many. I hope it will keep him from temptation to evil. Blessings on his head & may he ever be our pride. Manly R. is a merry, whole-souled boy & still there is little congeniality between them! God, send us a happy New Year! And may we be guided to opportunities better than those of the Past. May the Holy Spirit, Our Heavenly Father, be with us ever & guard our steps aright! And would'st Thou in the plentitude of Thy mercy bless our beloved country & shield us from the horrors of a civil war!———

j. Proverbs 3:17 KJV

[02/08/1861]
    Febru. 8th. A month, have I been silent, here. Little, can my pen boast of doing ever. Some, most have been working, hard. Farmers preparing to sow the seed of the coming crop. Death, our invincible enemy, has been busy in our midst.—

For months Mrs. C. Norris[5] has expected his unwelcome presence. Two weeks ago, the Dark angel, kindly relieved her, from long & extreme suffering. She expressed her resignation to the will of God; said she was willing to go; her only pang was in leaving husband and her two small children. I visited her twice, & watched beside her corpse, the night after her decease. Poor Mr. N. worn out with watching & grief, was pitied sincerely. Time alone, can console.—Just a week after performing the last sad offices for her dead friend, Mrs. S. Mims, universally known & respected, an old-settler,[6] was called hence, in the fifty-third year of her age. Her death was sudden, of congestion. Mc & I were there the day before & night of her death. Grandma present at the time. Oh! it was a sad scene; enough to melt a heart of stone to witness the grief of those six grown men & only daughter.[7] How could they give up their dear Mother! She was speechless, but extended her hand & shook all who gave theirs. Several of her children promised to meet her in Heaven.—They are wicked all of them. May God help them to turn from evil. A dozen years ago, old Mr. M. died,[8] leaving his wife & children heavily in debt. By industry & frugality she cleared her property & raised her children respectably. Long will she be missed! Calvin wrote Grandpa, to let him come home. Mr. B.[9] had required him to sign an article, containing numerous rules, pledging himself; to obey all the regulations, or any the President should see fit to make. To remain to stand an examination. To indulge in no revelry, night suppers, etc.[10] C. hesitated to sign. Whereupon Mr. B. talked of employing force. He then plainly told him he would not sign. Manly & several others refused, also. They were told not to return till they intended to obey. Mr. B. made public remarks in school concerning, the "little stumpy boy" as he was pleased to call C. Grandpa started Mond. to bring C. & M. home. Says he shan't be imposed on. The Pres.[11] is losing popularity! To-day we expect the travellers!

[02/13/1861]

Wed. 13th.—Tis a time for memory, and for tears! My *Birthday!* I can scarcely realize the fact! The "clock" of Time is striking the years of my Life. One, two, three—Till the last is tolled off; and I "sleep the sleep, that knows not waking."ᵏ Ah well! Providence shapes our destiny. I would not live again the years of my childhood! Let my fleeting Spring advance! I am in the hands of "Him who doeth all things well."ˡ May I be ever pure, in heart, in 'faith nothing wavering,'ᵐ then have I naught to fear. Strength will be given for the "warfare of Life!"ⁿ "O youth, in thy early years, how prodigal of Time; misspending all thy precious hours; thy glorious youthful prime."ᵒ Much have I lost. Many moments have been spent in idleness. Conscious of all this; still am I indolent. Habit is strong; stronger than resolutions of amendment! I will not believe in manual at the expense of mental labor. I probably sacrifice my health physically, by listless inactivity. Nothing to do. Have not energy to make work. Whose happiness have I ensured? In all my Life of *twenty-one* years, "what have I done that's worth the doing"? Last evening alone with "pale melancholy,"ᵖ despondingly I thought on these queries. And it is no new thought. I have often asked myself; to "see (myself) as others see me.". . . When the last preparations, were being made, for Mrs. M's interment, I confessed my inability to assist. I had never arranged crepe on hats or pinked edges. Yet I knew I could do it, but like to do it as well as others. E. N. wished the rising on her finger was well, she could help. Afterwards looking over the Family Bible, asked my verse in Proverbs. I told her, remarking that it was not very applicable. "She seeketh wool and flax, and worketh willingly with her hands."ᑫ "No indeed," she replied, with marked emphasis "you do not love to work." I then enquired her verse. "She shall do him good, and not evil, all the days of her Life."ʳ She expressed herself well pleased with hers, and believed it would be true. I then proposed, since mine did not suit me, and hers might possibly apply (to me), to exchange. No! she liked her own best. All this transpired in the presence of Leo. & S. M. She thinks the latter gentleman "so handsome"! I certainly will not stand in her way, if she wishes his favor. Her maneuvers are entirely transparent to me, as well as others. I'm not speaking disparagingly of E. I would like to see her married, to the *one* of her choice.—Mc & I spent the day with Jose Mond. She is not going to school; must become housekeeper; could not come home with us. I am indignant at A's selfishness. She, poor child, acquiesces willingly. Davie will

k. From *Charles O'Malley* (1841) by Charles Lever (1807–72)

l. Mark 7:37, also "He Doeth All Things Well, or My Sister" (1847) a ballad with lyrics by F. M. E., music by I. M. Woodbury

m. James 1:6 KJV

n. From "Our Heroes" by Phoebe Cary (1824–71)

o. From "Man was made to mourn: a dirge" (1784) by Robert Burns (1759–96)

p. From "The Passions: An Ode to Music" (1747) by William Collins (1721–59)

q. Verses in the thirty-first chapter of Proverbs were assigned to young ladies by their birth date. Since Sallie's birthday was February 13, her verse was Proverbs 31:13.

r. Proverbs 31:12 KJV

s. Chappell Hill, Texas[12]

t. Matthew 7:1 KJV

u. "Grandpa," Sallie's grandfather

v. March 4, 1861, was the date of Lincoln's inauguration.[16]

go alone to C. Hill.[s] Not unmindful of the warning "Judge not, that ye be not judged,"[t] yet I cannot help thinking J's brothers, A[13] in particular, think of their own comfort & convenience first. That child must stay at home alone. Instead of continuing at school several years. C. is now attending school at *la maison*. He left I. before Grandpa arrived. G.[u] found Manly there, had a talk with Mr. B. came on and overtook "little stumpy" awaiting him in Houston. We all say "they did right!"——

[02/23/1861]

Sat. I've felt & worked well this week. Mc, myself & sometimes Ma, accompanied by *Bernardo*,[14] have taken a walk, immediately after Breakfast, several mornings. I imagine I feel better, in consequence of the air and exercise. Have been embroidering a brand-new style. Mc has realy made herself, a flounced-dress, all alone.—Cousin, Em & Miss Angie were here, one night. This latter personage is fastidious to a fault. And the heartiest laugh I've enjoyed in many a day was occasioned by the involuntary commission of an impropriety, by NC. Mr. R. is coming here to school. Also, a Mr. Dixon;[15] he boards with us. Our folk went to town to-day, to vote for *secession*. The 4th of March[v] is almost upon us. What a revolution will that day see!—The boys are pleased, to receive new-*saddles*. Archie is unwell again. Eat too many oysters, perhaps. Received several valentines, very flattering ones; wrote none. The negroes caught alive, a species of Swan. He is easily domesticated. From my perch, at the back windows, I can see him stalking majestically, in the rear of a flock of geese; looking as if he thought, he was among them, but not of them. We suppose that he is not entirely grown. His long neck is of a grayish hue. A motley crowd of mules & horses are collected around the stables, enjoying a brief respite from their late occupation of plowing—very hard work I suppose. Brothers and "*that* boy" (as the stranger is called) are flourishing *lassoes*, in the attempt to 'rope' some of the knowing animals. A dull, leaden day, that is 'drizzling' at intervals, now the wind is rising; its hoarse whispers increase as every 'gust' sweeps by, sending the rattling rain-drops against the panes. Probably Old Boreas, will end, by favoring us with a 'Norther.'

9. This unfinished carving, an artifact found in the slave/tenant quarters at the Levi Jordan Plantation, may depict the swan mentioned in the entry for February 23, 1861. Courtesy Dr. Kenneth Brown, University of Houston.

[03/01/1861]

Frid. 1st March.—To-day is ushered in the new month. . . . stirring times in Washington—our far away Capitol . . . Abe Lincoln will be inaugurated, as President of the United States. Much to *Old Buch's*[w] satisfaction; who will gladly transfer his responsibilities of action, to the shoulders of his unenviable successor. For us *Southerners*—we are, will be, *independent.* Jeff. Davis is our President, as nominated by the Southern Convention, held at Montgomery, Ala.[17] Texas is again free. Only one Union ticket, was found at Brazoria. Judge Bell's vote.[18] Abe "will run the machine as he finds it,"[19] and will probably try coercion. Well let him 'try, try again.'[x] We are prepared. I hope, earnestly trust, that we may part in peace, without bloodshed. There is no use in

w. James Buchanan, 15th president, 1857–61

x. From *Teacher's Manual* (1840) by Thomas H. Palmer (1782–1861)

GOD HELP OUR CAUSE 97

war. May Providence avert the impending calamity!—Went to Church Sund. Saw Jose there in company with Leo. and E. N. Rcd. an introduction to the eldest Miss Patton.[20] She has auburn (red) hair, friendly and lively. Quite a Congregation. Mr. A. will preach there twice a month. Came home with us to give a Sermon to our Blacks. Mond. Mrs. Adams & E. R. rode up with Manly. Soon after a gentlemen from Brazoria, came for Bob S. to go over to look upon the murdered corpse of his Father. Such a shock. Poor fellow! we pity him! Mr. Stanger was a sot. He must have been deranged by *Drink,* to contemplate suicide, and court an awful Death. We do not know all the particulars. He was found hung, with the veins in his wrist, arms and throat cut, and sixteen wounds from a knife in his heart. Poor Bob returned the same night. All respect his grief, in silence. He has disgraced his children for years,—given all away. If he could only have died a natural death, it would have mattered little. I wish something could be done for his daughters. They are sewing at the Tavern, a bad place. I think I will ask Bob to write to his family in England after a-while.——

[March, 1861]

Thurs. Went over Caney to see Mrs. B. & E. Sat. That Miss Bassett,[21] a music-teacher accompanied Ma & Addison to Mr. Rowe's. Mrs. Jones' baby girl and the Strattons were there. Emily is quite friendly & young. Madame is youthful, good-looking and quiet: appeared easy & good-natured. I should suppose as much, in consideration of the fact, that she is the wife of an old man of threescore. What did she marry him for? Maybe we'll know someday. Not for love, I am sure. Oh! but I would beg or die in preference! "An old man's darling!" She has two pretty little children, and is the Major's[22] *fourth* wife. I look upon her, with *curiosity.* Leo. M. and Mr. Russell came Sat. eve. The latter gent had promised Miss B. Carter of La Grange, that he would visit me, while in Brazoria. Bettie had described my person & *good* qualities, so that he knew me, well. Said B. was a warm friend of mine. I remarked that 'Friends were partial & B. was in the habit of coloring pictures too highly.' He had seen my name in her Albums. Possessed of a handsome exterior, good manners and a good education I suppose, Mr. R. might be an entertaining beaux, to say the least, were it not for an unfortunate hesitancy in speaking. It is painful to see his efforts to overcome this defect. Enough of him, I shan't fall in love with his fine person. And Leo threatens to expose his antecedents in case his attentions should be turned to the ladies of this vicinity. Mc says she will not believe anything *he* says of a young man. Attributes his ill-will to Envy. I believe, though he generally confines himself to the Truth. He is coming with Joe to go to Mr. R's with us Frid. he says. M. Gibson was at Church with the Winstons. Mr. A. was unwell, & did not preach well. I mean, there was nothing eloquent or *new* in his sermon, to fix attention. He tells us the duty of each, and preaches Gospel. We complain that, we always have poor ministers.—I was thoroughly vexed this morning; about a trifle 'light as air.' Mc making an experiment would cut out my riding sacque. I wanted it loose, & after trying & finding she couldn't succeed just threw it aside & started something else. She ought to fit it after spoiling the pattern. Little cares if it isn't her own. Thinks I can take everything. Then she gave me her embroidery for me to work. I pushed it aside saying, 'I won't do it!' 'I don't care if you don't!' and she took it away. I rocked a good while, thinking it was foolish to care and finally commenced reading, and then betook myself to my pen. I wanted to make the Basque to wear Frid. & she wore out my patience with trying-on yesterday. She is real mean—selfish, about such things, sometimes. Always wanting me to sew for her, and won't cut for me occassionally. I never tried to cut—don't know one pattern from another, hardly. While she prides herself on her straight eye & is always cutting at random.—Enough of complaints.

[03/22/1861]

Frid. 22d.—A misty, rainy *matin!* Rumor says we—the South—are to be left in peace. The North will not listen to war. Our interests are too nearly identical. I rejoice at this good news, & must write to Coz M. A. and abuse old N. C. for her tardiness or *cowardice*.[y] The majority are unionists and many coercionists. Now it is too bad.—Last week went home with Manly, thence to see the Pattons & Strattons. Returning Sat. to witness the Negro wedding. On my way home called at Norris's a few minutes. Mc remained till Mond.—

y. North Carolina did not secede until May 21.[23]

[03/30/1861]

Sat. 30th.—Am in a matter-of-fact humor to-day. Can't appreciate sentiment. Wrote a few 'April-fools' in answer to 'Valentines.' Tired of the nonsense.—If it isn't drizzling! And Ma, Mc & Missy visiting. However they have the carriage. I didn't want to go. But would have accompanied Calvin fishing on the Lake, if the horses were here.—To-night Sam & Irene, a girl of hardly fifteen, are to be married. This is the fourth marriage, since Christmas. The ice once broken & others follow in rapid succession! Several of the lately married have already had matrimonial quarrels. Like a Negro!

[April, 1861][24]

Walked all around the new-ground yesterday, a distance that seemed miles; thoroughly tired were we. Burnt my dress . . . ! Grandpa is taking in so much land! Intends to buy more (land) & negroes also. I'm too indolent to write here. Mc & I, by our lone selves, rode to Mrs. H's one evening. Half a day runaways were in the woods & Grandma tried to frighten us from going, but we had no idea of confessing cowardice. Came home in a Gallop! looking suspicious on every side for '*Boogers.*' Well-a-day! what shall I do, to pass away idle time? I'm out of conceit with myself! I wish somebody would read me my character. What makes me *so* lazy?—There's the dinner bell! I don't wish anything & yet I'll go & eat as much as anybody! Is this fact the secret of my customary indolence?—

[04/22/1861]

April 22d—Resume my pen after this long silence, feeling still that I've nothing worth recording! Don't know what I've done in the time! Yet these weeks form a part of my *Life;* they go into the Past, burdened with my ill-spent hours; for my deeds and thoughts I am accountable! How solemn I should feel in view of this indisputable fact! Why do I not always remember, that God see's me? Alas! Shall I walk blindfold ever: shall I never do or feel better? I want to do right, to accomplish some good. Not to hide away my poor little 'talent.'[z] 'When we would do good, then evil is present with us!'[aa] How great is the depravity of the human heart!

z. Parable of the talents, Matthew 25:14–30

aa. Romans 7:21 KJV

Years only tend to make it worse! Sometimes I shrink from the contemplation of my pictured self, at fifty! In my own strength I can do nothing. Commit our ways to the great 'I am' and our feeble steps will be guided aright. May we give up our hearts unreservedly to Thee, Our Father! Keep us from temptation & carnal security! May Thy Peace ever be our portion and consolation through this 'Vale of Tears'! The cross of Christ is our only refuge. Thy Holy Spirit gave strength to the martyrs of old, to the sainted Ann H. Judson[bb] in a foreign & barbarous land. Conscience weighs heavily. What return have I made for the unmerited blessings and mercies showered on my unprofitable Life? My heart is sick at the review! Hundreds around me are outside the Ark of Safety. Do I shew that I care for their souls; or warn them of their danger? Why do I shrink from this duty? I try to set a good example, but Religion is often a forbidden subject, or spoken of too lightly. Sinners avoid serious thoughts, they bring unpleasant recollections. I do not attend Balls as some of our Christians do, yet I withhold censure for fear of giving offense. Is this right? I fear not. We had quite a fishing party on the Lake Sat. at Mr. Hinkles. I talked with many, but cannot remember one word, that will benefit any. I do not love immortal souls as I should. 'Out of the abundance of the heart, the mouth speaketh.'[cc] Christians rarely speak of their chief good to each other. How lukewarm the most of us are; what little progress we make! Life is made up of strivings and failings.

'Nothing in my hand I bring,
Simply to thy cross I cling.'[dd]

[04/25/1861]

Ap. 25th—Archie's birthday—He is just six years old. I told him he must have a cake to celebrate the anniversary of his little Life. But I haven't been out to attend to its composition. Sometimes Grandma don't care to have us attempt cakemaking; again she will complain at our want of interest in the Culinary Department.—Grandpa started for Gal. with Mr. E. & J. Mond. intending to go to N. O. But since the reported arrival of six men-of-war (belonging to the U.S.)[ee] off our coast, we hardly expect him to cross the Gulf. The war is getting unpleasantly near us. The U.S. troops

bb. Ann Hasseltine Judson (1789–1826) was the first American woman missionary to go overseas.[25]

cc. Matthew 12:34 KJV

dd. From "Rock of Ages" (1776) by Augustus M. Toplady

ee. On April 19, 1861, Lincoln ordered a blockade of all Southern ports.[26]

ff. They did not actually land there until November 1863.

gg. A literary allusion to mourning or being forsaken.[29]

have or intend landing at Brazos Santiago.[ff] Thirty-five volunteers from our vicinity marched by here Tuesd. on their way to Indianola among whom were S. & D. Mims,[27] and several of our other acquaintances. The Mims' came in to say farewell. We were all surprised & sorry to see D. go. Poor fellow, he is only nineteen.[28] We did not then anticipate any fighting & laughingly considered the trip a pleasant one. But if six thousand of the enemy have landed on our coast, there will be a battle, undoubtedly. God help the poor Soldiers! A heavy responsibilitie rests on the authors of this civil war!—Mc & I propose to wear the "Willow Garland"[gg] till the safe return of our Volunteers.—For several days Ma has been petting a little wild grey rabbit from the woods. Such a timid, soft little creature! It is hopping about my chair, as I write. She can't keep it, & will set it free soon, if Grandma don't kill it in the meantime.—Calvin tied his mule in a thicket last eve, & could not find him. This morn he has gone out in search, but has not returned though it is wearing on to noon, and the rain is falling. Little does he care I suspect, loving hunting & disliking school as much as he does. I am afraid he will never accomplish a great deal at study! I read his 'Cicero' daily & encourage him all I can, but he is too willful & perverse to be influenced. Bob complains of scalded feet. Missie had one fever, Arthur[30] several. I must write to my ever good friend, 'Miss Mary'!

[05/11/1861]

May 11th—Yesterday was Bob's nineteenth birthday! I asked him if I should congratulate him? What for? was the wondering reply. He hadn't thought of it! I wanted to make him a cake, but couldn't get enough eggs. And an attempt at candy-making, resulted in lumps of sugar; however it was liked sufficiently well.—Our Co. must furnish 100 men for the general Government. Many of our neighbors are enlisting. Boys of 17 are required. Bob will volunteer rather than be drafted. Oh how tired I am of the war already! We suppose Washington has been at [work.] The Mails fail to come.[hh]—Grandpa returned about two weeks ago, bringing the latest news. Virginia has seceded & we confidently hope to gain the other slave states.[ii] . . . I trust one battle will be decisive. At the cost of thousands of lives, probably. We

hh. Montgomery Blair, Postmaster of the United States, ordered U.S. mail service to cease on May 31.[31]

ii. Virginia was admitted on May 7 as the eighth state of the Confederacy.[32]

believe Justice is on our side. May we not rely on an arm of flesh, but invoke the 'God of Hosts' to fight our battles & protect our homes!

[05/19/1861]
 Frid. 19th—No change—the usual monotonous routine! Still I manage to be content, when I find work enough.—Read the N. O. Bills, am disappointed in getting only half the books ordered. None of the Bills are complete. Some things Grandpa left off, purposely, others Clerks neglected. Submission is the only alternative.—Have been to the Sugar-house twice to gather green grapes for pies! Johny climbed for Magnolia flowers, yesterday. The pure waxy whiteness of the bursting bloom, and its delightful fragrance, inspires admiration in every beholder. Dr. R carried some "below"; as he designates his Cousin's place.—Sunday, at Church the Miss P's. & S's promised to visit us this week. Mr. G. McNeel[33] gave a Party last eve in honor of his son's marriage. We did not accept our invitation. Calvin saw Pleasant in B. He insisted that he should come.—the Miss Williams came with the Bates, Sund. The eldest is a tall showy girl, generally admired. The youngest, dark and *petit* in form, but the better girl, I suspect.—Calvin rode a little mule hunting the other evening. On his return late, Grandpa asked him if he 'got any meat'? 'Yes,' he composedly answered, 'mule meat.' I, at first thought he had found a stray mule, but he soon undeceived all by declaring that Jenny Baka was dead. She had proved stubborn, whereupon he tied her to a tree & proceeded to whip her. At every stroke of the lash she ran around the sapling, becoming almost strangled then C. not willing to cut his rope, attempted to run her in the opposite side, when she sprang back, breaking her neck. No one offered a word of rebuke. Grandpa said she wasn't much loss. I told him he was a cruel bully and couldn't help crying, not for the mule's death, but for the spirit in which C. did the deed. I know he was angry enough to have shot the beast. He hated the act badly. Said he wouldn't have killed her "for five times her value." I hope the effect will be lasting!—Yesterday he did not come to learn his Cicero till two o'clock, then listened with a divided attention. I read the lesson several times, and then desired him to try, and upon

his refusal closed the book, & took up Grandma's dress, to sew on. He also threw down his volume & remained all the evening, idly looking out of the window. I almost despair of his becoming at all intellectual.——

[06/13/1861]

Thurs. June 13th. Long have I neglected writing. And now, with what feelings do I resume the pen. "A change has come over the spirit of my dreams"; the world is darkened. Our Missie, my favorite Sister, is here, no longer, brightening Life with her dear presence. Nevermore shall we behold those beautiful grey blue eyes, upraised to meet our faces! And with her, perishes my almost dearest hope. How could I realize the possibility of her Death? How could I do without Missie? Who would love 'Sis' as she did? Inexorable Death claimed his prey, and we are left to endure. Nothing to cherish, but the memory of our *brightest one.* I think I am resigned to the will of 'Him who doeth all things well.'^{jj} Still but cannot grieve to miss my *darling*. When the children are going to or are returning from school, imagination pictures the dear form as of old, in neat dress, with her books balanced on her head or wrapped in her arms. With what secret pride did I ever look upon that sweet child, and indulge in fond hopes for her future. Always deeply interested in her studies, and very fond of reading. Her regular Friday compositions were given to me for inspection and safe-keeping. A general favorite with her teachers, and of everybody who knew her. But I cannot enumerate all the virtues of my little Sister. She suited and was in many respects like me in disposition. Her temper was passionate, yet a word from me was generally sufficient to quell her impatience. She departed this Life at sunrise Mond. June 3d after an illness of one week. On returning from school at noon the Mond. before, she complained, that her leg pained her. Someone suggested that the cause was rheumatism. Mrs. Jones asked laughingly if it wasn't lazytism? I thought it was the effect of the unusual exercise of the day before, in searching for a pet fawn. That evening she had fever which continued till Wed. Tuesd. Ma noticed her leg, but could discover nothing but a scratch, from the bite of an insect, which being inflamed,

jj. "He Doeth All Things Well, or, My Sister, a ballad," by I. B. Woodbury, published in 1847, was a song about the loss of a little sister.[34]

she imagined was the cause of the fever. Next day a swollen red spot appeared on the limb, which she & Dr. Rowe pronounced 'St. Anthony's Fire.'[kk] And treated accordingly. Wed. night she was watchful and delirious. Calvin started for Dr. Sandford before day. By Breakfast she was better; the Dr. remaining only about a half hour. Next morning, still continuing wakeful & delirious Dr. S. was again called and to my astonishment left in an hour. That evening he was sent for the third time, the child had not slept for 36 hours. He remained all night & next morning Dr. Chinn came. 'But human power could not avail, our darling to save.' We lost all hope Sat. night, & thought she was dying. After application of some stimulants she rallied and lived till Mond. How gently and tenderly did Ma & myself nurse our little darling, little noticing the loss of sleep in our own anxiety for her. 'Sister' was her constant call. . . . She was always sensible of the things & persons around her, and several times she prayed audibly, & would ask us if she must not ask God to ease her pain? Mond. night she spoke the Lord's Prayer, with great correctness & deliberation. We asked her if she was afraid to die, & her reply was 'no.' Many times she said, she was 'going to die,' her time had come. I would have liked to have talked to her more but the Dr. forbade unnecessary words, and held out hope till the last. Sat. night we called the Boys, thinking she was dying, when she asked if Bob was there. And Sang a few sentences of 'Nellie Gray'[ll] & 'Saw ye my Savior'[36] in a clear sweet voice. Sund. we endeavored to keep her asleep, and on awakening and taking refreshment or ice, I would tell her, "shut your eyes and go to sleep." Towards night she grew weaker. I gave up all hope & went down stairs, she asked for me, & I returned, but I could do nothing more, but sit by, and soothe her. What agony it was to watch her labored breathing, and wipe the cold dew from her forehead & know she was dying. Yet Ma, Mc & myself sat there even smiling at the Dr's feeble attempts to believe there was hope. Conscious to the last, her expressive eyes were raised to Ma's and her lips would move and yet no sound come forth, from those pale lips. Our neighbors were kind. Everybody said she was a lovely corpse. I never saw a sweeter face & never shall again. We laid her dust by the

kk. Often used to refer to erysipelas, a spreading, hot, bright red skin infection caused by the streptococcus bacteria.

ll. "Darling Nellie Gray" (1856) by Benjamin Russel Hanby (1833–67)[35]

side of 'our Father's' whose especial pet she had always been. Vale.—

Brazoria, Lowland, Texas
Received Letters from—
Febr. Cousin Barbara P. McNeill N. C. Dund
Febr. Cousin Mary Ann McNeill N. C. Dund
Febr. Mrs. Mary L. Herndon, (McKellar) Tyler Texas
March Mrs. Rachel B. Stewart, (Barry) Marlin Texas
March Miss Angie Rogers, Montgomery, Texas.
Apr. Miss Mary Davis, Independence Texas
Apr. Miss Sallie Pier, Travis, Tex.

The third section of Sallie's diary ends here with this list of letters dated 8/10/1861—a list which seems to be out of sequence with the surrounding entries. The fourth segment of the diary is the most heavily damaged, with a large triangular piece missing off the upper right hand portion of the page. The dates of the entries are sometimes missing and portions of each page are missing several words. If the sense is apparent, a few words have been supplied. Words and phrases have been deleted if her meaning seems obscure.

[06/20/1861]

Thurs. 20th June—I must write to Miss M. and send it by Mr. Rowes, who will start Sat. to attend the Examination. Yesterday Dr. R's "Snake" threw him & escaped . . . encumbered with Bridle, Saddle & halter. As Mc and I were taking our morning's ride, we encountered "Snake," running off divested of Bridle & rope. "The Boys" have gone back to camp. Last eve they ran horses & dogs down chasing beeves. Bernardo can scarcely creep.—Here comes 'old ____,' quietly following 'Lucky Willie!' There, he is in the clearing. Charlie & Dixon are shouting in triumph. Dr. R. limping from his fall is examining his saddle.—Archie is sick, with cold & fever; Ma far from well; she has almost concluded to go to the "Lampasas Springs"[37] for a few weeks. Anxiety and watching together with the enervating effect of Summer heats, produce disability in a brain worn with disease. Her complexion always sallow, has assumed a greenish tint, while her cough is greatly increased. I have long thought a sea-voyage would be beneficial and have urged a trip to Ala. and N. C. However Ma is a poor traveller and dreads leaving

'Home.' Mc & I have had quite a discussion as to which one of us should accompany her. She declares she will not stay here alone, while Ma says I must stay & try to take *her* place. Now *I* think the children can be left to Grandma for a few weeks, while Mc, fat and healthy, might allow me, poor and almost Sallow, to have the benefit of a change, when I've been stagnating for nearly three years. I have really fallen off considerably, and need travel. Notwithstanding all this, if necessary I can cheerfully remain, though unwilling to have Ma go alone with Calvin. She would not enjoy her stay, without a female companion, and *without* vanity I would be a better one than Mc. Our mourning habiliments have not arrived or she could start now & attend the Examination. I dislike Black. However, it is necessary to show respect for ones dead. None mourn with greater sincerity, than we. Outward Life continues on, yet something is wanting. I feel a change. I realize I am talking almost as much as of old. . . . I miss my 'precious little sister.' Mornings we all *feel* her absence; and when we gather around the table her bright eyes are nevermore seen from her accustomed place. When the Sun is leaving us grouped on the veranda, then most I miss her, while pacing up & down the floor as of old, or seated watching the gathering twilight, thinking of my lost 'Darling,' till the bitter tears rise to my eyes, to be wiped silently away. Oftentimes she would sit by me at that hour, and lay her head in my lap, sometimes silent, again talking with animation or asking numberless questions. Then her Fawn, her little pet, 'Fan,' approaches the steps in expectation of the warm milk regularly brought formerly by her devoted Mistress. Now Mollie only is left to pet the little animal. Shrined in my heart forever is the memory of 'my Missie!' This, mournful pleasure only remains. Would that I had loved the little Darling more. I have no 'Missie' to share my room and bed now! Probably my life will be lonely and loveless, heretofore my consolation was the assurance of her unchanging affection; she never would forsake me. Now I must suffer and be strong. We are but six, like Wordsworth's little 'maid,' fain would we exclaim, 'nay, we are seven.'[mm] 'Tis but a little while and we follow our *brightest one* to the land of spirits. May our affliction be not in vain O God, may

mm. "We are Seven" (1798) by William Wordsworth (1770–1850)

nn. From the service for the Burial of the Dead, *Book of Common Prayer*

oo. *The Hidden Path* by Mary Virginia Hawes Terhune (1830–1922), pseudonym Marion Harland. She was a very popular and prolific author who was brought up in Richmond, Virginia.

pp. At Manassas, Virginia: First Battle of Bull Run, July 18, 1861

qq. Jeremiah 17:9a KJV[43]

rr. Matthew 7:1 KJV

we draw nearer to Thee, in humble resignation to thy will! And watch and pray in expectation of our summons from Earth! Frail is the tenure of our mortal breath, yea, "In the midst of Life we are in Death."[nn]

[07/29/1861]
Mond. 29th July—I'm forgetting how to write, answered a few letters. I've had considerable sewing to attend to, have read little or nothing except two novels by Mr. Harland, ... enjoyed The Hidden Path.'[oo] The 'Boys' have just returned from a several days camp near Houston, bringing the glorious news of a Southern victory[pp] in a general engagement occurring near Manassas. Scott[38] is beaten badly. Our loss is severe, causing sorrow in many a happy home. Dearly bought victory at the cost of thousands of lives, among whom are three Southern generals.[39] The good news spreads fast & joyfully. Manly joined us at Church, eager to impart the glad tidings. Oh! that this bloody combat would suffice. Wharton[40] is going to Virginia with a portion of his company in spite of the danger of an invasion at home.——

[08/05/1861]
Aug. 5th.—A cool, windy morn, the harbinger of a sultry noon. Drouth does not prevail as it did last year, therefore the weather is more comfortable. Ginnie C.[41] has returned home, delighted with her month's stay in our "Bottoms." Her Father was very anxious to reach I. on account of Church disturbances. Watching for the absence of the most prominent members, the Burleson-party dismissed Bro. Ross from his office as moderator and taking matters into their own hands, reinstated 'A. Lipscomb,' who has been excommunicated a year, gave themselves Church letters, preparatory to their removal to Waco.[42] Mr. C's life is even threatened. How sad the condition of such a Church. 'The heart is deceitful above all things & desperately wicked!'[qq] Judge not, that ye be not judged,'[rr] but it does seem that Mr. B. & his Faculty, have indulged a spirit of Envy and revenge, till they are morally blinded to the uncharitable spirit, pervading their own hearts. I would not willingly believe their wickedness, intentional. May strife & evil depart with the 'celebrated Faculty!'[44]

[September, 1861]

Another month over and gone. It has been the saddest three months of my life, I may safely conclude! . . . a portion of my cheerfulness has fled . . . Sometimes my heart aches so bitterly, I'm just so miserable. And yet I know it is wrong to grieve . . . At times I cannot help feeling depressed . . . No one notices my moods but Bob, and I do not need his enquiring glance or spoken question to realize that his quick penetration observes my clouded spirit. My interest in him never diminishes, and I will not believe he will disappoint my hopes (for him). Three months has 'my Missie' lain in the silent church-yard. I have looked upon her grave twice, only. I do not need to see it, not that I remember her loss always, no, for Sund. I called Mollie 'Missie,' the name that is no longer spoken, but the effect of her absence—the weight on my heart is rarely lifted. When necessary I talk, even animatedly, but I cannot enjoy anything as formerly. I've always professed to be stoical, and cold-hearted, and bitter has been my punishment for the falsehood—false I knew it to be ever, when my heart was concerned. Silent endurance only is left me now, & patient waiting for the Future. I did not know that I could feel so deeply; still am I ignorant of myself. "We are fearfully & wonderfully made."[ss] I did know that my 'little Sister' was my dearest one, God 'loveth a cheerful giver'[tt] & I strive to be resigned. Dr. R has written some sweet verses in memory of 'our Darling,' & though I'm grateful, yet shrink from acknowledging it, when I recollect his apparent indifference to her when ill, he neither prescribed nor gave advice. And my judgement must be, that his ineffectualness was a result of ignorance, yet I regard him coldly, rarely vouchsay him a word; but I must at least say 'thank you' for his kindness.

ss. Psalm 139:14b KJV

tt. II Corinthians 9:7b KJV

[09/29/1861]

29th Sept.—I heartily wish I had kept back my response to his 'kind acknowledgements,' since the 'old Bach' presumes on my correspondence to not ask or require an answer & there it is, pages and pages long! Eh bien! it seems my fate to be misunderstood. I wonder if most men have such dull perceptions where a lady is concerned! Such is my experience. "Cupid is blind."[45] I verily believe its truth.———Men are vain mortals—self-deceived; if a lady treats one of her would-be admirers with cold indifference, her motives are attributed to bashful modesty. Few *can* or *will* take an open hint. I must set it down on the score of *vanity*. Why will a man subject himself to the pain of refusal when reason warns him his suit is hopeless. "Youth & childhood are vanity,"[uu] so are old Bachelors on one *subject* I can testify.——I mean to send his unwelcome communication back with a laconic reply to his egotism, and sympathetic appeals.

[uu. Ecclesiastes 11:10b KJV]

[10/12/1861]
Oct. 12th—This week we have been visited by the first regular Norther. The cane-fields are beautifully green and ripening now. While the snow white cotton, pendant from the brown stalks, presents a fine sight. So I thought when riding one morning on the margin of the dewy fields. And remarked to Bob that "Miss Townsend could say something prettily descriptive of the scene spread before us, if blessed with a view of it." Pecans are abundant. Johnnie Nuckols[46] teases me daily to accompany him on excursions for grapes & nuts. He runs up to the head of the stairs to call out "Miss Sarah" whenever he needs my help. My first attempt at shirt mending has been on one of his ragged ones. Yesterday I, Mollie, and the little 'niggers' Promise & Ange went with him . . . when he climbed a tree and thrashed down the Pecans for us to pick-up. It was work for indolent I, but I persevered, securing a basketful and dividing with J. Returned home to find that Manly had called and announced that Mr. Leo Mims would be married to Miss Fannie Patton on the 6th Nov.[47] My good wishes attend him, however undeserving!—M. Reese has been here all the week and we expect others to-night to witness "Hulda's marriage to Black Jim." Grandma is sick, Mr. Jones and old "Mr. Snead, the negro hunter"[48] also. So I do not anticipate any pleasure in having company. The Hounds caught 'Mose the runaway' who was fettered with a stiff-leg of iron, so that he could neither outrun the dogs or climb out of the way, consequently was bitten in several places. Poor negro! he is idle at work & runs to escape it and the lash. And is treated with severity when he is caught, besides half-starving in the woods.[49] Our

negroes are treated well in general, much better than those of most of the surrounding Plantations they say themselves, yet discipline must be maintained. The tears rose indignantly to my eyes, when 'Mose' was led up that evening ragged and bleeding. I could say or do nothing, for he brought the trouble & pain on himself. Words of abuse & ridicule only were given him. Mr. S. highly elated at 'catching' him; Bob likewise in good spirits, Calvin quieter as if disgusted with the affair. I learned the next day, that he was severely whipped to make him tell the truth . . .—moaning, and confined in the stocks without food or water. I am disappointed & angry to find so much of the cruel master in Bob. And much to his surprise no doubt, dismayed him by word or look, for several days. Poor boy! He is hurt by my manner and pretends ignorance of its cause, but I tell him; he knew well enough, that he must have done something wrong to merit my anger for the first time after an intercourse of three years. I have petted and made so much & more of him in respect to favors, than of my Brothers. It is painful to lose confidence in one we trust implicitly. B. says I've been "mighty good" to him since we've made up. The impression of wrong has faded, but I haven't altogether forgotten.—Last month we were invited and went to 'Sallie McNeel's marriage to Mr. Van Dorn.'[50] Such a mixture of folks of all classes, from the 'would-be aristocracy' of the vicinity to 'cow drivers'! Small pleasure the crowd gave me! I went there against my better judgement, just because it has been a long time since I attended a Party. Mc was indignant because she was not taken to the first table, and did not go till the last, I, refusing to eat without her. Our party comprised the Rowe's, who neglected us & their sisters, to wait on the others. In fact, there were few young men there. It did not hurt my pride to be unnoticed almost, by them or Leo. My estimate of myself is not drawn from their appreciation. I do not feel it. L. apologized to Mc using such taken for granted assertions, that she indignantly declared she cared not for his or the attentions of anyone at the gathering. The Brazoria Rangers have disbanded and formed a guerrilla band. Col. Bates[51] is commissioned to raise a thousand men for the coast.

[November, 1861]

Leo Mims has been married to Miss F. Patton, a pair who became *engaged* at the last wedding. Their wedding was quite a pleasant one. I had several interesting talks. (Dr.) Capt. Veasey[52] and several Officers of the regiment were included in the invitations————Attempted making lager of green cane. Weather warm. . . . Joe & Mollie here this week. Mrs. McGrew[53] to-day; Mrs. Chinn yesterday—Good Sallie Pier has written me again; she deserves true friendship. Mc has Cousin Maggie's ambrotype. We pronounced her fine looking, if not handsome—Oh! I can't begin to write facts and opinions here. I've almost given up the attempt. This year is fading: and where am I? Alas! Poor I! Can pity myself sometimes! I find that I am not stoical, but so indifferent, when I should be grateful for manifold mercies, bestowed by "He who giveth to all willingly and upbraideth not."[vv] O Father, may I be strong for Life's battles, through faith in the "Lamb of God which taketh away the sin of the world"![ww]

vv. James 1:5 KJV

ww. John 1:29b KJV

[12/09/1861]

Dec. 9th—Little did I, poor shortsighted mortal, forsee the trial of my strength, so near at hand, when penning the above. Then "Mollie," my only little sister, seemingly in perfect health, flitted here & there, enjoying in her own active way, her Holidays. Rarely did I look upon the child, without thinking of our "lost Missie." And ere we could cease mourning her, relentless Death has snatched our "last one." Suddenly, after an illness of two days, she expired. Poor little one! suffered intensely from nausea & inflammation of the stomach. Sunday she exercised & ate more than usual, partaking freely of Pecans and wild grapes. I reported to Ma, that "Mollie" had fever. Then she began vomiting like a lava flood till evening when the terrible illness bore her hence, from this "vale of tears" . . . "of such is the Kingdom of Heaven."[xx] Sisters are spared the bitter experience . . . thus early unfolded to the sorrow of our once happy band. Archie is our only little one. What a gap! Everywhere their bright forms are missed. Our home is lonely, desolate. In less than six months to be stripped of the loved Beings of so many years. This new trouble takes its place in my saddened heart

xx. Matthew 19:14, Mark 10:14, and Luke 18:16 KJV

so naturally. Yet! oh still! I cannot realize the truth . . . they never return! I almost fancy I can hear their footsteps!

[12/16/1861 Undated entry, December 1861]
    Dec. 16th—A wet, gloomy day. The fog without seems to be a type of the one within my brain, settling heavily just above my eyes. I've done all I can towards fitting "Bob" for a soldier and have nothing to do but write letters, a long defered duty. I've been reading "The Mill on the Floss," am almost shocked at the tragical end of the unhappy Bro. & sister. There are some truths in the book, but the whole has left a bad impression on my mind. I suppose chiefly because I would fain believe better of 'human nature.' But does not truth exceed fiction? For a week past, Mr. Lum Mims[54] has been & is still very ill, scarcely expecting to recover, closely tended by all his relatives but Leo, who has not been to see him at all. The supposition is that they are at enmity. How can he rest away, alas! for cruel pride! Poor Rivers Erwin[55] is vacillating between Life & Death!———Grandpa is summoned to B. to attend a meeting of the Citizens in order to 'try' suspected Abolitionists. I pity the offenders! Calvin & I yesterday almost agreed that we sometimes felt like crying out against slavery. . . . but his perverse obstinance grieves me. . . . Oh! this horrid war! . . . There is a vague report to the effect that we will be abandoned to the depredation of the vandals. Coastal residents must retreat to the interior. Why will we waste this short life in such unholy strife! Calvin came, bringing Bob after an absence of several hours. He had started early, on a Camp-hunt, coming by to say 'Merry Christmas' before he went. Several of the others went upstairs, for the same purpose. It is a useless gesture to wish me a 'happy Christmas,' said I, & felt, what a sad, lonely day in prospect. I was contrasting this holiday, with last year's, thinking so longingly of the merry voices, which awakened me, then. Archie only was left to meet 'Santa Claus.' Poor little boy! found the old man poor, enough! I hadn't energy to dress, when I heard Bob's voice, around the corner. Oh! there's Bob! I called out, gladly and, running to look at him, as he rode up. Ma shouted 'howdy,' from the window, & I dressed in a hurry; while Mc lay still & read a novel, not

even appearing at the Breakfast-table.—Cousin was here for two days, & Mc & I accompanied Bob, to Mr. R's on his return to Camp. This week the Rowes & Mollie have been here. Mc is at Norrises 'till Ma & I go, or send for her. Miss Mary wrote me such a *good* letter; & dear little Mamie, thanking me for the Pantalettes I sent her.—Calvin visited the 'Camp' Sunday, not at all pleased with a soldier's life, as he had imagined. Says indignantly "They are treated worse than Negroes, insulted at every step." The ladies of the vicinity visited the soldiers twice. Grandpa wouldn't consent for Mc to go, I wasn't inclined to visit soldiers, but wanted to deliver things & call on 'the boys.' We must risk the displeasure of the volunteers, for the camp is not a fit place for ladies!

[02/11/1862]

Tuesd. 11th '62 Febr.—For the past few weeks have been reading Dickens inimitable works. Furnished by the kindness of . . . & Mrs. H., Johnny also is delighted to bring the books over to us. It is my opinion that 'David Copperfield' is his masterpiece. My eyes are tired from constant application to those closely written pages, yet still engrossed enough to be impatient at the interruption by Charlie's recitations. Poor boy! gets a long slowly, alone and unaided by good teachers. I wish he could go away, but times are so unsettled. Calvin oversees in general . . . Bob visits home occasionally; spent nearly a week horse-hunting. A doz. Cavalry horses escaped from Camp. All are recovered, but one. So many letters to answer. Dear Miss M. wrote me such an encouraging letter, who else ever praises me as she does. I have at last tried to deserve her good opinion.—No news from Mr. Evans, much to Dr. R.'s perplexity. Thinks it 'very cruel to be kept in suspense.' Poor Davie Mims[56] is dead, (of fever, far away from home), and his Coz. Benji McNeel.[57] Always from childhood entertained kindly feelings for Davie, his mother's pet. Poor, poor boy! Requested his Bro. Sam to bring his remains home. Alas! for the wild & wayward one! how well I remember his half-reluctant good-bye. I could not wish him success, looking into those brilliant black eyes.—Our Texians are suffering greatly, in those cold climates. May the Time be short!

[02/14/1862]

Frid. 14th—Yesterday was my birth-day, passing unheeded, Grandpa reminding me of the fact this morning. I know I'm just so old; know I should regret my many deficiencies! Go to, I will be wise! and forget the resolution in an hour. Such is Life and destiny. Thanks for an overruling Providence! Bob is here, with a broken ankle. Mr. Hinkle kindly brought him up to Mims' on a Skiff. Mr. W. Rowe fetched Pegasus, the ungrateful cause of the accident. Ma saw him approaching, and exclaimed, "Bob's dead!" I looked out of the windows, saying to myself that it must not be so, yet my heart beat anxiously. We all heard the good news, thankful that his neck was spared. I tried to read the note, but couldn't read understandingly; my nerves were so distraught. Bob is here now, patient and uncomplaining, glad to be at home, injured from jumping off his horse while running, . . . fearing that Pegasus would dash into the flood, he had no alternative but to jump off, or be drowned.

[March 1862]

A year has passed since our secession. The Lincolnites make desperate efforts to recover last year's losses. Still we are hopeful of gaining the next battle, if the odds are not too great, as they have heretofore been. 'Victory or death' is the general sentiment. We must be free. God help our cause! Mr. Stribling and another young minister preached Sat. & Sund. Oh! that we had such ministers often! Prone to forget our eternal interests, how sinful and wicked is the heart! I am sick of vanities and vexations, struggles for the right and find only wrong. Without aid from on high, how can the misery of Life be borne? I feel like hunting a solitude, knowing that even in a hermit's cell I could not be contented. And why should I shrink from trials of patience and temper? Sorrow is our portion here; long ago I have seen that pleasure is but a name, and Life is stern reality. Not being free to do as duty prompts, I do nothing, trammeled by the will of others, and the opinion of the thoughtless crowd. "Honi soit qui mal y pense."^{yy} Motives are misunderstood as well as the person. Yet, why! should I complain, when perhaps I judge others as harshly as I myself am censured. Oh! for knowledge to widen

yy. "Shame on the one who thinks evil of it," the motto of The Most Noble Order of the Garter, the oldest and most important order of knighthood in Great Britain.

the narrow contracted minds of those who measure others by individual standards.—Eh bien!

[04/22/1862]

April 22d—To-morrow week some of our soldiers leave for the seat of war.... to join Van Dorn.[58] We fear for their safety. Missouri is far, and out of reach.... I trust another general better.... 'the Boys' can participate.... Calvin will go with Bob.... he will not wait a year, and all of them are impatient to be off.... Charlie would accompany them if he were allowed. All of our neighbors go, all except William. Poor boys! how much will they suffer!—M. Reese is wed. To a little soldier-boy of eighteen, called ... Willie Williamson. We attended the wedding, held at her guardian's.[59] Few were there, and none of her distant relatives.[zz] Mollie has risked the most, knowing little of her Bridegroom,[61] probably supposing him to be rich, or marrying for a home. She has gone to his home at Eagle Lake. In twenty days he departs to join Capt. Veasey. Willie as he is universally called, is a gentlemanly little fellow, of pleasing appearance, not particularly handsome, however.

zz. By "distant relatives," Sallie means those who lived out of state, rather than those who were not closely related.[60]

[05/25/1862]

25th May—Brown's Batt. was ordered to Arizona, much to the general dissatisfaction. Now ere they reach Columbus, are recalled to defend Gal., the surrender of which is demanded within four days.[62] The long-looked for invasion is at hand! Two weeks ago, "our Boys" bravely bade us 'good-bye,' strong in hope and pride. Few tears were shed—all courageous. Mr. R[63] realized the separation from his family, they remain with us. Calvin was quite unwell for days past, but with his usual quiet determination was deaf to entreaties to remain at home till his health was restored. In striking contrast, to his manly response to Duty, is the conduct of Mr. J., under thirty, keeping his room for a cold, while his Co. is busily organizing for service.... Under a variety of excuses managed, to escape duty. Now is awaiting a dentist to extract an aching tooth. Mr. R. came last eve, shorn of his mustache & immense whiskers.—E. Norris has wed A. Burkhart, the lover discarded, ... 'Now takes him to escape being an old maid,' says Mc. He is quite poor & indolent.[64]

... M. Alcorn is united to _____ a young recruiting soldier; Emeline engaged ... from a two days visit, below with Joe M., ... J. here, looking extremely upright in his drilling uniform. Have just rec'd our first letters from the 'Boys': are awaiting orders near Harrisburg. C. says "Don't let Charley join the army," and not to be frightened, at the near approach of an invasion. The enemy (can) will not advance further than Virginia Point. Mr. R. writes their mess is the only moral one in the *Co.*, is disgusted with profanity, a sad truth.

[07/16/1862]
    July 16th—The Battalion changing from place to place, is now at Chocolate.[65] Calvin came home for two days. Bob visited us three times. Having horse hunting for an excuse, he slips home. Both boys are growing rapidly. There is no certainty with regard to their movements. Pobe Rowe, getting a ten-day furlough; married Ginnie Cleveland the same week she graduated.[66] Frank & Joe Mims are engaged, & thereby hangs a tale! William will marry Miss Cooper, I suppose.—Poor Mrs. Erwin is dead. So pleasant & agreeable, we'll miss her. At her Funeral it was reported that Geo. Weekley was dead. "It is not so," was my instant reply. I was anxious about it, though & Sat. night sitting in the moonlight talking to Dr. Rowe & listening to Mc's confidential talk to Bob. Dr. R., in answer to Grandma's enquiries, said that the rumor was certain. Captain Fly had written the particulars of his Death in Camp of sickness. Gerald & wife were then in Wharton. Dead! George! dead! How my heart thrilled as I heard the dread intelligence & began to realize, that my childhoods firm friend was indeed, no more. Oh! Shall I see him never again. . . . my earliest, best friend has perished, . Never shall I have another such friend again, known from the days of my childhood, together at school, studied from the same books, then, three years ago we parted & his last words of that time, adding as he left us, that he wished could live down here. Now he is deaf to his friends, his eyes are closed forever, the thick brown hair, such a peculiar & bright a tint, was put away from his broad forehead by kindly, but rough hands of soldiers! Ah! Little did we realize in those happy & careless days of old what a sad fate was

reserved for our merry-hearted Boy. I too was happy, then. Never was there a harsh word or look exchanged between us. I thought of him as my adopted brother. I grew still, looking out on the dim moonlight, . . . with the tears slowly dropping over my face. My sleep was unrefreshing, and an aching void in my heart. I had intended wearing white that morning, but with the thought that only sad colors suited my feelings, I resumed the black, garb of mourning. Mrs. Jones opened the Piano to play several pieces; at the first note, the remembrance of the passionate love for music felt ever by George, came over me sorrowfully. Never again, would he waken music from his loved violin. A sad duty is mine, to write to his Sister! Friend of the brightest portion of my quiet Life, your memory will ever be cherished by your true friend & Sister. Would that I could hope, he were spared!

"He, the young and strong, who cherished,
Noble longing for the strife,
By the road-side fell and perished,
Weary with the march of life!"[aaa]

aaa. From "Footsteps of Angels" by Henry Wadsworth Longfellow

[09/22/1862]

Sept. 22nd.—Summer is over, and gone. A long, dry and dusty one. For two weeks the rain poured daily, causing much sickness in Camps. Calvin came home convalescent, looking ill, but with a ravenous appetite. Bob did not seem well; I accused him of indulging a 'sullen fit.' Frank R. was also ill enough to obtain a furlough, to Mr. Alex' extreme dissatisfaction, not wanting any opportunity for F's visits to Joe. Dr. R. gave a minute to imitate the expression of his face, looking like a 'thunder cloud. . . . from Sandy- Point have changed their location to near Wharton. Mr. Rainey will rejoin them there. . . . Went fishing Sat. at Mr. Churchill's. Bennett's invited us to a gathering at the Capt's, only five ladies in attendance . . . Charlie representing a lady, took his first bow, delighted with his success. . . . Calvin don't care for such gayeties. . . . In spite of recent glorious victories, gained by our brave soldiers, . . . a second time, the scene of an inglorious rout of the enemy.[67] God grant that it may soon cease! This terrible strife among a people, who should be friends. Nevermore can I harbor kindly feelings for Yankees;

their delusion is almost beyond belief. Dick Haynes! fell before Richmond! And Sam Mims reported to be dangerously, if not mortally wounded, at Murfreesboro,[68] while fighting by Col. Wharton's side. Friend after friend departs, who has not lost a friend? I have so few, ill can I spare one. Peace, peace is the universal prayer! Sometimes the end appears distant to my desponding heart, again hope will brighten at the glad tidings of numerous victories achieved by us. The Grand Army has been driven back, hopeless of gaining Richmond, & soon will we threaten their own proud Capitol.

[09/30/1862]
Sept. 30th—Feel impatient and cross, am heartily sick of *selfishness*. Oh!, I don't want to be mean and little souled, but generous and just. I sigh for independence of thought and action. Weak woman can rarely attain either. I must submit with what patience I may, feeling that Life will be ever a struggle. I rarely visit or talk, without regretting something said, or done either on mine or others part. I can't be still and stupid in company, as there's little to entertain one, here. Oh! dear! I fear I shall be a complainer. Gerald Weekley & Bride are stopping here, and at Mim's, a few days. I was glad, & yet sad, to see them. The remembrance of old times is almost painful now. Julia is a sweet woman, not near as pretty as of old, though. Mr. Rainey has returned to Camp with Pegasus. We expect Calvin in a week or two. . . .

[11/04/1862]
Nov. 5th—Yesterday was Calvin's eighteenth birthday. He wished to be at home on that occassion. All can come, but he was too independent to ask leave of absence from duty. . . . . Bob gets off on a horse-hunt, suffering from the jaundice this time. . . . For several weeks the regiment has been encamped near Matagorda, in which place, illness has broken out fearfully, for the first time. We fear the contagion will spread. 'The Boys' would as soon face the Yankees, rather. Yankee ships are cruising off the coast. Gal. has fallen![69] Contrary to the wishes of the citizens a defense was not even attempted. Resistance was pronounced untenable; and surrendered to eight gun-boats, with not men enough

on board to garrison the city. Sugar-cane is badly frosted, ere preparations are completed for grinding.

[12/03/1862]

Dec. 3d.—Sund.—Bob took away Calvin, after a stay of three weeks. Col. Brown was kind to allow C. and F. Rowe to assist in sugar-making. Frank availed himself of the opportunity to marry.[70] Mr. Alex made little or no objection, and the wedding came off at his house.[71] We all went—an informal assembly. Jo behaved with more dignity than I thought possible, for her. Dr. Green came at Mc's invitation, and fatigued me. Calvin accuses me of acting deceitfully towards him. I know I felt dull and indifferent. He asked me instead of Mc to ride with him. I wanted to refuse, but couldn't. It was the darkest night; I thought we were driving in the woods half the time. Charlie & Mr. Wm. Rowe last Thursd. were on the Prairie hunting bears. The Yankees had landed, and partially destroyed Mr. Winston's salt-works, on the coast. Anticipating another visit from the vandals, scouts from Bate's Reg. & Brown's Batt. to the number of fifty concealed themselves behind some sand-hills on the Beach, a mile & a quarter below the Salt-works.[72] Just before day Mr. R. & C., anxious for a fight, joined the scouts. The Yankees sent two launches ashore. . . . Our men kept hid, till the enemy were at two hundred yds. distant, from them, and with wild yells gave chase. Before the marauders could regain their boats, our Rangers were upon them. Instead of surrendering, the Yankees opened fire on 'our boys' still fighting desperately. When last seen, only three remained alive in one boat & two in the other. Several prisoners were taken, who failed to reach the Launch. . . . But others were shooting at him, & C. was inexperienced & did not see him hold up his hand in token surrender. Capt. Mosely put C. & Mr. R in the rear much to their displeasure, but when the race began, they being better mounted, distanced the others & had the first shot at the Yanks, ere they could push off. In return for a shot through the nose of his horse Mr. R. felled the Lieut. in command. Oh! but that was a wild race over that log strewn shore. One of our soldiers was shot in the leg,[73] another had his horse killed. I tried to quarrel with Mr. R. for taking C. into danger, said they could not stay away.

[02/16/1863]

Febr. 16th, 63.—"Tis a time for memory and for tears."[bbb]—I am twenty-three, and begin to realize that I am growing old. Still I am content: I would not be younger. If I could only feel, that these years had not been spent altogether in vain. I can bitterly regret misspent time, without an effort to reform for the Future. My natural indolence has been fostered by indulgence, till I have little or no energy left. Idleness is with me a besetting sin. Not that I do nothing; I generally pretend to work at something; embroider, knit or do plain sewing. This sort of work does not satisfy me, however. Yet I am fast becoming a human drudge, resigned to my fate. I seldom can get a new book, or take pleasure in my love of reading no longer. . . . Alas! for me. . . . Ah; well! I'll try not to speculate. . . . The Present only is mine. If I cannot achieve great deeds, and words, I will at least avoid any wrong intentionally, committing myself to Him, who erreth not. May I so walk so as not to bring reproach on thy holy Cause, O God! . . . Our new Year was ushered in with the cry and shout of Battle. Magruder deferred till darkness, the attack upon Gal.[74] The short conflict ended in the glorious recapture of the Island, and a portion of the artillery of their Boats. All honor to our brave leader! Ere this year has completed its months we confidently hope for Peace. The hand of God is with us, and may we never forget the thanksgiving due to "Him who giveth us the victory."[ccc]—Our darling Archie is just recovering from a month's illness. For days we were almost hopeless, of his restoration to health. What a weary time, was that. The Boys came to nurse him. Calvin is a darling Brother, so gentle and assiduous in his attentions to the restless invalid. Mr. Weekley[75] is here for the first time in years. The Batt. will be dismounted in Matagorda. Mrs. Wm. Rowe is as natural as ever; spent two days with us.

bbb. From "The Closing Year" by George D. Prentice (1802–70)

ccc. I Corinthians 15:57 KJV

[03/12/1863]

March 12th—This morn there is a cry of Measles in the quarter. I haven't been sick so long, I don't want to have the disease. I am afraid we all will. Calvin wrote to me for the first time, since he has been in the service. Orders are strict, not to grant Furloughs. Manly returns to camp, reluctantly.

Visited Mrs. Burckhart yesterday with Mr. Weekley. Sent Miss Mary D. a pink calico: wanted to give her a prettier one, but rather than have a fuss in the Family, gave up the idea. Grandma had the keys.

[Possibly March or April, 1863]

The Yankee threat has withdrawn to our surprise, leaving the Batt. to guard the coast, much to our delight & their dissatisfaction. They left three weeks ago. Measles has been severe, killing, several negro babys. In some cases, there were two and even three eruptions at each spot, and two kinds. Archie & I were not very sick. Many were lost to the disease in Gal. Mose also died. Forgive our complaint! We should thank God, that more were not fatal. Bettie & Hulda have professed Religion. In the months since, two backsliders are reclaimed. All around us, the white dove still finds no resting place, in our midst . . . My heart sickens, at the dreadful prospect!

[Possibly November, 1863]

. . . Months have elapsed, since I have written here or answered my few letters. Days and weeks have fled, burdened by the hopes & fears of this unholy strife. We count it a blessing that 'our Boys' are still in the vicinity, though in imminent danger . . . from the Yankees who are now in possession of Matagorda Peninsula. We are hurrying preparations to leave our home in compliance with Magruder's orders, to fall back into the interior. Houseless, penniless wanderers, seeking a refuge from the Vandal horde, so closely threatening our Coast. But the trouble of leaving our Home is as nothing to the pain of abandoning our soldiers. I shall certainly remain as long as possible. Poor boys! stole off home, for a few hours yesterday. Archie too is ill, has been for a week & Dr. Chinn's too much scared to be of much use, even when he dares come over. Simon, Grandpa's foreman, died last night. He will be a great loss, but thank Heaven! was an unob[tru]sive[ddd] Christian. Oh! If my Brothers were only in the Ark of safety, I could be resigned to their danger. Charlie, I'm afraid we cannot keep from joining Calvin, soon. In the hour of adversity we can only trust in Divine aid.

ddd. The middle of this word is illegible.

[02/21/1864]

Feb. 21st, 1864—Another New Year and still this struggle continues unabated! "Hope deferred maketh the heart sick."[eee] We no longer look for aid from abroad, or present Peace. The all enduring South has buckled on her armor of defence and wear it ever, till Liberty is regained. Texas has been waiting all Winter, to welcome, with bloody hands her ruthless invaders. Brown's Reg. have been sent, guarding the Mouth of Mat. Peninsula, where the Foe has quartered. From our home Circle, we miss a valued friend. Bob is a prisoner. On the 29th Dec. the daring Boy volunteered to scout far down the Peninsula. A Gunboat of the enemy, cut off all retreat.[76] Our brave soldiers are no longer exchanged, but languish in Northern dungeons, far from home & friends. In their adversity, may they look aloft to Him, who is always near, and a saving help in times of need. Poor Bob! Would that he could write to us of his safety. Ma is slowly recovering, from a severe illness of a months duration. Her sudden sickness recalled Mc from a visit to Old I. whither she had gone with Joe Haynes, who spent several weeks, with us. It was a trial to useless, inexperienced I to nurse. I did not know before that I could. Grandparents are old, and almost helpless,[77] & to me Ma could only look for assistance.—The last Page of my neglected book. Hard times will no longer allow paper to scribble on.[78] The days are speeding on un-chronicled by word or deed of mine. Silently but swiftly they depart to Eternity. I have almost ceased to regret the passage of Time. Peace of heart, and Life is my greatest aspiration & humble prayer. Vale.

eee. Proverbs 13:12a KJV

The fourth portion of the diary ends here, with the wartime paper shortage causing the longest break in the diary. Sallie resumes her journal entries a few months after the end of the war in the fifth segment using paper and ink of much inferior quality. Although the paper is not damaged, the ink on at least four pages is so faded that most of it is indecipherable.

[11/10/1865]

Nov. 10th 1865.
Sat. eve:—'Tis long since I've felt like journalizing. The days, and weeks of the last two years, have been spent in anxious suspense, or patient waiting. Heroically the South

Nov. 10th 1865.

Sat. eve. — 'Tis long since I've felt like journalizing. The days and weeks of the past two years have been spent in anxious suspense, or patient waiting. Heroically the South struggled against adverse fate, and endured all ills, 'till exhausted and "overpowered" by numbers, she surrendered her gallant little Army, and the Confederacy was no more. Suddenly, and with scarce a word of warning, the dread news reached distant Texas, reducing all to despair. The bitter suffering, the sacrifice during four long years of bloodshed, has all been in vain; all is lost save honor. The agony of suspense is over, and endurance only is left to the humiliated, but not disgraced Southerner. Slowly we are awakening from the feeling of utter despair, which overwhelmed all classes, upon receipt of the news of the fall of the Confederacy. The realization of the change is bitter indeed, but Time the consoler is healing some of the old wounds — necessity, inexorable necessity teaches patience and submission. 'Twas hard to be resigned — we had hoped and prayed for the success of our Cause. Never had a doubt of victory been entertained. I had a proud faith in the justice of our cause, and in the nobility of the South. Doubts were traitors! And to the last the Patriot hoped against

10. Page of Sallie's diary. Author's personal collection.

struggled against adverse fate, and endured all ills, 'till exhausted and "overpowered" by numbers, she surrendered her gallant little army, and the Confederacy was *no more.* Suddenly, and with scarce a word of warning, the dread news reached distant Texas, reducing all to despair. The bitter suffering, the sacrifice during four long years of bloodshed, has all been in vain; all is lost save honor. The agony of suspense is over, and endurance only is left to the humiliated, but not disgraced Southerner. Slowly, we are awakening from the feeling of utter despair, which overwhelmed all classes, upon receipt of the 'news' of the fall of the Confederacy. The realization of the change is bitter indeed, but Time the consoler is healing some of the old wounds—necessity, inexorable necessity teaches patience, and submission. T'was hard to be resigned—we had hoped and prayed for the success of our cause. Never had a doubt of victory been entertained. I had a proud faith in the justice of our cause, and in the nobility of the South. Doubts were traitors! And to the last the Patriot hoped against hope, that perseverance would win. But the end came and we have lost. Oh! how dark grew the world! How still, and quiet everybody, and everything seemed. Soldiers hurried silently, and sadly homeward, not to receive the triumphant greeting which has been anticipated, for four long years, but to be welcomed with sadness and tears. We are mourners, for the dead, and living; for the miserable Past, and hopeless Future. No! not altogether "hopeless." We are growing resigned. The God of Battles has decided against us—we were not worthy; we are punished for our sins. We must realize that "the ways of Providence are not, as our ways." That "He doeth all things well."[fff] The proud Southerner is humbled. We are but dust.—May not the sacrifice be in vain! as gold purified in the flames, may the South come forth from the furnace of affliction, purged of all dross. We see through the glass darkly"[ggg] we grope in the dark. Without aid from on High, we are lost—teach us O God! the error of our ways, and "lead us to the rock that is higher, than I."[hhh]—

fff. Mark 7:37 KJV

ggg. I Corinthians 13:12a KJV

hhh. Psalm 61:2b KJV

No Concessions to Make

*S*allie begins her record of life after the War with a complaint about the difficulty of dealing with freedmen rather than slaves. Many other changes begin to take place in her world. Their neighbors, the Rowe family, depart for Washington County, and her brother Calvin moves to their plantation. Her sister Annie has married, her brother Charlie has gone to North Carolina to school, and an orphaned child, Kate Jackson, has moved in with the family. Her cousin, Barbara Rainey, and her children, who stayed with them during the War, also move away, and her dear friend, Miss Mary Davis, dies. During this time of upheaval and loss, Sallie makes another trip to Washington County, and still manages to write about once a month. The final change occurs during the summer of 1867, when she and some of the family join friends for an extended stay at the beach. There she begins to write every few days until her last entry, exactly one month before her death on October 28, 1867.

> [11/28/1865]
> Nov. 28th.—The last night of sugar making. And everyone rejoices that the cane is cut, and this grinding season over. The Freedmen have tried Grandpa's and Bob's patience to the utmost. The institution is certainly a "trial;" the theme of every tongue and the subject of busy thought & speculation for the past six months. Next year, the experiment will be made, of free Negro labor. I only wish the Yankees could have the insolent indolent Blacks in their midst! Poor Nigger is ignorant, and unfit for the care of himself. Manly Rowe has been, and is still very ill. Ma and A. visited him yesterday. He asked to have me come and I could not choose but go. Poor fellow! I forgot my hardness toward him, as I thought of his danger, and realized the frailty of human strength. I do feel, that the Past is inexcusable, but I'll try to forget—to remember his especial weakness, and to believe he erred from no bad motives. He was instrumental in

bringing bitter suffering on me, but he has repented and I forgive him, I hope. I need too much forgiveness myself, to withhold pardon from others. "Forgive us our debts, as we forgive our debtors."[a] Can I breathe this prayer without condemning myself? I am afraid not, sometimes. "Charity suffereth long, and is kind."[b] I can multiply texts to prove that "hatred is death and Love is life."[c] It hurts me to feel bitterly towards anyone, and yet pride cannot brook insolence, or presumption. 'Cleanse us, O God, from secret faults.'[d] May we follow the example of our blessed Savior, who was "meek and lowly,[e] and when He was reviled, reviled not again."[f]— I have lost a valued friend. Miss Mary[1] no longer suffers in this world of woe; we weep, but well we know that 'our loss is her gain.' My almost best friend—I do not realize, that I will never behold her again. I'm thinking of her throughout the hours of the day; gathering up olden memories, every word and act of affection, bestowed upon me for years past; I who often felt unworthy of her anxious solicitude. Dear dear Miss Mary! who will hear and sympathize with my troubles now? No one appreciates me, as did Miss Mary! I shall not want to visit Independence again; I would miss her so constantly; I should be miserable.—When Calvin wrote me, she was very ill; I felt anxious, a dim foreboding of evil, seemed to haunt me for days and when the dread intelligence came, 'Miss Mary is dead' I tried not to believe and yet I knew—felt too surely that t'was truth. She was indeed no more. Slowly, I came up-stairs, and gave way to bitter tears, and oh! have I not cause for heart ache? I have lost my friend—an unselfish, devoted friend. I have so few, ill can I spare one. "Cousin Sallie! what ails you," "what makes you cry" pleaded Katie,[g] affectionate little creature, while I felt that my heart was indeed hard, not to grieve more, for such a friend. Calvin had asked Miss Mary! to come down with him Christmas, and I had planned to keep her with us during the coming summer and now I shall see her *no more*. Little did I think last summer, as I bade her adieu at Mr. Clark's gate, that last lingering farewell was forever. My only consolation is that she is now happy; freed from the ills of Life, she rejoices in Heaven. "The Lord giveth and the Lord taketh away, blessed be the name of the Lord!"[h]

a. Matthew 6:12 KJV

b. I Corinthians 13: 4 KJV

c. I John 3:14 KJV

d. Psalm 19:12b KJV

e. Matthew 11:29b KJV

f. I Peter 2:23a KJV

g. Kate Jackson, born in 1859, was orphaned and came to live with the Jordan/McNeill family.[2]

h. Job 1:21b KJV

[12/4/1865]

Dec. 4th 65—Calvin is home, grew tired of school, and must have a holiday; as he intends returning to Chappell Hill next session.[3] Charlie can't afford to lose so much time, says Calvin, is younger than himself; he doesn't expect to come even during Christmas week.—Mr. Rainey has moved to his new home; we miss them again and again. I think I hear Cousin's step on the stair. And the noisy children, who have been with us nearly four years, the house seems very quiet. Cousin's room is desolate, a step across the floor echoes mournfully, even the servants shun the room. Dear Cousin! swift to say "good bye." "Why, you are not going to stay away always Cousin!" said Calvin consolingly as he mounted the bay pony, and took Cal on his lap. Collin too looked sober as he held out his little hand for 'good bye.' Yesterday we had company, so that only Grandma and Archie attended Church. Dr. Rowe brought the Ladies who were so cruel, as not to notice their escort, after arriving. Mrs. J. Rowe gave an animated description of a fall the dignified Dr received from his horse. His very name has become a signal for laughter and ridicule. Poor man! I would pity him, if he had any charity for others. His sweetheart, Emma R.—of whom he dreams by day and night, rarely vouchsafes him a word or look, still he is an humble devotee at the shrine of her beauty. He must worship, even at a distance. How sad he was yesterday, to observe her smiles and words bestowed on another—the object of his cordial dislike.—Miss E. R. is rather fine looking, and amiable I believe. Amiability is a scarce quality now-adays, belongs to the gentlemen more particularly, now they are so completely *subdued.*

[1/10/1866]

[J]an 10th 1866. Jordan Plantation, near Brazoria, Texas. A New Year! And what do the coming months promise? Alas! as I recall the trials, and afflictions of the past Year, my heart sinks in contemplation of the Future. "And if we judge of time aright, the Past and Future in their flight, would be as one."[i]

[2/8/1866]

Feb 8th—"There is nothing new under the sun."[j] Not that there isn't change enough in the world. In my world—

i. "Coplas de Manrique" by Jorge Manrique (1440–1479), translated by Henry Wadsworth Longfellow in 1833

j. Ecclesiastes 1:9b KJV

which is certainly a limited one—the few changes are not for the better. I dread change; though reformation be needed. Away with moralizing—I'm too indolent——spiritless to write—Have just edited a gossiping letter to "the Boys;" with an unspoken threat, in case they failed to consign the same to oblivion.—Ma has been visiting a week, at Mc's[k] and Mr. Raineys; bad weather has detained her. I was glad she couldn't return sooner; she needs change. And I enjoyed the rest, with nobody but Katie to fuss. Down-stairs was only Grand-parents and the talking Bachelor. I could escape from this company, whenever I chose. Though I've spent the evenings in Grandma's room, as usual. I hope, I'll never be selfish, though I doubt, that I'm wanted sometimes, when my Brothers are away. Bless "the Boys!" Bob—quiet Bob—is away too; has gone West for mules. But Bob has lost some of his old tacumity. Free niggers try men's souls, and render the most silent eloquent. I banter him, not a little on the subject! And he, and Calvin tease me unmercifully, about the "little unruly member" belonging to my sex. I've declared my intention to "quit talking to them," and expect this terrible threat will silence Mr Bob, since he tried to mollify my feelings, by allowing that I "was improving;" I didn't talk *much,* as I once did. Ah me, I haven't the spirit for anything I once had. I have the consciousness, that I don't do my duty even in my limited sphere. And yet make no effort to shake off this pond like existence—my faculties—of body and mind are rusted; with folded hands I sit by the fireside, and dream away Life. Because my friends do not care—do not make me exert myself—I have not the energy—do not care enough for myself—for health of body or mind—to do aught but knit, sew, and walk the gallery in the evening perhaps,—go down to my meals, see the few people who call, and average a visit not more than once in three months. Well! I forsee the end. I think, but I do not resolve—well knowing that I have "the wish, but not the will to act." Ma has practiced obedience and self-denial all her Life. And I cannot feel, that her course has conduced to the happiness of herself, or others. On the contrary, her uniform practice has brought trouble, and annoyance to the Family. Life, health, and her children's every wish is sacrificed with scarce a murmur, to her Father's whims. Grandpa don't see this—she scarce acknowledges

k. Her sister Annie married Robert F. Martin on March 9, 1865, but it is not known exactly where the couple was living, perhaps near the James G. Rainey family in Matagorda County.

this fact to herself. And yet I feel, too truly, that it is truth. In bitterness of spirit, I realize the consequence of Ma's amiable weakness—for weakness it is; and possibly a *wrong*—to prefer the happiness—no! not happiness—that is a myth—welfare of her own children, to the narrow wish of others, who if persuading themselves to be in the right and allowing good motives—err much, both heart, and judgment pronounce. Alas! for human errors and human ills! An orphan's lot is ever most always a hard one. A father's place cannot be supplied. If I had less, of the spirit of my Father—if I were more a Jordan in feeling and temper—I would care less. But the spirit of freedom is an inborn one. All my life I've been trammeled, by the wish and opinion of others—even of my neighbors, and the world, in general. Hope for better things! Alas! I do not. The Present only is mine. If I could fill it with good deeds, and thoughts, I should be content. Eh *bien!* Life is the old struggle. Trials and crosses are good for us—sent in mercy, lest we should wish to linger—God has in mercy, "Called for a cloud, to darken all their years" And said, go spend it in the "vale of tears!"[1]

[3/30/1866]

March 30th—At last, we hear from Calvin, after enduring anxiety concerning the state of his health, for over a week. Charlie wrote he was suffering from a cold, merely. Grandma prophesied that he had the Measles, which is prevailing, and sure enough this disease has confined him to his room for fourteen days. Poor Boy! how home-sick he must have been, though he writes that the Ladies were overwhelmingly attentive: sending Bouquets, etc., to use his phrase 'the womenfolk are doing their best to spoil him with profuse compliments and attentions.' Still he repines—is home-sick—can't be content with his book, longs for home. All in vain I fear we try to keep him at school. He knows the importance of an education, still is too restless to be satisfied. Well! have his own way he will—with him the decision rests. I worry too much about his waywardness. Selfishness would prompt me to wish him home, but self I've ceased to regard the claims of self. 'Tis a shame for Calvin to neglect the talents God has given him for usefulness, while Charlie with a less gifted intellect patiently struggles on determined to

1. "An Epistle to an Afflicted Protestant Lady" (1781) by William Cowper (1731–1800)

gain an education. Sometimes I'm afraid we underrate Charlie's abilities. Study was ever difficult for him, and yet he perseveres—Calvin acknowledges that he is distancing him in the race for attaining knowledge. Manly lingered late, last eve to hear from '_____' he said. Poor Manly! I'm sorry for him. I know he is restless, and unhappy oftentimes. Says he feels, that he must "go to school, or get married soon." Asked my advice, which horn of the dilemma should he take? I laughed, ridiculed, and declined counseling him at all. He insisted—would abide by my decision—was in earnest, and complimented me to such an extent, that I talked to silence him. Really, I would not listen to such flattery from another. I know my candor wounds his feelings, but what can I do? I am sorry to treat him badly, and I no longer do, though I can't be as cordial, as I used to be in 'the long ago.' Only to think, that for a year I treated him with marked coldness, and too often with contempt. And he did not resent such treatment; thinks as much of me as ever. I don't understand his nature, or my own perhaps. "We bear within us mysterious things."—

[4/14/1866]

April 14th:—A damp rainy day. Mud and water abound. Lt. Masterson promised to come over this morning, to escort Grandma and I to Brazoria, in order to have our Ambrotypes. The artist remains but a short time. Now the rain has prevented the Lieut's arrival, much to my satisfaction. I don't care to trouble him, to gallant me, and then he would expect us to dine at his Brother's, which I should decline doing, as I am unacquainted with the Ladies of the family. I like Lieut. Masterson, but I do not wish him to be considered, as a beau of mine. He is such a tease—insists on having me go in Town, 'till I feel ashamed of saying 'No'—calls me contrary, etc. Sometimes I feel desperate enough, to almost resolve to "go," whenever I am asked, independent of my own wishes. Manly is just another torment. I suppose people think strange of me, stopping at home so much. I'm so in the habit, I scarcely will go, when an opportunity presents. Went with Bob to see Mc, for a wonder this week. I hate to go there, and its wrong to stay away, altogether—Mc looks so badly, it's small pleasure to see her.—Grandpa is talking outside to John, who has just returned from a cow-drive. Poor hampered horses will suffer now, that stock is bought.

[5/2/1866][4]

May 2d [Ma] is composing herself and Grand parents have returned, Dr. _ has betaken himself to his Office. . . . Alas! for human blindness. "Not your fault, but my misfortune," says one disappointed lover. Then he spoke truth, and though I expressed the deepest regret, he must think me a monster of ingratitude, to turn so coldly from the devotion of a warm heart, which with all its waywardness has ever loved me too well. Poor boy! bitterly do I regret his infatuation—he will never learn how much his evident misery affected me. I who can do so little for the good of others to be even accidentally the cause of unhappiness to anyone, is a source of grief to me. Hard hearted I confess to be, incapable of returning love I freely acknowledge—but insensible to the misery of others—never. I would purchase the happiness of my friends, by risking much of my own. But my peace of mind I'll never part with willingly. I depend not on my own strength. May that Light from on high illumine my pathway, and the spirit of God direct my erring steps aright! Oh! that we were pure in heart, "create in me a clean heart O God! and renew a right spirit within me."[m] "When all others forsake . . . Blessed be the name of the Lord! Another disappointment—Calvin is home. 'I am not glad to see you' was my greeting as he walked quietly into the Parlor one night. And he is not sick. I tell him he would not take anything for that opportune illness.

. . . crazy Boy has scarcely his own consent to marry. Insisted we all should go to Br. to the wedding, . . . knew not the arrangements . . . I helped . . . embroidered the shirt front . . . safely married. Poor, poor Manly, he has my best wishes and prayers for his welfare! . . . Polly is a sweet, pretty girl, but I'm afraid not the right disposition to manage M. Rowe. Love alone overrides all things. Hope for the best.

____, Archie, & Bob are weary. . . . We all went to Brazoria to have our Photographs taken. C. Rowe and Lt. Masterson were here and were to accompany us. . . . such a gathering, so much talk and confusion, asked Mr. Masterson if the scene did not remind him of John Gilpin's [ride.][n]

m. Psalm 51:10 KJV

n. "John Gilpin's Ride" (1782), poem by William Cowper (1731–1800)

[5/25/1866]

May 25th 1866. A bright morning—all Nature rejoices. The birds, happy songsters are caroling folk-hymns of praise for the bright sunshine and exhilarating breeze. Especially does the mocking bird, 'wildest of singers,' pour from his little throat floods of delicious music. Night, and day his glad cry is heard. Never before have I thought him so enchanting, and if the air and the woods are not silent to listen, I certainly hear his varied notes with pleasure. At intervals the mournful coo of the gentle dove mingles with the twitter of the rest of the feathered race. The mingled sounds are indescribable, from the triumphant crow of chanticleer, to the sharp *chee, chee* of the crested wood-peck from the neighboring pecans; golden butterflys are seeking the sweetest flowers to rest upon, and the bright hued humming-bird darts from flower to flower of the mimosa tree, rarely pausing to rest its tireless-little-wing. Pigeons too of gay plumage flash across the sunshine. And at a distance is heard the ploughman's voice, bidding his patient mule. "haw, woa." Looking forth from the window, the scene is fair to behold; the green tasseled corn waving in the wind and the darker hued foliage of the wood beyond, forming a deeper background, with the white clouds floating over all. See from another point, and you trace the sluggish waters of the slough, by its willow-fringed margin meandering through the plantation—there is the cane field with its lighter green blades, swaying and rustling with every passing breeze, and beyond in the dim distance the cotton weed is beginning to cover with a carpet of still deeper green, the dark soil. Nature is fair, and only man is vile. Sad conclusion. Man, the noblest work of God! Ma and the Boys are gone—Katie, I & grandparents are alone. The Boys cow-driving, and Ma visiting Sister Mc and Cousin. I wish I had somebody to do away with the monotonous present, and inaugurate something new for the Future. The warm weather is enervating—all feel lazy, and lifeless-without feeling really ill—still I am losing my flesh—was never so thin before—weigh less than a hundred lbs. We are anxious to spend the Summer on the Beach, but under the present system of free labor it is difficult to obtain laborers to do the requisite work. Calvin would come home, and impose on him the duty of making arrangements. We torment him enough about his fickleness—tell him he learned it of Manly—Manly & bride were here *en route* for Wharton Sat. but broke their Buggy a mile from here and returned. Sis is looking better, than when she first came. There is something charming about the little graceful figure. Manly ought to be proud of his Bride. I know he bitterly regrets talking as he did before his marriage. It seems neither party had confidence in the other—each expected the other to break faith. "Truth is stranger than fiction."[o] Maria certainly loves Manly devotedly, to be enabled to forgive him for the many slights, and mortifications he caused her. I feel relieved about his unhappiness—think he is contented now, as he told C. he loved her 'better, than he thought he would.' Who else could we excuse, as we do Manly; were it not for old associations sake I could neither trust or like him. But I judge him not by common rules, and I of all others should excuse him, when 'tis possible. He cannot help being wayward.—Well! must write to N.C. Our relatives happily escaped the perils of war.

[7/2/1866]

July 2d—Have just returned from a three weeks absence. Visited Chappell Hill, Independence, and Brenham.[6] Found a warm welcome everywhere, but sadly missed loved ones in the old accustomed places. A year brings changes. At the Clark's the contrast was marked. Calvin and myself dined with Tilda, that day of our arrival, and then proceeded to Maj. Haynes. Only Joe & her Mother were *a la maison*. I was tired and dreading the change at Mr. C's, decided to stop with Joe. Soon Mamie came in to see Kate, and suddenly appearing in his doorway, sprang forward with a burst of hysterical tears 'Oh, sis Sallie!' affectionate child, she never forgets me. Of course I had to go with Mamie, who was half beside herself with delight, as we drove up the well remembered hill, leaving C. to walk with Joe. Meeting Bobbie, who peered curiously under my veil, she exclaimed 'you don't know who this is' recognizing me Bobbie sprang from his horse, almost pulled me out of the buggy and would have a kiss. 'Where's Calvin?' was his first inquiry, and off he hastened to find him. We passed several well known groups, 'who wondered who that was'; drove to the front

o. "Don Juan" (1823), canto XIV stanza 101, by George Noel Gordon, Lord Byron (1788–1824)[5]

gate, and sprang out, with mingled emotions of joy and sorrow. But when I turned to behold Mr. Clark's mourning dress, my tears would not be repressed, 'why Sallie! is it you darling,' and I was folded in a warm embrace. Grandma too came to meet me arrayed in the same 'weeds of woe!' I was completely unnerved and sobbed in bitterness of spirit. Miss Mary was no longer there to welcome me, and the contrast to the joyous welcome of last year was painful indeed. I missed her everywhere, every room was haunted with the presence of long ago. Where, Oh Where! was the constant cry of my desolate spirit! I would have avoided the well remembered room but grandma led the way and I made the effort. How can I enter this room, where every object recalls my lost friend. Poor Grandma how desolate she is, and with what apparent fortitude she bears her great sorrow. Often she talked of Miss Mary's last illness, gave me a lock of the once beautiful brown hair, now slightly threaded with silver, pointed out her last resting place in a clump of Live-oaks, but would not allow me to visit her grave, 'till it was properly cared for. Mr. C. has not had time to erect a tombstone. Mrs. Clark with tearful eyes spoke of the last hours of her devoted sister—she knew she was going to die and was resigned, nay eager to leave this world of sin and woe, though as she looked upon her sisters many helpless young children she felt that she ought to be willing to live, to aid in caring for them. Her pure spirit has passed to a brighter sphere. And the void left in our aching hearts can never be filled, 'till we too meet on that bright shore, where parting and sorrow is unknown. May we so live, that we too shall receive a summons from this world with unshrinking faith in the merit of a blessed Savior, to atone for our unworthiness. Our righteousness is as naught before Thee O God! "Simply to thy cross we cling, Nothing in our hand we bring."[p]

[p]. Paraphrase from "Rock of Ages" (1786), lyrics by Augustus M. Toplady

[1/4/1867]
San Bernard, Jan. 4th 1867.
A New Year! The Old is dead, and with it our roses, and delightful weather. The first of Jan. was ushered in by a snow Storm, which continued for two days, till the snow was six inches in depth. I wonder if it followed the Yankee thither. Christmas was dull—duller than usual. Not even a darkey

claimed "Christmas Gift." Grandpa was unwell and though we had the customary egg-nog, and Turkey, everybody was lifeless. On the evening of that day, Calvin, Bob, and myself rode to Mr. Rowe's to make a farewell visit, as the family intended starting on the morrow. Met Mc and the Col. there, also Mr. & Mrs. Bryant. Remained several hours, started our return late, and had a wild gallop home. Not a week before I passed over the same road by moonlight on our return, from the Beach, where a party of us remained two days. We caught a quantity of fish, and enjoyed some fine oysters. I shall long remember this excursion, as it cost me a fit of real anger. The trip was proposed on account of the intended departure of the Rowes, as they wished to visit the Beach once more. On our arrival, we were coolly informed by the considerate ladies, that they were too busy to accompany us—was sorry, etc. Oh! but I was angry, still said little, while the Boys begged and they quarreled till Miss Mary & Emma concluded to go. They have spent several days here since, and are as pleasant, as usual, though they knew how angry I had been. In fact I told them, I was never treated with more *cool contempt* in my life. I excused Fannie—she did not promise to go at all. Manly came from Wharton yesterday, and to-day Calvin goes up to secure the hands, he says are so plentiful. Thence John his striker accompanies him, for he can't condescend to bargain, or persuade Negroes. No letter from Va. in two weeks—Charlie a poor correspondent.[q] Poor Charlie, laments Ma as she watched the drifting snowflakes. Jim Rainey came to day to announce the birth of a little brother. Ma has gone to see the stranger. Jane and Fannie leave us—and none to fill their place. Fannie goes to the Rowe place with Calvin, and Jane to keep house for Mr. Hood on Caney. At first I hated to give them up, now don't care, as twas their free choice. I dread the experiment of this year for Calvin. Seven miles away from home, alone with freedmen. He thinks I would be lonely, and he will be too busy to need society. Nearly every building on the place will have to be rebuilt. I wish the Rowes could have kept their own place.[7] With them go our last of society. And I fear, they gain nothing by the remove. Work—money is the universal desire. Mammon is the object seemingly of every mind. Well! I can't but protest at so much time serving, if

q. Charlie attended Hampden-Sydney College in Virginia from 1866 to 1868 but did not receive a degree.

this world were all—the affairs of the soul and forgotten quite. Was the sacrifice of the thousands of our best and bravest all in vain—did the war produce no good results. In many respects we are wiser, and sadder in all, still are we no better? Was I to answer from surrounding facts I should say worse—worse. Public opinion is not regarded—no man cares for another—All is for self. Like the ignorant Negro, he seems to fear that each neighbor wishes to *cheat*—no confidence—small respect everywhere! Oh my heart sickens, at the bare contemplation of so much evil. All is vanity, and vexation of spirit."[r] "And you are not as good as you used to be" replied Bob to some such lament of mine. Is it even so? Well! I'll not excuse myself, I have been troubled, and disappointed till I have lost much faith in man—am old in spirit, and sometimes so weary—The imagination of man's heart is only evil continually. Strengthen us O God for the warfare of life.

r. Ecclesiastes 2:17b KJV

[3/6/1867]
    March 6th 1867.
    To-day I'm alone. Only Grandparents down-stairs, and Bob in the Field. Ma, Archie, and Kate at the Rowe place. The Col.[s] is sick, and sent for his Grandmamma. Calvin, and Mr. Rainey spent the day here, yester-day. This morning recd. a letter from Charlie, who is improving mentally, physically, and we hope morally. I have just written to Sallie Pier-Wiley. And draw out this almost forgotten journal, to record What! I'm always unsatisfied with myself, and often with others. I sometimes wonder if everybody has the same experience. Not that I repine at my lot, in comparison with others. Oh, No! I feel that I'm blessed in many respects. Yet am oftentimes cross, and impatient of censure, and hindrances, in the accomplishment of trifling things. My besetting sin. The 'little member will prove unruly.' I have plenty of sewing to keep me still; now Jane is gone, and Ellen our new servant, so slow, if good-natured.
    Have been to see C. but twice, since he established a Bachelor's Hall. However, Mc is staying with him. He makes himself ill working. And I fret to see him so preoccupied with farming, to the exclusion of all other things. An ignoramus, he is a monomaniac on the subject of Crops. Ma

s. Her sister Annie's first child, Royal Furniss Martin

and I tell 'tis no use to kill himself working, if he is in debt to Grandpa. Has only six hands, and nearly every building to be renewed. Take time. We fret all in vain about the perishing things of this world. And I realize, as never before the curse pronounced on Adam "In the sweat of thy face, shall thou eat bread."[t] Mary Stratton is mourning over the loss of twenty bales of cotton and Sugar house, which were consumed, by accident. The old man cursed and raved, and his wife fainted it is said, on beholding the burning ruins. The labor of many days vanishing within a night. Does the thought cross the mind of the profane old Maj. that the misfortune is punishment for his wickedness. His son Acy has just married Lou Walderman,[8] and bargained for a Place on Caney. Recd. a letter from Cousin Mary. She is glad to think Charlie will be with them in vacation. Wish I could go on then. Calvin too much occupied. Don't even expect to visit Wash. Co. this Summer. Wrote to E. Rowe. Their cousin lives near them.

Well! I'll quit scribbling, and go down to dinner, and then to work—Sewing I'm afraid engrosses too much of my thoughts, for me to complain of C's attention to vanities. "What is man that Thou art mindful of him, or the son of man that Thou takest knowledge?" "Lord! Cleanse Thou us from secret faults."[u]

[4/20/1867]
April 20th A quiet time this week—only Kate to run around me, while Ma and Archie are at the Rowe Place. I should not repine for the want of society. I enjoy the undisturbed companionship of self too well. I'm afraid I'm growing selfish—in fact profess to be learning to care for nothing but *self*—in self defence. Nobody wants my help—interest is felt sometimes as meddlesome interference. And the bare suggestion of obtruding my notice upon anyone is humiliating to my pride. So I too often do nothing. Well! 'If we could only see ourselves, as *others* see us!' Work! I find plenty of sewing. And bend over the machine, till, as C. remarks I'm growing round shouldered, and am often tired enough to sleep very soundly. Sleep. I wonder how I can slumber away so many hours. I suppose the brain has not sufficient excitement to arouse it to exercise. I suppose I overlook the

---

t. Genesis 3:19a KJV

u. Psalm 8:4; Psalm 144:3 KJV; Psalm 19:12 KJV

work, that is nearest to. Very little energy is wasted—wasted in activity. The laziest creature I ever saw! is Ma's comment often when I sit idly by in utter unconcern of housework. Ellen was sick this week, and I made beds and swept, and dusted 'til my hand was actually blistered.

This morning while reading a Chapter of Jeff Davis' Prison Life,[9] Grandpa caught up Prom's neglected Broom, and swept the Hall and the Piazza, and I only interrupted him to suggest, that he should also take up Prom's neglected Paddle. 'Tis a shame to pet that nigger, as Grandma does. I certainly won't be instrumental in his ruin. Calvin is away horse hunting, and Bob Cow-driving.

They returned last week from a trip to Galveston. Mr. Alex and Joe Mims are gone to Mexico. Tuxpan[v] is the goal of their hopes. While Cad was at her Father's, her House burned one night, leaving only the Chimneys to mark the ruins. The servants saved nearly all her clothes, and most necessary articles. We are sorry for the misfortune. Caddie[11] returned home, and is occupying a Negro cabin. I want to go, and see if I can do anything for her, but cannot till Ma returns, with Archie. Mr. Stapp confirms the report of Mrs. Harrison's *outre* marriage. 'Commend me to a widow.' A stranger came in during a stay of three months in Gal. marries a twenty three year old Boy, while she is fully thirty seven. And to cap the climax, he is a Yankee. Ugh! I think she should emigrate northward. Mrs. Stapp is inconsolable, as she well maybe.

Mrs. Joe Frank actually made us a visit recently. In order as she said to deliver Manly's message, that he had a name-sake for me in the person of a beautiful little daughter, but a few hours old. Am I not enough lamented? I don't deserve Manly's good opinion, either. Have a long letter from E. Rowe and Florence. Must write to Charlie, and Cousin Mary Ann McNeill. And Mr. Rainey shot my dog because he ran after Turkey. Alas, for Bernardo! I hope your enemies, who were many are satisfied. 'Love me, love my dog'[12] and I don't excuse the act—cruel as it is and disrespectful to me.

v. Many Confederate veterans from the area and their families moved to Tuxpan, Mexico, in the state of Veracruz, after the Civil War.[10]

Sallie reaches the end of the fifth section of the diary here and concludes her entries on the plantation. After a break of a few months, she resumes her pen while she and her family are visiting the beach. Despite the rather primitive conditions at the beach, these last two segments are in fairly good condition with little damage. She writes the first section at the beach in the month of July, beginning on the first and concluding on the last day of the month. After a break of almost two weeks, she begins the final section on 8/13/1867.

[7/1/1867]
[Beach]-side, Monday, July 1st 1867.

Another rainy day; everything damp and dismal. Just a week since leaving home. Now all sick, or complaining. Sat. was the first day I felt like walking out, or doing ought save sleeping, or lounging. And then I was somewhat alarmed about Ma, who had worked, till she suffered a slight hemorrage of the Lungs. For a few hours she complained of weakness and was content to rest, but soon the irrepressible spirit of industry was again active. No use, she is incorrigible. We might work every minute in the day, and yet she would find something to busy herself about. Archie, Kate and myself came down in good time to save ourselves perhaps from a serious indisposition. All have had a pain in the side—an attack of the spleen, Ma says. Mc has neuralgia from exposure to the heat, in her efforts to care for troublesome chickens. And too our Cook shed is leaky. We find our house far more comfortable and roomy, thanks to Bob's goodness. Effie would do very well if she could be contented. But the constant cry of her tender soul is for "my Mammy"! She cries every day and almost all day sometimes. Neither scolding nor coaxing avails much to dry her tears. I've interested myself in all her relatives and friends in the laudable effort to soothe her wounded spirit and she will smile and talk, and anon have recourse to tears, till I can scarcely distinguish her sobs from the wail of the wind and waves. Old Ocean seems brimful, this Summer. And our miniature Lakes are overflowing their grassy banks. Old Mr. Uzzel[13] called here last evening. I did not see but I heard him express his Yankee sentiments; or I could have heard, but I wouldn't listen. Sick and tired, I could ill hear those insolent triumphs of the renegade Unionist. Mc was angry and Ma politely differed with the old—I pulled my bonnet over my ears, and confined my attention to a newspaper. Now and then his harsh voice would grate on my nerves. I began to feel only pity for the old man who could entertain as bitter envious thoughts as evidently filled his heart to the exclusion of all good. He was anxious to borrow a newspaper, but nobody had a late one. Yesterday Mrs. Lum M. called, and was duly entertained by Ma and Archie.

[7/5/1867]

July 5th:—Yesterday was the once celebrated 4th. Archie complained of a poor dinner. I told him, we should fast, instead of feasting, on this formerly honored day.—Have had rain every day. Sewed and read trashy novels. I was so fretted awhile yesterday morn; wanted to braid Grandma's Cap and after sending again and again to Gal. found I did not have the right material—too bad, and too much for my philosophy, with Kate's lesson at my elbow too. I am ashamed of my fretfulness; and I'm cross before I half know the reason. My Mammies temper exactly, Calvin's too and yet I've no patience with his undignified fits of ill humor. "Lay aside every weight and the sin, which doth so easily beset us, and run with patience the race before us."w A part of my Bible lesson. *Patience* and *humility!* if we lay our hands on our mouths, and repent in the dust, remembering our frailties, what is man that thou art mindful—. . . Made our first visit to Mrs. Sweeney last evening . . . Mc, Kate and myself were feasted, and failed to return till the sun had set, much to Ma's discomfort in her efforts to get supper and nurse Colonel, whose birthday it was. Effie was standing over the fire, but didn't feel well enough to assist. Archie had gone fishing and failed to reappear at the proper time. In the midst of Ma's scolding, he broke the lamp chimney, and this disaster served to silence all parties. Mrs. S. has an excellent cook and stove, though how she manages to keep dry in her begging shed when it rains is beyond my ken. Miss Uzzel is about to marry H. Armstrong[14]—the Hog-calf is being fatted for the occasion.

Nobody from home yet. Calvin and Bob came Sat. and caught a fine lot of fish in the Canal. C. & Grandpa were going to Gal. this week—we hear the Yellow fever[15] prevails there, would like to spend the week with Grandma, but Bob said my presence "might do more harm than good" so I content myself with the doubt. Such a turbulent element, I am surely. Finished Grandma's cap, but couldn't trim it to suit

w. Hebrews 12:1b KJV

myself, or others much to my vexation. Am trying another. Today adjusted my mask for the first time this season. I had fancied my new room would keep out the sunburn—but alas for my hopes, when powder would not hide tan and freckles yesterday in preparation for calling.

[7/19/1867]

19th—Just as C. had sent Archie to leave to "go fishing to the Canal," Ma discovered the boat descending the River; which C. has been awaiting for some days, to take him to Gal. He gathered himself, and traps as he would say, getting ready for departure. I looked over his list, added a few items, and erased 1 Bbbl Whiskey. All ridicule my scruples and encourage him to get the liquor. He smiled, and don't pretend to excuse the action only as a matter of interest—'and Bob wants half.' 'Yes, uses you as a cats' paw; he didn't dare get it himself, and Grandpa disapproves,' was my indignant response. Maybe, if I was called on to practice my theories, I would do as others do! Oh this Curse of Mammon. I will say 'tis wrong; and I will veto the wrong at home. I clear my conscience at all events. Why not give Coffee, as harmless, and better, if there must be stimulants needed during Sugar making. "Oh, less trouble, and customary"——Grandma protected by an Umbrella, stationed herself on the Beach to watch the sloop clear the Mouth. After C. had gone, I discovered he had forgotten his gloves, and Jimmie ran to overtake him. Upon looking up from the newspaper— that Bob was good enough to send, together with Charlie's letter—my eye rested on C.'s Bills. Ma hastily snatched them, and started in pursuit, while I ran to exchange bonnets and handkerchiefs with her, with the injunction that she 'must call and see Mrs. S. Mc had joined Grandma, and I and chickens were in undisturbed possession of premises. Mc returned tired; while Grandma joined Ma at the S. I suppose they will spend the day there.

[July, 1867][16]

Was sick all night from overeating half done oyster frying. Sleep disturbed, and as a consequence, late rising generally—Grandma dressed for her bed provoked a general laugh. Exhausted in efforts to sweep the floor. I threw myself on bed to rest, and listen to Grandma's stories of olden days. I wonder if a verbatim account would not be different.

Read 'The Land we love'[17] and 'Leslie's Magazine.'[18] Hope C. is able to remember all our commissions. As soon as we descried a Boat coming in Sund., we were out on the Lookout to see if C. had returned. Directly it stopped we descried a figure coming over the Hill, which proved to be himself—still lame. Could only stay half an hour—long enough to shew Bills and get a Cup of Coffee. We accompanied him to the sloop, where each were loaded down with packages. I could but laugh at the ridiculous figures we cut, trudging homeward. C. in his hurry to disembark Ma's store slipped into the water, 'Confounding his luck,' and shaking the water off the Boot that contained his package of Greenbacks. I wouldn't go on board the Boat, and he was in such a hurry I missed seeing our new bonnets.—Last eve Mrs. & Miss Uzzel called—very pleasant. Mrs. U. told Ma 'Texas was going to be married soon,' and asked the loan of crockery, etc. Miss U. wished to know if Mc wasn't 'a good cake maker.' There sails in a graceful schooner over the calm waters.

[7/25/1867]

25th All gone to Mr. U. but Archie, Kate, and myself. Read them two love stories from the Herald, to while away the lonely hours. Now Kate walks on the Beach, while bad Archie busys himself in putting the stove to rights. Last eve sent him to invite Mrs. U. to bathe at the mouth. He pulled on his new boots and trudged off. Mrs. U. met at the mouth. We talked over the wedding, enjoyed the water, and returned to find Archie still gone. Waited til twilight deepened into dusk when Ma could no longer be restrained from searching for her Baby. As soon as I could, putting on hose, and shoes I roused Kate from her cot where she had lazily thrown herself, and then saw he and Jimmie, down the Beach. We could perceive the returning party; the lost one in advance, walking rapidly, his boots thrown over his shoulder. To the query, why did you stay so late? Came the brief reply 'couldn't come.'. . . though nobody was really uneasy but Ma. Yesterday recd. formal invitations to the wedding, accompanied by the present of a piece of fresh beef. Have 'nothing to wear,' not secretly am glad of an excuse; don't care to go. Surely I'm the laziest most insensible of woman kind, not to be roused to interest by an approaching wedding—and too on a desolate, isolated Beach! But I'm so used to loneliness, I rarely look beyond myself, and the Home Circle for companionship.—Mc is crazy to go—will go home, and remodel her silk—in short dozens of impossible plans flit through her busy brain.—Kate runs in exulting, "O Cousin Sallie! I've found a quiet piece of sea wax; Grandma wants it." I look up, to nod and answer; and wonder how small a thing can give happiness to her; and my own childhood seems far off, this dreamy evening. The Summer is rapidly passing 'and no good accomplished' is the accusing cry of conscience. Indeed myself with everybody, and everything around me seem to be growing worse instead of better. We want to attribute all ill, to 'those evil times fallen to us.' But I sometimes dimly realize these are simply the occasion for bringing forth of the evil dispositions, which have laid latent in our hearts. Truly, 'the heart is deceitful and desperately wicked.' I despair of ever knowing myself—even of seeing myself 'as others see us.' The 'besetting sin of the tongue,' is I often think the peculiar temptation of my sex, a source of evil, even in the most charitable and purehearted. Grandma and Mc laughed in wonderment at some of my peculiar views of women's organizations, that struck me, as I was spreading the cloths for dinner, while Grandma knit, and Mc was attending to the baking of that particular piece of veal Mr. U. brought us. Enough—I'll moralize no further, but betake myself to braiding Kate's gingham. I fear 'twill not be finished in time for the *wedding*.

[7/26/1867]
26th—C. has come for Grandma. Mr. Sam[19] had called to borrow our cooking vessels; Archie was pointing the pots out to him, in the Porch, when there was a delighted cry, 'Oh Buddy Calvin,' and a rush for the horseman. Ma dropped her sewing and caught up the Coffee pot, 'he must have coffee!' The considerate boy brought us some butter. I had an eye to this latter fact, and aside to Mc with a nod toward the bucket, 'We'll have some cake now.'—Have a letter from Fanny[20] and C. one from E. Rowe. They are sorry we were not at the Ex. F. is going away—is gone to Dallas

again—why I do not know, 'tis strange this move. She would have come, but could not afford the expense of the trip. Fear F. is too restless to be content, sent me some of her verses for criticism. Poor orphan homeless—almost hopeless—

[7/30/1867]

Tues. 30th—Yesterday, . . . an object suddenly appeared in the door calling an energetic 'Good morning,' with a start of surprise recognized Bill,[21] who explained his presence with the announcement of Mrs. McGrew's arrival, glad of this addition to our little circle. Hope Miss McKinney will teach, and relieve Ma & I of the education of Archie and Kate.—Colonel, mischievous infant is tugging at my dress, and peering into my face as if to see that my mask had disappeared. Lazy—oh how lazy I am! I could easily sleep half the day. Here is a spot to dream away life. I came to rest, do little save set the Table, spread the Beds and sometimes sweep.

[7/31/1867]

Wed.—Called on the newly arrived ladies. Very pleasant if not pretty. All tired of slow travel on a flatboat. Miss Lottie will not teach—is ill, and needs rest. To my surprise Mrs. Uzzel invited Mrs. McGrew & Family to the exclusion of Miss McKinney. Mrs. Rutlege[22] advised her not to invite them, as Texas was not acquainted with either of the ladies. Miss Lottie overheard the confab to this effect. I thought I would, by intimating that these ladies danced, show Mrs. U. that we considered them invited, but she coolly replied, that they 'were not acquainted, and there would be plenty to dance.' Well, concluded I, you'll not have the pleasure of my company either. Only Mrs. U. recd. us this morning. The ladies were busy and asked to be excused. I explained that I called to excuse my non-attendance at the party on the plea of 'nothing to wear.' She gave us a nice melon—showed some cake—fancily trimmed, even childishly arranged baskets of flowers on the dark surface of brown sugar cake. Don't want to criticize—

[8/13/1867]

Beach-hills Tuesd. 13th Aug. 1867.
After an absence of a week, returned Sat. Nothing has

transpired of importance, since the *wedding*. We—rather the Freedmen—had quite a meeting on the Bottom. Only three ladies in attendance at the Old Church Sunday. Mr. Vandevere[23] baptized seventeen colored converts. Archie witnessed the immersion and described the scene as laughable—how they shouted and wriggled in the water. Poor ignorants need a pastor like Mr. V. who explains doctrines and takes so much interest in teaching them 'the way.'

Mrs. V. is a confirmed invalid—her condition excites my sympathies. She thinks, she has consumption. Last evening two of the Ladies called with Mr. Holmes. How difficult it is to receive strangers, and especially Gentlemen in our generally disordered rooms! Retired early after a pleasant bath in the surf, to be awakened by the sound of an approaching carriage. And Miss Lottie's voice explaining they had called for Miss Sallie to ride with them. Ma and I called out that we had retired—was afraid would rain, etc., I managed to thank them for the offer and laugh to myself at the utter disregard of propriety in talking from bed to a gentleman. Ceremony is difficult to maintain on the Coast, when we are simply camping. Propose to Ma to go up and make amends for last eve's rudeness by, calling on the Ladies.

[8/15/1867]

Thursd. 15th—Met Ladies by appointment at 'the Point.' Went alone. Kate refusing to appear in her torn gown, and Ma and Archie busy righting the Coop, which they had upset, in a vain attempt to kill a snake. Wanted company to stay over night, as Mc is gone 'to the settlement' as our neighbors would say. Oh No! wasn't prepared. Mr. S. stopped on his way home to take a message for us, this morning. Walked up the Beach and sat watching A. fish before breakfast. Only caught a Cat.

[8/16/1867]

Friday—

Miss Sophie & Olivia staid over night with us. The former lady is cold, quiet and tall, with a colorless face and sad expression in her eyes. Olivia is short, chubby and talkative, evidently 'looking up' to wealth, in her estimate of people and things. Miss Lottie was too unwell to come. Mr. Holmes seems as meek as a lamb, and nothing to say, or do but bring the horses, and mount the Ladies.—Ellis came to see his wife and child, bringing some vegetables from Grandma, butter from C. and letters, paper & note from Bob. He writes to relieve my anxiety concerning the settlement of the curious question between C. and Maj. S. Very considerate— has had fever every day since Sund. Manly is down—hardly expect a visit this far. Cousin Barbra writes after a long silence from N.C.—don't know that Charlie is in her vicinity. Yesterday and today amused Archie by reading "St. Elmo."[x] He is impatient, of a pause, and eagerly listens—

[x]. Novel by Augusta Jane Evans (Wilson) (1835–1909), published in 1866[24]

[8/17/1867]

Sat.—Went last night to "the Point": captured Miss Sophie and home to find Archie and Ma dispatching Supper. While we set down to ours, minus our shoes, Mc suddenly entered behind Ma, dropping Colonel on her lap, startling us no little. Pronounced her tiresome trip foolish. 'Just as I told you' I scolded. Miss S. did not sleep last night, but was so quiet I could only guess the fact. She was trying to take a nap, when Mr. H. came for her.

[8/19/1867]

Mond. morning.—Walked to 'the Point' before breakfast. Read my daily chapter of sacred writ. Lolled in bed while Mc & Kate dressed for a call on Mrs. U., to deliver a long detained letter. And now shall I sew, read, or "sit in reverie and watch the changing color of the waves that break upon the idle seashore of the mind." Archie will decide for me, when he remembers "St. Elmo."

[8/22/1867]

22d:—Almost through Aug. and we propose lingering til Oct. Fear so many Northers argue an early winter. Though Mrs. U. thinks differently, as long accustomed to a life here I allow weight to her judgement. Called with Mc at the Mouth yesterday. A schooner just arrived. Report yellow fever fearfully on the increase in Gal. Relieved to hear of Dr. Chinn's convalescence. Dr. Salmon died—relapsed from eating ham. Poor humanity ushered off the stage of life so rapidly! Ladies coming to bathe.

[8/28/1867]

28th—Rain all day yesterday; all night long the winds howled, and showers dashed, through every crack and crevice. Was aroused at midnight by cold mist sprinkling my face. This morn still the skies are dripping. 'What a spell,' we exclaim and pity our less comfortable neighbors. Stay till Oct. To-day suggests thoughts of leaving the Coast. Messengers from home came yesterday, and returned to-day in the rain—brought B___ looking badly, 'Mrs. Joe Mims at the point of death.' Am sorry I didn't see her as I intended before coming down. Calvin spent Sund. with us—brought beef and delicious honey. We think only of eating, it seems. Wrote to Charlie, but couldn't send letters up, through the rain.

[9/6/1867]

Frid. 6th—Continued rains still, 'till we wish ourselves at home, in the midst even of bottoms miasma. Surrounded by water, how we shall escape from our island, is the frequent query. The Canal was almost swimming when Calvin came for Ma.

[9/7/1867]

Sat. And too our supplies are getting beautifully less everyday. Are reduced to corn bread and bacon for the first time in my life, I think. We breakfasted on these two dishes, and a bowl of honey. In spite of my warning Kate eat so heartily as to be sick ere noon. We fortunately have plenty of good coffee, and white sugar. Pet duck and chickens will I fear, fall a prey to our ravenous appetites, if succor does not arrive soon. Ma promised to send Mond. Will come herself if Grandma is convalescent. However, I do not expect her, while the rain continues and care not how soon we can go home, if she and Archie do not return. Our neighbors ignore our existence, since Mc "missed her chill." Mr. S was kind enough to aid Ma in prescribing for her. She looks ghostly still. Mrs. Uzzel and daughter came one evening. They furnished Col. milk several days; refuse to sell potatoes to us, even if we are half starved.

[9/9/1867]

Mond. 9th—Despatched a line home per Uncle Sandy, made no complaints of neglect and hard fare since it rains daily in the Bottom, he writes. Mr. McG. came through yesterday, wet and tired. Was relieved to hear of Grandma's convalescence. Ma intends returning when she can. We are ready to leave the Beach. The last week has been a dreary one. I don't feel well. Yet am more apathetic than usual. Mc cross, Colonel troublesome, Kate provoking. Sarah maintains her cool philosophy through all the 'rainy days' though she is overheard wishing herself 'off the Beach.' We are waiting dinner for her return with the Beef killed this morning by the half-starved denizens of the Beach. Mrs. U. exchanges potatoes for coffee with us. The Ladies came Sat. Misses Lottie & Olivia remained over Sunday. We had only fowl and potatoes to offer them, but 'tis all they have *a la maison*.

[9/12/1867]

Beach-Cot, Thurs. 12th:—A bright sunshiny day. We had rains, so constantly, that we hail with joy the appearance of 'the king of day,' who has hid his cheering beams behind gloomy clouds so long that all things betokened the advent of the "melancholy days." 'So lonesome, Mc says, without Ma, when it does nothing but shower.' Col. cries to go out. Kate watches the clouds, and runs to the Beach, 'when it's only misting,' rarely returning without a shell, to hold up for general admiration. Within doors, she pleases one moment, and tantalizes the next. And what do I 'that's worth the doing,' this 'dripping weather?' Sew sometimes—oftenest sit on the bed, looking out upon the tossing waters, and dream idly of bygone days, while fragments of rhymes pass through my mind descriptive of 'the deep blue Ocean,' and 'rainy days.' "Into each life, some rain must fall, Some days must be dark and dreary."y In the face of threatened starvation, I passively eat hard bread, 'till I was shocked to discover that I have broken a tooth. 'Only a little piece,' Mc consolingly remarks, but upon further investigation decides that another of my eye-teeth needs a 'plug.' I have such a horror of decayed teeth. And complain, that Bob might have sent us hominy, he knows we don't like bread. Uncle Ellis came Tuesd. with supplies. Last night tied a drag to blind mule, who is missing

y. From "The Rainy Day" (1842), stanza 3, by Henry Wadsworth Longfellow

this morning. Miss Sophie & Olivia came on the beach, yesterday 'gathering shells.' We sat on a log and talked over 'the situation.' Couldn't prevail on them to come in, not with their draggled dresses, and bare feet.

[9/14/1867]
Sat. Eve—Spent yesterday at Mrs. McGrews. Enjoyed, what seems to be a first consideration hereabouts, a good dinner. Much to the regret of the Ladies, and delight of gentlemen, the schooner came in to take them home. They wish to remain till Oct. Such fine days the last few. And Miss Lottie's health isn't restored yet. I offer to keep her with me—share my uncertain fate. Mc has called this evening. I suppose their final arrangements are being made. Mrs. McG. sent Mc some pickles & she returns the compliment with a duck, which is Mr. McG. favorite dish. I insist that Mr. S. must have one too.

[9/16/1867]
Monday:—A lazy dull day with sun. Was aroused last night by a dash of rain, hurried to close the door and window, and returning to my pillow found 'the drowsy god' would not be coaxed to grant me "Natures sweet restorer, balmy sleep,"[z] Consequently am moping to-day, watching Mc and Kate do most of the house keeping. Sarah is still lame from 'water-poison.' Mc grows daily more impatient for Ma's return. I am as apathetic as usual. Those Boys, are certainly not intending to test my boasted independence. I will only care less with the lapse of time. Expect to depend on self, during Life, so never allow myself to feel lonely. Yesterday read Tennyson & Pilgrim's Progress. Fear my Progress toward the Celestial City, slow if at all advanced in 'the way of righteousness.' Yet the thoughts inspired by the sublimity of the scene before me, should raise my soul in gratitude and wondering humility to Him who, holds the sea in the hollow of his hand.

[9/21/1867]
Sat. 21st, 67:—Slept ill last night—wonder at the cause—have no particular reason for disquiet. Yet for several nights am awake for hours, listening to the roar, and rush

z. From "Night Thoughts" (1742–45), Night I line 1, by Edward Young

of the ever moving waters, and thinking, thinking—what countless thoughts pass through my mind, leaving only an indistinct memory of the same, when morning dawns, and the garish light of day bids the shadows flee. "Then the dreams depart, then the fading phantoms flee; And the sharp reality, now must act its part."aa Ah, but mine are open-eyed visions! and real stubborn facts that bring salt tears to my eyes sometimes,

> "When the hours of the day are numbered
> And the voices of the night
> Wake the bitter souls that slumbered (not often),
> To a holy calm delight."bb

aa. From "Beads from a Rosary" (1843) by Thomas Westwood, English poet[25]

bb. From "Footsteps of Angels" (1838), stanza 1, by Henry Wadsworth Longfellow

My troubles—I have none comparatively speaking; do not fret, as I once would, at the seeming desertion of myself by home-folk: Left to depend upon self, on this bleak Coast, for three weeks, with scarcely anything to eat, and the little we have the starved fowls dispute the possession of it with us. Pshaw! These are minor trials. I can passively submit to them, if it wasn't for the one *nuisance*—and they all *know* at home, that it is hard for me to bear, when Ma is here. I resolve again, and again, that I will be selfish enough not to expose myself to the infliction any more. Yet I cannot plan for the future—helpless, and hopeless almost of the whole subject, 'tis the one great grief—the rarely lifted shadow that throws a somber color across my sky—away with such thoughts—only the old repetition.——

[9/23/1867]

Mond. 23d.—Breakfasted on beef and bread; set rooms to rights. Taken the usual walk on the smooth beach, and return to prop myself in bed, and ask, 'what shall I do to-day.' I thought, I should have a nice time reading the bundles of Yankee papers Mr. U. dropped here last eve, but on examination find I have seen them all before. Have plenty of sewing to do for Mc, but conclude to 'write letters' this morning as I am entirely alone, save the presence of Servant, dog and fowls. The rest have gone fishing and shelling across the river. I generally keep Kate, when Mc goes, but she was so eager to see 'the other side of the river' that I consented upon her promise to be amiable.

C. came Sat. bringing supplies for the week. A week before I should have been glad to see him. Now I 'didn't care a straw,' but met him with the anxious enquiry, "how's Grandma?" 'Getting well,' was the answer, 'but Grandpa has been very sick.' Just as I feared, somebody's ill. C. looked searchingly at me, and abruptly demanded 'What's the matter?' "Nothing" I said. He thought I wasn't looking well. Perhaps I was pale, as I slept little the preceding night. He wanted to know, when I wished to go home; but I disclaimed wish, or voice in the matter. I had not expected to go; but thought he might have come down before, to which he coolly replied, "I am neglecting business now to come." Oh this business of these men absorbs every thought, as well as moment of time. If we had comfortable winter quarters and Grandparents would come, I should propose to Ma to leave the Plantation. Give the men folk the indifference and solitude they covet.

[9/27/1867]
 Beach-Cot, Mouth—Bernard River, Gulf Mexico 1867
 Friday 27th Sept.
 Delightful weather, this week! Mc goes fishing and nearly every day. Can't persuade sluggard to go out alone, often. The supplies we predicted would last a week, failed to-day. It seems that each day provides for itself. Yesterday recd. a note, and potatoes for schooner from home. Bob without excusing, has saved himself from utter condemnation, by this late notice. He "don't want to hurry me home—would have come, but business and sickness prevented." Why not be honest, and—but I care so little, 'tis not worth talking of. If they don't want me, I would not go for the world. Indeed, if 'twere not for Ma and the vexations of my present position, I would not care! Bob is very considerate; to forget me for a month—three weeks for his note dated Sunday and then ask—doubt that I wish to leave this desolate Coast, when they all know & I said I did not want to stay if Ma could not return—especially when our neighbors left. And almost dependent on our poor permanent neighbors for scanty supplies. Well! I can imagine how much I would have felt a year, or two ago. Now I haven't feeling enough to be indignant. Have learned a lesson, or two. Know how much

I can depend on self, and others. I'll take truth at any price. Believe they would let them all die at home, and never show me respect enough, to send for me to the Funeral. Oh, but I wouldn't interfere with Corn gathering for any consideration. "Can't send the waggons for two weeks but will come with the Boat, if I will only let him know," continues Bob, trusting of course to my generosity to say 'I'll wait your convenience,' or knowing I would not have an opportunity of letting him "know." No! And I'll starve before I say 'Come.' This don't look as if I were as indifferent as I claim to be. And yet I think, if I don't feel that I ought to be indignant; in spite of my philosophical notes to Ma. They were intended to quiet her, for I am sure she can't send for us. I'll dismiss the subject, perhaps I am *too exacting;* we must drop the mantle of pride, and bow to Policy.

One part of Bob's tidings gave me deep pain. Why did he tell me Emmie Rainey was dying. Jimmy had just come for Ma. Cousin wrote she feared she would not live for Ma to arrive. I cling to the hope, that the mother's fears overrated the danger. Only sick three days. Calvin did not know of her illness Sat. Our Emmie, of whom we are so proud—the only daughter. God forbid that death should claim our bright one! We begged to have her with us this summer, but Baby couldn't spare her, and now—And in the face of all this, Bob can doubt that I wish to go home. I am not so selfish even if the lesson of self is forced on me. I'm not tired of the Gulf. I can exclaim with Byron

"*There is a rapture on the lonely shore;*
There is society, where none intrudes.
By the deep Sea, and music in its roar."cc

But I cannot 'keep my spirit to this height,' and would go, where I need have no thoughts of what I shall eat. Mc grows desperate. We have three meals each day, but little variety. Killed the broken footed chicken for dinner. Mc sighed over Aunt Abbies fate. Sarah 'just wishes Mars Bob would come, she'd set him down to a bare table.' I told Ellis, now Miss Emilie was home they wouldn't care for the rest. "I'd think they would for Miss Sallie too." And when I answered that I had not insisted on being sent for. He wondered "You didn't! Well, you ought to stay!"

cc. From "Childe Harold's Pilgrimage" (1812), canto IV, stanza 178, by George Noel Gordon, Lord Byron

[9/28/1867]

Sat.—Walked to 'the Point' as usual. No trace of the sick Lamb of yesterday; perhaps the cruel waves bore away the helpless one. 'Meek as a lamb.' Patient and moveless; but for the slight breathing, I would have thought it died. I stood over it and moralized. Deserted by its own 'kith and kin.' At some distance, motionless, but for the wise looking goats who are ever chewing the cud,—was the Flock gazing seaward with the usual apathetic appearance. Sheep always recall to my mind the beautiful comparisons of the Bible. We are as 'Sheep having no Shepherd'[dd] to care for the weak and suffering. Christ, the good shepherd. "The lamb of God," which taketh away the sin of the world."[ee]

We watched two sloops, ploughing their difficult way through the breakers into the smooth water, beyond, and away for Gal. The question arises are they not afraid of the Yellow fever? What will not a man risk for gold! And "what shall it profit, to gain the whole world, and lose his own soul?"[ff] Verily, 'all is vanity, and vexation of spirit.'[gg] 'Somebody will come today,' confidently repeats Mc as usual. And I reiterate 'don't care; they understand the situation,' and we can but accept the clemency of the Northern party. President, Congress, and Grant can let us stay out of the Union. I offer to return when they choose, have no concessions to make.[26]

dd. I Kings 22:17 KJV

ee. John 1:29b KJV

ff. Mark 8:36 KJV

gg. Ecclesiastes 2:14 KJV

Epilogue

Exactly one month after her defiant last entry, Sallie died on October 28, 1867. The cause of her death is unknown, but she may have fallen victim to the yellow fever that she had mentioned as "fearfully on the increase in Galveston." The disease was not confined to the Island City, but became a devastating epidemic that afflicted towns and cities all along the Texas coast before spreading inland. Thousands were stricken with the disease in Galveston, with about 725 deaths already recorded by early September.[1] While yellow fever is a possibility, some family stories attribute her death to diphtheria. Another possible cause of her death could have been a hurricane that moved up the Texas coast less than a week after her last entry. The storm hit the coast near the mouth of the Rio Grande, and moved up the coastline to the Brazoria County area by October 3. The area experienced a high storm surge, which destroyed most of the docks and flooded the business area in Galveston, causing monetary losses of $1 million.[2] If Sallie and other family members were still at the beach, she could certainly have died in the storm. However, it seems unlikely that the final section of the diary would have survived if the hurricane were the cause of her death.

The next death in the family was her grandfather, Levi Jordan. Although Sallie says in 1864, "Grandparents are old, and almost helpless,"[3] Jordan seems to have remained active in business until his death on February 3, 1873. His death at the age of seventy-nine came while on a business trip to New Orleans, and he was buried at the Cedar Lake Cemetery, just a few miles from his plantation home. Jordan's will provided for the plantation to pass to his youngest grandson, Archie, as he had already provided for the two older grandsons, Calvin and Charlie, who were named executors of the will. The will also had some unusual provisions that were to cause problems later. Jordan did not leave any property at all to his granddaughter, Annie, but did specify that $5,000 be set aside for the education of her children. In addition, the will provided for a home for his wife, Sarah, and their daughter, Emily, but with the stipulation that Emily was not allowed to bring Annie, or her husband, R. F. Martin, into the house or onto the plantation without Sarah's consent.

Jordan's death was soon followed by happier occasions, including the marriages of the two older brothers. Charlie married Ella Hinkle on October 22, 1874, while Calvin married Sarah Reese on January 1, 1875. About this time, Calvin and Charlie were working together to operate the plantation that had formerly been owned by Shadrack Rowe. Their younger brother, Archie, was operating the original plantation after returning, in 1874, from two years of attendance at Virginia Military Institute. His mother and grandmother continued to live with him in the Jordan home.

Within a few years, however, more losses followed. Annie seems to have been the next loss, though the exact date and cause of her death are unknown. A letter written by her mother in 1880 indicates that Annie died about 1877.[4] Emily wrote to Kate Jackson, who had lived with the Jordan family, saying, "Many have been my sore afflictions within the last 3 years. First I was made to grieve over the sufferings and decease of my only daughter dear Mc." In the same letter Emily also describes the untimely death of her youngest child, Archie, in 1879:

> But Oh! The greatest affliction that was ever my destiny to bear was the painful sufferings and death of my darling Archie, my all, my only hope to nurse me and dear blind Grandma in our declining years. Oh! How my poor heart aches while I try in a feeble manner to tell you of the unfortunate accident which has blighted so many days of my anticipated happiness in his dear company and at home.
>
> Well, you know Archie did not enjoy good health, although he grew to be a tall stout fine looking man. Being one day not very well, thought that he and little Boys Furniss and Willie Martin would clean up his guns and was in the act of pulling the fated gunn from a chair, when it fired, striking him in the right knee, and passing through the joint, and entering the left and going to the bone, being so near that his pants caught fire. My dear child begged to amputate the limb, which the Dr B thought they could save the limbs. But alas, his frail constitution sunk under so much agony in three weeks. His grief like all my other children was to leave me. He said he said he was not afraid to die, and I trust that his dear soul is at rest with the people of God.[5]

Archie's death was the beginning of many changes for the family and the plantation. After his death, his mother and grandmother were no longer able to live at the Jordan plantation home, so they then made their home with either Charlie or Calvin. During this time, Emily helped to care for her elderly, blind mother and some of Annie's four sons, Furniss, Willie, Charles, and Cal. Emily and Sarah lived with Calvin until his house burned down early in 1880. They then moved to Hinkle's Ferry on the San Bernard River to stay with Charlie. By 1881 Emily and her mother were again living with Calvin, but at Mims Ferry, as he had purchased the old plantation home of their former neighbors, Joseph and Sarah Mims. Emily and her mother lived there until their deaths. Sarah died in 1882, just a couple of months before her ninetieth birthday, with Emily passing a few years later, in 1885, at the age of sixty-six.

Although Jordan's will had not left any property to Emily or Annie, Archie's death changed everything. He died without leaving a will, so the plantation was divided according to the state law concerning inheritance of intestate estates. In December of 1879, the court partitioned Archie's property, with the northern half of Jordan's original plantation going to his mother, Emily, and the southern half of the plantation being divided into thirds, with a third going to each of his brothers and a third being divided among his sister Annie's minor children. Emily, who may have felt that Jordan's disinheritance of Annie was unjust, deeded her portion, the 1107 acres comprising the northern half of the plantation, to Annie's children in 1884. So despite Jordan's disinheritance of Annie, her children came to own over half of the original plantation. As the boys came of age, disagreements led to the filing of numerous lawsuits that divided the plantation and fractured family harmony.

For almost a century, the descendants of Calvin and Charlie, the McNeill boys, had little contact with the descendants of their sister Annie's sons, the Martin boys. Then in 1987, interest in the archaeological excavations on the plantation prompted descendants of both the Martin and McNeill families to plan a reunion of the descendants of Levi Jordan. Family members, many of whom had never met one another, gathered together to reunite the family and learn about the excavations as well as more of the history of the plantation. The archaeological excavation, which had begun in 1984 under the direction of Dr. Kenneth Brown of the University of Houston, continued for over fifteen years. This excavation, which focused on the site of the slave and tenant quarters on the plantation, uncovered one of the richest deposits of African American artifacts in the United States. Several of the carved bone items that were discovered were included in the Smithsonian exhibition, *Before Freedom Came: African-American Life in the Antebellum South*.

The reason for the existence of this extraordinary deposit is unclear. The Quarters on the Jordan plantation seem to have been continuously occupied by residents of the enslaved and freed community from 1848 until around 1891, after which they were left undisturbed for almost a century. After their abandonment, the cabins eventually collapsed, sealing this rare record of nineteenth-century life. The type and location of the artifacts discovered indicate that residents were evicted or abandoned their belongings in haste, apparently leaving behind nearly all of their possessions. They may have been forced to leave their belongings under the terms of chattel mortgages that favored landowners over sharecroppers. Their eviction may also have resulted from animosities brought about by the McNeill and Martin lawsuits, or they may have abandoned everything in flight from racially motivated persecution.

Whatever the chain of events, this abandonment came at the cost of great personal suffering and loss for those tenants living on the plantation at the time. Yet this tragic situation left a remarkable record at the Levi Jordan site, revealing much information about the culture of the enslaved people in the plantation community and their transition to tenants. Although the importation of enslaved people from Africa was illegal by the time Jordan came to Texas, illicit trafficking was still taking place on the Texas coast, and many of the enslaved people on Jordan's plantation were African born. Some of the artifacts discovered in the Quarters show connections to African symbols and rituals, making the site even more significant, as the artifacts illustrate some of the ways the enslaved community preserved their customs and cultures and adapted and adopted those of the Anglo society.

Brown's study of the plantation history sparked increased interest in the transcription of Sallie's diary and fueled concern for the preservation of the antebellum home. Within a few years, Brown, along with former graduate student and fellow archaeologist Carol McDavid, Ph.D., joined Jordan descendants Dorothy Cotton and Ginny McNeill Raska to organize the Levi Jordan Plantation Historical Society (LJPHS). Before taking any further steps, however, they invited descendants of the former slaves and tenants to join them in the organization. From its inception, therefore, the Board of Directors of the society included representatives of descendants of *all* of the members of the plantation community, both those who had lived in the Quarters and those who had lived in the Big House. This inclusion marked the first time in the United States that a plantation historical society had involved representatives of both black and white descendants from the beginning of their organization.

Initially, the LJPHS leased the property and began offering tours to share information about the history and culture of the plantation community. McDavid collected and published much of the information and research about the plantation on a Web site. Funds raised by memberships, donations, and grants were used to help preserve the deteriorating house as well as for other projects of the society; nevertheless, progress toward restoring the house and developing the archaeological site moved slowly. Eventually, however, the significance of this site, this untold story of the journey to freedom of an enslaved people, attracted the interest of the Texas Parks & Wildlife Department (TPWD). In 2002, TPWD acquired seventy acres of the original plantation, including the plantation house and the archaeological site of the slave and tenant quarters, from descendants of Will Martin, one of Annie's sons. Additional acreage purchased later brought the state historic site to about one hundred acres. At the beginning of 2008, the site was transferred, along with other state historic sites, to the management of the Texas Historical Commission. The LJPHS has worked collaboratively throughout this process to help plan the development and interpretation of the site.

The story of plantation life has usually focused on the owners, those who held the purse strings and thereby the power. The history of the Levi Jordan plantation, however, offers a rare opportunity to view the past with a new perspective, by exploring the *terra incognita* of the nineteenth century through the inner lives of one particular woman and many people of color. The diary reveals the inmost thoughts and spiritual searching of a daughter of the Big House, while the artifacts tell the story of a community in the Quarters, searching for meaning in a frightening and harsh new world. The two worlds of the Quarters and Big House were physically located fairly close together, but they were separated socially by a tremendous gulf, one that Sallie was unable to bridge, imprisoned by the racial misconceptions and rigid class rules of her society. The societal and economic upheaval brought about by the War and Reconstruction only served to widen the gulf, with Sallie's racial attitudes shifting from a paternalistic belief in the childlike inferiority of blacks to animosity and impatience with their perceived shortcomings.

The plantation community was based on racial and gender inequalities. With the destruction of those rigidly defined roles and relationships, a tremendous tension resulted as roles were redefined and symbols of status were reshaped. The dramatic disruption of the plantation community created by the sudden emancipation of the slaves left many planter class women totally disoriented, unable to seize a similar emancipation from subservience to patriarchs and restriction to the domestic sphere. Many slaves seized their freedom and eagerly moved out of the plantation community to make new lives for themselves, but others stayed on the plantation, perhaps fearing the unfamiliar frontier of constructing new ways of fitting into society. Many of the plantation mistresses also continued to cling to the community that they knew. Their ventures into the masculine spheres of farming and plantation management during the War had left many of them feeling frustrated and inadequate, ready to relinquish the reins of responsibility and retreat into the comfort and familiarity of the domestic sphere. Some, like Sallie, had never really moved out of their spheres, whether due to lack of opportunity or initiative.

The destruction of slavery, the cornerstone of the plantation economy, did not just rend relationships in the community; it ripped apart the very fabric of daily life. Many tried to mend or patch the tears to reconstruct the old mythology of Southern honor and Confederate glory, but it could not be refashioned. Society needed to be unraveled and rewoven into a new whole. Sallie's untimely death ended any opportunity she might have had to fashion a new life for herself, to reconstruct her identity as the South tried the same. However, her young charge, Kate, gives us a glimpse of the sort of possibilities that were available in the postbellum period. Letters written in the early 1880s by Sallie's mother, Emily, clearly indicate her desire for Kate to remain in the domestic sphere by letting the family provide a home for her. Kate, however, had other ideas and went out on her own to earn a living. This tension was mirrored to a certain degree in many of the newly emancipated people who went out to earn a living in a new environment, while others stayed on the plantation to try to earn their living as tenants among familiar surroundings and circumstances.

The cataclysmic event of the Civil War created dramatic social upheavals, many of which have yet to be fully reconciled. As we seek to better understand this seminal event and its far-reaching consequences, we find it necessary to continue to explore the past. Sallie's diary offers a glimpse into one aspect of the plantation's history; the slave and tenant artifacts provide another. As we explore their *terra incognita,* we may find hope for our *terra firma.* Already, descendants of both sides of a fractured white family have come together to hear excerpts from the diary and the story told by artifacts left behind by people of color. Board members of the LJPHS representing the enslaved community have sat down, talked, and made plans with those representing the plantation owners. Visitors have come to stand near the excavation pits to hear about the artifacts, while others have traveled through cyberspace to visit the plantation on its Web site. Each person, enslaved or freed, rich or poor, male or female, old or young, all have, to quote Sallie, "left footprints on the sands of time," and have contributed to our shared history. Perhaps by walking in their footprints and listening to those voices once silenced by racial and gender inequalities, we will further our understanding of the *terra incognita* of the nineteenth century and begin to heal the scars of the past.

Appendix A
Baylor Classmates and Faculty

Sallie listed the names of her classmates in the second section of the diary after the entry for May 28, 1860. Except for the first two names, Sallie has placed them in the "singular & noticeable" order in which Mr. Clark arranged them for commencement.[1] The italicized listing gives the names as they appear in the *1859 Baylor University Catalogue of the Female Department*, but in her order. This was the first graduating class of some size.

Graduates of Baylor University, Independence, Texas, Nov. 1858[2]

M. T. Whiteside	*Mary T. Whiteside, Retreat*[3]
(Mrs. Ashford 1861)	
F. A. Rogers	*Fannie Alabama Rogers, Houston*[4]
Julia A. Robertson	*Julia Ann Robertson, Independence*
Dora A. Pettus	*Eudora Pettus, Marlin*
M. L. McKellar	*Mary A. McKellar, Palestine*[5]
(Mrs. Herndon, Dec. 1860, Tyler)	
B. B. Carter	*Bettie B. Carter, La Grange*
S. McNeill	*Sally McNeel, Brazoria*
R. Barry	*Rachael Barry, Marlin*[6]
(Mrs. C. Stewart, June 1860, Marlin)	
B. Skelton	*Rebecca Skelton, Huntsville*[7]
K. Clark (Higham)	*Catherine Clark, Independence*
S. Chambers	*Sarah F. Chambers*
now Mrs. Kavanaugh 1859, Jan. Bellville,[8]	*(Mrs. Kavanaugh), Bellville*[9]
E. Allcorn	*Emeline Allcorn, Brenham*
M. Allcorn	*Mary Allcorn, Brenham*
M. Eddins	*Mary A. Eddins*
(now Mrs. Breedlove 1859, Jan.)[10]	*(Mrs. Breedlove), Independence*

Baylor Faculty & Staff of Female Department (from *1859 Catalogue*)

Board of Instructors
  Horace Clark, Principal, Moral and Intellectual Philosophy
  Mr. B. S Fitzgerald, Ancient Languages and Mathematics
  Miss Mary R. Davis, English Language and Literature

Miss Liane De Lassaulx, Modern Languages
  Mrs. Sarah J. Scott, Preparatory Department

Music Department
  D. W. Chase, Principal and Professor, Vocal and Instrumental Music
  Miss Mary E. Chase, Harp, Piano and Vocal Music
  Oscar A. Chase, Piano and Guitar

Ornamental Department
  Mrs. Carrie L. Chase, Drawing; Painting in Oil and Water Colors, and Wax Work
  Miss L. DeLassaulx, Embroidery

Gymnasium
  Prof. W. Willerich, Superintendent

Boarding
  Mrs. B. S. Fitzgerald, Mrs. H. L. Fitzgerald
  Mrs. Mary T. Fitzgerald Sr., Matron
  Mrs. Martha D. Clarke, Governess

A number of the faculty were related. Horace Clarke's wife was Martha Davis, daughter of Rev. Abner Davis, founder of Shurtleff College in Alton, Illinois. Her sister, Harriet L. Davis, was married to B. S. Fitzgerald, and they were both on the staff. Another sister, Mary Russell Davis, who died unmarried, was particularly close to Sallie, who referred to her as "Miss Mary."

Appendix B
Letter to Sallie McNeill from Charlotte T. Nuckols

August 1857
Brazoria, Texas

Dear Sarah,

    I have Come to the conclusion that you do not intend to write me until I make the beginning. I therefore seat myself for that purpose. tho I am a poor hand to compose, as you will see in this letter—I was at your grandfathers last week and found the family all well and in good spirits for they had just heard from you through a chalenge to Mrs. Durant, you put us all to our studys to find out who that was who was born before his mother and dyed before his father, now I should like for you to tell me as I have given it up————

    We had quite a pleasant time of it. Mrs. Keen went out with us, I say us for the whole party went out together to carry Mat to school, for I must tell you that your kind grandfather and grandmother and your Excellent mother wrote me that Mat could go to school free of charge, which heaven will reward them for and which I ever shall be grateful for she was delighted to get back. I think she will lern fast as I think Mrs. Durant is a excellen teacher and Mat likes her very much

    The new house is almost done, it looks magnificent. We had such a romp up stairs and often wished that you could join us. Please write to me soon, as nothing would give me more pleasure than to receive a letter from you as ther is no one in the world I esteem more than I do your family. I expect a scolding from your mother the next time I see her for not writing to you last Tuesday, it was my intention to do so but I was in bed sick all day and I am not well yet tho much better. Luther is not well and has not been this week. Mrs. Keen is well and sends her best respects to you. I hope you will excuse this poor apology for a letter as I have no news to write except what I suppose you have already heard. I suppose you have heard of the death of Mrs. Hoshren & babe. Her death was regretted by all who knew her.

    Please excuse this scratch out. I will write you a better the next time. Farewell and may you ever be happy is the wish of your friend

    C. T. Nuckols

Written in another hand on the outside:

Dear Kates Mothers only letter

This letter was written to Sallie while she was at school in Independence by her friend Charlotte T. Nuckols. Charlotte, whose maiden name was Crenshaw, married Martin L. Nuckols on December 17, 1844. Before his death, they had at least two children, Luther and Martha, called Mat, in this letter. Charlotte remarried on April 29, 1858, wedding Elisha S. Jackson. Their daughter, Kate, was born in 1859, and another daughter, Laura, was born in 1860. Apparently, both of Kate's parents died, and she came to live with the Jordan/McNeill family by 1867. Kate was very close to the family, as evidenced by letters from Sallie's mother, Emily McNeill. Often in those letters, Emily refers to herself as Kate's mother. The Mrs. Keen mentioned was probably Charlotte's sister, Parmelia, who married Robert Keen on December 13, 1855.

Notes

INTRODUCTION

1. Henry Louis Gates Jr., "Foreword" in Catherine Clinton, *Tara Revisited: Women, War, and the Plantation Legend* (New York: Abbeville Press, 1995), 11.
2. Levi Jordan's birthplace is often given as Georgia on the census records. His mother may have given birth at the home of her father Robert Wallace (or Wallis), who lived just across the river in Wilkes County, Georgia. Deed records Edgefield County, South Carolina.
3. Their marriage license is dated February 31, 1838, but as that is an obvious error, the date is most likely to have been January 31.
4. *The New Handbook of Texas,* 1996, s. v. "Census and Census Records."
5. Ibid., s. v. "Railroads."
6. Martha Doty Freeman, *An Overview of the Development of an Historic Landscape on the San Bernard River, Brazoria County, Texas, and a History of the Levi Jordan Plantation* (Austin, Tex.: Report for TBG Partners, 2004), 121.
7. David Lane Hedrick, "The Investigation of the Caney Creek Shipwreck Archaeological Site 41MG32" (Master's thesis, Texas A&M University, 1998), 36–37.
8. Freeman, *Overview of the Development,* 85–87, 112.
9. James A. Creighton, *A Narrative History of Brazoria County* (Waco: Brazoria County Historical Commission, 1975), 37, 48.
10. *New Handbook of Texas,* 1996, s. v. "Antebellum Texas."
11. Randolph Campbell, *An Empire for Slavery: The Peculiar Institution in Texas, 1821–1865* (Baton Rouge: Louisiana State University Press, 1989), 193, 274.
12. *New Handbook of Texas,* 1996, s. v. "Slavery."
13. Creighton, *Narrative History of Brazoria County,* 204.
14. *New Handbook of Texas,* 1996, s. v. "Banks and Banking."
15. Freeman, 114.
16. Ralph A. Wooster, "Wealthy Texans, 1860," *Southwestern Historical Quarterly* 71, no.2 (October 1967): 172.
17. Ralph A. Wooster, "Wealthy Texans, 1870," *Southwestern Historical Quarterly* 74, no.1 (July 1970): 27.
18. Lynn Z. Bloom, "'I Write for Myself and Strangers': Private Diaries as Public Documents," in Suzanne L. Bunkers and Cynthia Huff, eds., *Inscribing the Daily: Critical Essays on Women's Diaries* (Amherst: University of Massachusetts Press, 1996), 27.
19. Entry of October 23, 1860.
20. Entry of April 2, 1860.
21. Joan E. Cashin, *A Family Venture: Men and Women on the Southern Frontier* (New York: Oxford University Press, 1991), 120–21.
22. Frederick Law Olmsted, *A Journey Through Texas: or a Saddle-Trip on the Southwestern Frontier* (New York: Dix, Edwards, & Co. 1857), 123.

23. Entries for October 12, 1861, and December 16, 1861.

24. Entry for November 28, 1865.

25. Michael O'Brien, ed., *An Evening Alone: Four Journals of Single Women in the South, 1827–1867* (Charlottesville: University Press of Virginia, 1993), 3.

26. Anne Firor Scott, *Making the Invisible Woman Visible* (Urbana: University of Illinois Press, 1984), 192.

27. Christie Anne Farnham, *The Education of the Southern Belle: Higher Education and Student Socialization in the Antebellum South* (New York: New York University Press, 1994), 59.

28. Ibid., 174.

29. Anne Firor Scott, *The Southern Lady: From Pedestal to Politics 1830–1930* (Chicago, University of Chicago Press, 1970), 11.

30. Entry of May 9, 1858. This attitude was not unusual among Protestants of this era.

31. Mary D. Robertson, ed. *Lucy Breckenridge of Grove Hill: The Journal of a Virginia Girl, 1862–1864* (Kent, Ohio: Kent State University Press, 1979), 18–19.

32. Historical Census Browser. 2004. The University of Virginia, Geospatial and Statistical Data Center: http://fisher.lib.virginia.edu/collections/stats/histcensus/index.html.

33. *New Handbook of Texas*, 1996, s. v. "Religion."

34. Frederick Eby, *The Development of Education in Texas* (New York: Macmillan, 1925), 157.

35. Ibid., 114, 154, 141

36. *Catalogue of the Trustees, Faculty and Students of Baylor University, Female Department, Independence, Texas for the Year 1857* (Galveston, Tex.: Galveston News, 1857), 24–25.

37. These courses required additional fees. The fee for collegiate studies was $50, and each modern language required an additional $20. Piano training was as expensive as academic work at $50, and Oriental Painting was $30.

38. Farnham, *Education of the Southern Belle*, 86.

39. Ibid., 61.

40. The *1857 Baylor Catalogue* states that the exams were annual events while the minutes from the Board of Trustees meeting from October 28, 1858, dictated the composition of examination committees.

41. Lois Smith Murray, *Baylor at Independence* (Waco, Tex.: Baylor University Press, 1972), 384.

42. *New Handbook of Texas*, 1996, s. v. "Edwin E. Hobby."

43. Ibid., s. v. "William Smith Herndon."

44. Ibid., s. v. "Charles Stewart."

45. Farnham, *Education of the Southern Belle*, 131.

46. Warren, Kim. "Separate Spheres: Analytical Persistence in United States Women's History." *History Compass* 5/1 (2007): 262–277 doi:10.1111/j.1478-Q542.2006.00366.x. Accessed on October 3, 2007.

47. Angela Boswell, *Her Act and Deed: Women's Lives in a Rural Southern County, 1837–1873* (College Station: Texas A&M University Press, 2001), 7–8.

48. Breckenridge quotes from John Crowne's play "The English Friar," in Robertson, *Lucy Breckenridge of Grove Hill*, 167.

49. Erika L. Murr, ed. *A Rebel Wife in Texas: The Diary and Letters of Elizabeth Scott Neblett, 1852–1864* (Baton Rouge: Louisiana State University Press, 2001), 5.

50. Entry of March 29, 1860.

51. Laura F. Edwards, *Scarlett Doesn't Live Here Anymore: Southern Women in the Civil War Era* (Urbana: University of Illinois Press, 2000), 80.

52. *New Handbook of Texas*, 1996, s. v. "Civil War."

53. Historical Census Browser. 2004. The University of Virginia, Geospatial and Statistical Data Center: http://fisher.lib.virginia.edu/collections/stats/histcensus/index.html.

54. Clayton E. Jewett, *Texas in the Confederacy: An Experiment in Nation Building* (Columbia: University of Missouri Press, 2002), 267.

55. Entry for November 5, 1860.

56. Entry for April 25, 1861.

57. Entry for February 8, 1866.

Sallie's Family and Friends

1. *New Handbook of Texas*, 1996, s.v. "Joseph Mims."

2. Joseph Mims had three children by a previous marriage to Jane O'Neill.

3. *New Handbook of Texas, 1996*, s.v. "Thomas Jefferson Sweeny."

Two Years Spent at Independence

1. See *Catalogue of the Trustees, Faculty and Students of Baylor University, Female Department, Independence, Texas for the Years 1858–9* (Galveston, Tex.: Galveston News, 1859), 5. Mrs. Clark was the wife of Horace Clark, the head of Baylor's Female Department, and sister to Miss Mary Davis, instructor of English Language and Literature, and also sister of Mrs. H. L. Fitzgerald of the Boarding Department. Texas State Historical Marker, site of Baylor University at Independence.

2. Mary E. Jackson of Chappell Hill, undergraduate, daughter of T. J. Jackson, trustee of Baylor University, *1859 Catalogue*, 9.

3. No listing in the 1857 or 1859 catalogues.

4. Probably Fannie Alabama Rogers of Houston and Bettie B. Carter of La Grange, both 1858 graduates, *1859 Catalogue*, 6.

5. Probably Rebecca Skelton of Huntsville, Catherine Clark of Independence, both 1858 graduates, and Lucy Avery Atkinson of Washington County, the only 1859 graduate, *1859 Catalogue*, 6.

6. Mary T. Whiteside of Retreat in Navarro County, 1858 graduate, *1859 Catalogue*, 6.

7. Her cousin, Mary Ann McNeill of North Carolina, b. 5/2/1838, daughter of her father's brother, William C. McNeill, b. 5/5/1802, d. 7/31/1875 (Family records).

8. Mary A. McKellar of Palestine , 1858 graduate, *1859 Catalogue*, 6.

9. Emeline Allcorn of Brenham, 1858 graduate, *1859 Catalogue*, 6.

10. Annie Muckleroy of New Ulm, Orcene Gresham of Retreat, Martha Wilson of Vine Grove, and Georgia Owen of Fairfield, all undergraduates, *1859 Catalogue*, 9–11.

11. Rachael Barry of Marlin and Eudora A. Pettus of Richmond, both 1858 graduates, *1859 Catalogue*, 6.

12. Mrs. H. L. Fitzgerald, and her mother-in-law, Mrs. Mary T. Fitzgerald Sr., are both listed in the Boarding Department, *1859 Catalogue*, 5. Later, Sallie refers to the elder Mrs. Fitzgerald as Grandma Fitzgerald in reporting her death in the entry for 5/02/1860.

13. Undergraduate, *1859 Catalogue*, 10.

14. Oscar Hopestill Leland, Professor of Mathematics, Mechanical Philosophy, and Astronomy, 1856 graduate of the Literary Department, see *Seventh Annual Catalogue of the Trustees, Professors, and Students of Baylor University Male Department* (Anderson, Tex.: Texas Baptist, 1858), 4–5.

15. John Lewis Graves of Independence, senior class, collegiate department, law department, *1858 Catalogue*, 6, 20.

16. Her reference is unclear here, as she seldom refers to the Rowe boys who are students as Mr., yet she usually refers to Stephen Decatur Rowe as Dr. She could mean William Rowe, as she often mentions him with that form of address. Although he was not living at Independence, he could have been visiting up there.

17. Burleson was also Professor of Moral Philosophy, Belles Lettres, and Spanish Language. *1858 Catalogue*, 4.

18. Possibly Matilda S. Calloway of Wharton, *1859 Catalogue*, 7.

19. Whiteford L. Smith of Daingerfield, preparatory department, *1858 Catalogue*, 9.

20. Possibly Lemuel Lunceford Callaway of Wharton, sophomore class, *1858 Catalogue*, 6.

21. Susan P. Rhem of LaGrange, *1859 Catalogue*, 11.

22. Possibly Ophelia V. Jenkins of Independence, 1857 graduate, *1859 Catalogue*, 6.

23. Cicero Jenkins, 1857 graduate, *1858 Catalogue*, 5.

24. Possibly Cloana Oliphant of Huntsville, *1859 Catalogue*, 10.

25. Possibly Martha T. Anderson of Seguin, *1859 Catalogue*, 7.

26. Bettie P. Johnson of Fairfield, *1859 Catalogue*, 9.

27. Fannie Early of Long Point, *1857 Catalogue*, 8.

28. Emma Marsh of Independence, *1859 Catalogue*, 10.

29. Sarah E. Huckaby of Fairfield, *1859 Catalogue*, 9.

30. Dr. Jerome Bonaparte Robertson (1815–1890) came to Texas in 1837, served in the Republic of Texas Army, as an Indian fighter, a state legislator, and later as brigadier general and commander of the Texas Brigade (*New Texas Handbook*, 1996, s.v. "Jerome Bonaparte Robertson").

31. Vitula Clay of Independence, *Catalogue of the Trustees, Faculty and Students of Baylor University, Female Department, Independence, Texas for the Year 1857* (Galveston, Tex.: Galveston News, 1857), 5.

32. Probably Alfred Gee of Independence, parent or guardian of Courtenay A Gee, *1859 Catalogue*, 8.

33. Elizabeth J. Allen of Chappell Hill was a former classmate, *1857 Catalogue*, 5.

34. James Thomas Daniel, 1858 graduate, *1858 Catalogue*, 5.

35. James Brooke Thomas, 1858 graduate, *1858 Catalogue*, 5.

36. Probably Ashbury Daniel, parent or guardian of Delia Daniel, of Independence, *1859 Catalogue*, 8.

37. Probably Angeline Hendley of Washington, *1859 Catalogue*, 9.

38. Mr. Clark's son.

39. Probably Rev. J. A. Kimball of Bryan City, listed as examiner for the Male Department in 1867 and 1870. See Murray, *Baylor at Independence*, 377.

40. The Spring term was to begin on Tuesday, February 1, 1859, and to continue for five months, *1858 Catalogue*, 24.

41. Mrs. Sarah Mims, widow of Joseph Mims, an early colonist, who settled on the San Bernard River.

42. Sarah J. Mims of Brazoria, *1859 Catalogue*, 10, and David Mims of Brazoria, preparatory department, *Eighth Annual Catalogue of the Trustees, Professors, and Students of Baylor University Male Department, Independence, Texas, 1859* (Galveston, Tex.: Galveston News, 1859), 12. She usually refers to Josephine as Jose or Joe and to David as Davey or Davie.

43. Robert S. Stanger, b. 5/10/1842. d. Nov. 1881, not related, but treated almost as a family member.

44. Cornelia Woodruff of Post Oak Island, *1859 Catalogue*, 11.

SECLUDED AND REMOTE FROM THE BUSY WORLD

1. Probably Mr. Lumbert Mims, but possibly Leonard Mims.
2. Probably George B. Davis, brother-in-law of Horace Clark and B. S. Fitzgerald, brother to Miss Mary Davis. Texas State Historical marker at site of Baylor at Independence.
3. Sister-in-law of Horace Clarke, taught English language and literature, *1859 Catalogue*, 4.
4. W. S. Spencer, age thirty-seven, in the household of Joel Spencer, age sixty-five, planter, (1860 census, Brazoria County).
5. John Lloyd Stephens (1805–1852) was a traveler and archaeologist whose books were quite popular. The two books mentioned were published in 1837 and 1838, and he later published one in 1841, *Incidents of Travel in Central America, Chiapas, and Yucatan*, 2 vols., which created great interest in the Mayan ruins.
6. Alexander (1772–1851) was a Presbyterian minister who served as president of Hampden-Sydney College (1796–1807) and was the first professor at Princeton Theological Seminary.
7. Claiborn Holmes, sometimes spelled Clayborn, was enslaved on the Jordan plantation and later may have been a tenant after emancipation. See the Levi Jordan Plantation Historical Society Web site at http://www.webarchaeology.com/html/afamres.htm for more information.
8. Possibly an enslaved woman, Millie Williams, who was later listed in the 1870 census as sixty-three years old and living near the Jordan home.
9. Mary Rowe, daughter of Shadrack and Sarah Rowe, was married to Henry Jones on May 22, 1856 (1850 census, Brazoria County, Brazoria County Marriage Book I, page 44, license no. 270).
10. Possibly Isaac Holmes, who was enslaved on the Jordan plantation. He is listed in the 1870 census, age fifty-four, near the plantation with his family. For more information, see the Levi Jordan Plantation Historical Society Web site at http://www.webarchaeology.com.
11. The oldest daughter of their neighbor Shadrack Rowe, who married Wm. B. Wilson on September 16, 1854 (Brazoria County Marriage Book 1, page 22). She and her husband are listed in Wharton in the 1860 census. See other mentions in entries of 9/1/1859, 10/15/1859, and 2/2/1860.
12. J. H. Dance and Company of Columbia, operated by James Henry Dance and his brothers David Etheldred and George Perry, manufactured grist mills and cotton gins before the Civil War and pistols for the Confederacy.
13. Probably Cayce. Henry Cayce, forty, was a planter in the Columbia area, but possibly an S. Cayce of Wharton (1860 census).
14. Similar concerns about John Evans led Jordan to file suit against Evans at a later date for $10,000 plus interest, which money had been given to him on September 25, 1861, to purchase Negroes. However, in this instance, Evans did return. See entry of 10/5/1860.
15. Barbara Ann Rainey, her father's niece, presumably the daughter of his sister Margaret who married Daniel Malloy (family record). Barbara Ann Malloy married J. G. Rainey on March 28, 1849 in Union County, Arkansas (Marriage Bonds and Minister's Returns of Union County, Arkansas). She often refers to her as simply "Cousin."
16. James H. Rainey, son of Barbara Ann and James G. Rainey, three years old (1860 census, Matagorda County, Texas).
17. Probably George or Gerald Weekley of Wharton. For more information see note on entry of 2/2/1860.
18. Leo (Leonard) was the fifth son of Mrs. Sarah Mims, listed in the 1860 census as twenty-three years of age, and was unmarried at this time. She usually calls him Leo. See entry following 10/12/1861 concerning his marriage.

19. William and Manly Rowe. William, age twenty-seven, and Shad M. Rowe, age eighteen, called Manly, are listed in the household of Shadrack Rowe, planter, (1860 census, Brazoria County).

20. Rev. James H. Stribling, Wharton, is listed among the Examining Committee in the *1859 Catalogue*, 4. He is also mentioned in the entry of March 1862 as being a particularly good minister, and he frequently officiated as the minister for many marriages in the area.

21. Population statistics for the two cities are not available, but the free white population of Wharton County in 1860 was 646, compared to 2,033 in Brazoria County (1860 historical census data at http://fisher.lib.virginia.edu/).

22. Mrs. Veazy may have been related to their Rowe family neighbors. Sarah A. L. Rowe married John Veazy on July 1, 1850 (Wharton County Marriage records). See additional mention in entry of 8/14/1860.

23. Possibly the wife of S. J. Thomas, county clerk of Wharton County in 1860. Thomas and his wife, Jane, were living next door to Edmund, George, and Gerald Weekley. Jane may have been the sister of George and Gerald (1860 census, Wharton County, Texas). See also the reference to Thomas in the entry of 2/2/1860.

24. 1858 graduate of Baylor, *1859 Catalogue*, 6. See also mentions of Mary's failure to correspond in entries of 2/17/1860, 6/15/1860, and 9/17/1860.

25. Probably Stephen Decatur Rowe, first graduate of Baylor in 1854, *1858 Catalogue*, 5. He was a cousin of the neighboring Shadrack Rowe family.

26. After losing popularity, partly because of his support of the Union, Houston lost his bid for reelection as senator. The 1860 edition included Houston's farewell speech in 1859, which included his response to these criticisms.

27. Mercer was a long-time member of the Baptist State Convention, and a charter trustee of Baylor University (*New Handbook of Texas*, 1996, s.v. "Eli Mercer").

28. Houston was baptized on November 19, 1845, by Rufus C. Burleson, president of Baylor University at Independence (*New Handbook of Texas*, 1996, s.v. "Samuel Houston").

29. Ibid.

30. Margaret Moffette Lea married Houston on May 9, 1840, in Alabama. She was his third wife, and they had eight children (Ibid).

31. Sam Houston Jr., Sam and Margaret Houston's eldest son, was born at Washington-on-the-Brazos on May 25, 1843. He was a student at Bastrop Military Institute, and left to join the War in 1861 (*New Handbook of Texas*, 1996, s.v. "Sam Houston Jr.").

32. Foster A. Parks, eighteen, mail rider, in the household of D. J. Parks (1860 census, Matagorda County).

33. Eleanor M. Rice married Elsy Harrison on April 23, 1857, in Matagorda County (Matagorda County Marriage Book A, page 72). Their home was on Caney Creek on the league of land adjacent to the Jordan property.

34. Columbia was the first capital of the Republic of Texas.

35. Mrs. Henrietta Norris Mims. Lumbert Mims married Miss Henrietta J. Norris on November 17, 1846 (Brazoria County Marriage Book A, p. 218). Lumbert Mims was the oldest child of Joseph Mims and Sarah Weekly Mims.

36. Shadrach Rowe.

37. Cousin Barbara Ann Malloy Rainey had a new daughter named Emily Ann. See entry for 4/09/1860.

38. Susan Caroline Nuckols Mims, wife of Joseph Mims, Mrs. Sarah Mims's second oldest son. The 1860 census lists their children as Mary, two years old, and Columbia, less than a year old. They were married October 16, 1856 (Matagorda County Marriage Book A, p. 71).

39. Mrs. Sarah Mims.
40. See entry for 10/15/1859 for previous comment on Wharton.
41. Gerald Weekley, one of her particular friends. The Weekleys may have been related to the Mims, as that was Mrs. Sarah Mims's maiden name.
42. Mary A. (Puss) McKellar of Palestine was one of her classmates at Baylor.
43. Betsy is her father's sister, born September 11, 1788 or 1789. According to one source, she married a Danola McNeill in 1811 and went to Mississippi in 1835; she died a widow in Louisiana on November 2, 1857.
44. According to family records, her Grandpa McNeill would have been Archibald McNeill, also called Archie Gahr, born March 12, 1760, in Scotland and emigrated in 1774. He married four times and had at least fourteen children. Sallie's father was possibly the last of Archie's children by his second wife, Barbara Patterson. John was much older than her father, but was also a child of the second marriage. John was born May 31, 1794, and was fifteen years older than her father.
45. Sarah Copeland married John R. Dawson on August 2, 1858 (Matagorda County Marriage Book A, page 77). The 1860 census of Matagorda County lists J. R. Dawson, overseer, and his wife, S. J. Dawson, in the household next to John Duncan, a planter.
46. Tilphia Guthrie Fuller of Houston was one of the two members of the 1856 class, *1859 Catalogue*, 6. The report of her death was not correct. See entry for 2/27/1860.
47. Horace Clark, head of Baylor University's Female Department.
48. Clarence W. MacGreal, age twenty, in the household of Peter MacGreal, lawyer (1860 census, Brazoria County).
49. The 1860 census shows a count of 134 slaves for Levi Jordan, but Jordan did also regularly loan money.
50. In August 1857, Mrs. Durant was teaching at the Jordan home, according to a letter written to Sallie from Charlotte T. Nuckols telling Sallie, who was at Baylor, that the family was allowing Charlotte's daughter, Martha, to attend the plantation school. Charlotte calls Mrs. Durant an excellent teacher.
51. According to the *State Gazette* in 1849, a hogshead of sugar weighed about one thousand pounds. Cited in Abigail Curlee, "The History of a Texas Slave Plantation, 1861–1863" *Southwestern Historical Quarterly* 26, no. 2 (October 1922).
52. This poem is also the source of the title of her essay "Footprints on the Sands of Time," which she delivered at her commencement exercises, and recorded in her diary.
53. Sam Hinkle, age fifty-nine, planter, and Betty Bridges, age sixteen, listed in the same household with E. H. Moseley, age thirty-three, planter, and his family (1860 census, Brazoria County).
54. Wm. J. Maynard married Catherine Oafe on July 22, 1838 (Matagorda County Marriage Book A, p. 6).
55. Galveston was often called the Island City.
56. Probably Pinckney McNeel of Matagorda County, but possibly Pleasant McNeel of Brazoria County. The McNeel families, who came to Texas earlier, were not related to Sallie's family.
57. Pierce Junction was the connection between the Houston Tap & Brazoria Railroad on which she had ridden from Columbia and the Buffalo Bayou, Brazos & Colorado Railroad which would take her to Harrisburgh.
58. They took a different route home on the Galveston, Houston, & Henderson Railroad, traveling over the newly opened railroad bridge from Galveston Island to the mainland. According to a newspaper account (*Dallas Weekly Herald*, February 29, 1860), the bridge opened about February 19, 1860.

59. Catherine E. Winston, wife of planter Anthony Winston, with three children (1860 census, Brazoria County).

60. Sarah Josephine Mims, a student at Baylor, youngest and only surviving daughter of Mrs. Sarah Mims.

61. Her former classmate, Mary T. Whiteside.

62. Possibly Elizabeth J. Coleman of Marlin, *1859 Baylor Catalogue*, 8.

63. Her former classmate, Rebecca Skelton.

64. Gunn (ca. 1795–1863) began publishing his popular home medical guide in 1830, and various editions were produced. One of them was *Gunn's Domestic Medicine, or Poor Man's Friend; Describing the Diseases of Men, Women, and Children, and the Latest and Most Approved Means for Their Cure, and is intended expressly for the Benefit of Families in the Western and Southern States. It Also contains descriptions of the Medical Roots and Herbs of the Western and Southern Country, and How They are to be Used in the Cure of Diseases; Arranged on a New and Simple Plan, or Which the Practice of Medicine is Reduced to Principles of Common Sense*, 10th ed. (Xenia, Ohio: J. H. Purdy), 1838.

65. Julia Waldemann, aged twenty, born in Texas, household of N. Thompson, (1860 census, Matagorda County).

66. Mr. Lafayette Winston, age twenty-five, planter with $68,600 in real estate and $61,042 in personal property, listed with his wife and two small children (1860 census, Brazoria County).

67. Nearby community, northwest of Sweeny, in the area now called Old Ocean.

68. Nearby town in neighboring Matagorda County on Caney Creek.

69. Ann Chinn, wife of R. H. Chinn (1860 census, Matagorda County).

70. Caleb Letts, age twenty-eight, sailor (1860 census, Brazoria County).

71. The Sweeny family, led by John Sweeny Sr., came to Texas about 1832 and settled in the area of Chance's Prairie, near the present day town of Old Ocean. Sweeny, who died in 1855, had ten children. This seems to refer to his son, Thomas Jefferson Sweeny. The oldest child of Thomas Jefferson and Diana Frances Haynie Sweeny was Elizabeth Ann (Bettie), born in 1844 in Brazoria County. Miss Bettie apparently won the bet mentioned later in the paragraph, as she married R. G. Turner on March 10, 1864. Sallie also visits Miss Bettie in the entry of 9/17/1860 (Family records, Brazoria County Historical Museum, Brazoria County Marriage Book).

72. A. W. and J. S. Watts, females, ages eighteen and nineteen, and the minister T. B. Buckingham, age thirty-one, and his wife, age twenty-five, in the household of Mary McKinney, age sixty-three (1860 census, Brazoria county).

73. Mary E. McMaster, age thirty-seven, is listed with her husband, William, age forty-one, a merchant (1860 census, Brazoria County).

74. Mrs. Louisa Banton, age thirty, listed in the household of Joel Spencer, age sixty-five, planter (1860 census, Brazoria County).

75. Mr. W. S. Spencer, age thirty-seven, also listed in the household of Joel Spencer (1860 census, Brazoria County).

76. Her former classmate, Sarah Chambers. Marriage notice in the *Texas Baptist*, January 27,1859: "Wed. Jan 12 at residence of Mrs. Rebecca Chambers, Austin Co., by Rev. H. Clark. Mr. Charles T. Kavanaugh to Miss. Sarah F. Chambers."

77. Probably Sarah Huckaby of Fairfield, *1859 Catalogue*, 9.

78. Probably Pincknie Harris of Fairfield, *1859 Catalogue of the Male Department*, 7.

79. Elizabeth Eddins of Independence, *1859 Catalogue*, 8. Her sister, Mary A. Eddins, was one of Sallie's former classmates.

80. Possibly Angeline Hendley of Washington, *1859 Catalogue*, 9.

81. Possibly Rosella E. Rowe, daughter of Shadrack Rowe of Brazoria County. Although she

is not listed in the Catalogue, two of her brothers, Benjamin F. and Napoleon B. Rowe, are listed in the *1859 Catalogue of the Male Department.*

82. Probably Florence Davis of Independence, *1859 Catalogue,* 8.

83. Mrs. Adams was twice widowed. The 1850 census of Brazoria County lists her as Eliza A., in the household of B. B. Binion. After Binion's death in 1853, Mrs. E. A. Binion was married to Gideon W. Adams on July 24, 1856, by M. C. Conoly according to license no. 273 in the Brazoria County Marriage Book 1, page 47. Adams died in 1857, and Mrs. Adams married again on November 9, 1862, to Lemuel Callaway by J. H. Stribling.

84. "George W. Adams June 4, 1820–March 27, 1857 He sleeps in Jesus" inscription listed for his marker in the Cedar Lake Cemetery (*Brazoria County Cemetery Book*).

85. "Burton B. Binion Feb. 5, 1817–March 21, 1853 To live is Christ, To Die is gain." Inscription listed for his marker in the Cedar Lake Cemetery (*Brazoria County Cemetery Book*).

86. Her sister Annie was at Baylor with their brother, Calvin.

87. Benjamin F. Rowe and Napoleon B. Rowe

88. Miss Mary Davis, instructor in the Female Department, and a particular friend of Sallie.

89. Probably C. C. Bell, age twenty-seven, planter (1860 census, Brazoria County). The Christopher Bell plantation was on the San Bernard River, near the Rowe plantation.

90. Annie, Sallie's sister, is listed in the *1859 Catalogue* on page 12, as being in the Music Department. Sallie is not listed as taking music, and declares in the entry of 5/31/1860 that she has "what is called a good education; possessed of no accomplishments."

91. Probably William Rowe, aged twenty-seven, listed in the household of Shadrack Rowe (1860 census, Brazoria County).

92. R. H. Chinn, age forty, of neighboring Matagorda County. His occupation is listed as planter, not physician.

93. Mrs. Mary Rowe Jones apparently left her son Arthur with the Jordan/McNeill family.

94. Probably Virginia Hawkins, age nineteen, listed in the household of James B. Hawkins, age forty-six, planter (1860 census, Matagorda County).

95. Probably Francis S. Bowie, age thirty-three, listed in the household of George J. Bowie, age, forty-one, planter (1860 census, Matagorda County).

96. Probably Mary Duncan, age nineteen, in the household of John Duncan, age sixty-two, planter (1860 census, Matagorda County).

97. Samuel Sheldon Fitch, *Six lectures on the uses of the lungs; and causes, preventions and cures of pulmonary consumption, asthma, and diseases of the heart; on the laws of longevity* (New York: H. Carlisle, 1847). Various other updated versions and editions were available.

98. Mrs. Mary T. Fitzgerald Sr., matron in the boarding department, *1859 Catalogue,* 5.

99. Gerald Weekley.

100. William Rowe.

101. Lucretia M. Davidson (1808–25) and Margaret Miller Davidson (1823–38).

102. C. C. Millican was the tax assessor-collector for Brazoria County. He was named as defendant in an injunction that Jordan and others filed in April of 1861 to restrain him from selling property for nonpayment of the Railroad Tax which many of the Brazoria County planters opposed. See entry of 4/10/1860.

103. Henrietta Catherine Lafitte Norris, age sixty (1860 census, Brazoria County). See also the entry for 6/20/1860.

104. D. C. Rathburn, age twenty-six, overseer, in the household of Levi Jordan (1860 census, Brazoria County).

105. John L. Cochrane, age thirty-six, physician, in the household of Andrew Churchill, planter (1860 census, Brazoria County).

106. Sarah Tate Mims, daughter of Lumbert and Henrietta Mims, born July 24, 1849, died May 17, 1860. Buried in the Mims family cemetery at their plantation on the San Bernard River. The inscription on the tombstone reads, "Dear Sarah dwells with God" (*Brazoria County Cemetery Book*).

107. Charles Stuart married her former classmate, Rachel Barry. See entry for 5/21/1860, which describes a letter from Rachel telling her about the upcoming nuptials.

108. Classmate Rebecca Skelton.

109. Mary Russell Davis, instructor at Baylor.

110. Joseph Bates, a former mayor of Galveston, moved to a plantation on the west side of the San Bernard River in 1854 (*New Handbook of Texas*, 1996, s.v. "Joseph Bates"). The 1860 census of Brazoria County lists him with his wife and four children. The daughters are mentioned in the entry of 5/19/1861, and Bates is mentioned in the entry of 10/12/1861 concerning wartime duties.

111. Emmaline or Emma Norris, daughter of Henrietta Catherine Lafitte Norris and Joel Bradford Norris, sister to the wife of Lumbert Mims.

112. Probably Maggie Bennett, age seventeen, in the household of Charles H. Bennett (1860 census, Brazoria County). She is mentioned again later in the entry of 10/15/1860.

113. Mary Ellen Reese, also called Mollie, attended Baylor University. Emma, though close to her own age, was her aunt, and the mother and brother mentioned were Mollie's grandmother, Henrietta Catherine Lafitte Norris and uncle, John Hancock Norris. Another of her aunts was the wife of Lumbert Mims. For mention of her marriage, see entry of April 22, 1862.

114. Her former classmate, Bettie B. Carter.

115. Mrs. Mary T. Fitzgerald Sr. of the Boarding Department.

116. Mrs. H. L. Fitzgerald, sister of Miss Mary Clark.

117. The report of the Examination in the July 24, 1860, issue of the *Houston Weekly Telegraph* agreed with Sallie's assessment, saying "The Senior Class underwent a thorough examination, and proved the justice of their claim to the honors conferred upon them."

118. Mary Davis.

119. Horace Clark.

120. The 1860 census for Matagorda County lists the Rainey family as living on Kenner's Prairie.

121. Leonard Mims.

122. Benjamin Franklin (Frank) Rowe.

123. Oscar A. Chase was instructor of piano and guitar in the Music Department of the Female Department of Baylor. *1859 Catalogue*, 4.

124. This panic, known as the Texas Troubles, led to the formation of vigilante groups and the lynching of suspected abolitionists and slaves. According to many rumors, a widespread uprising was scheduled for Election Day, August 6, 1860 (*New Handbook of Texas*, 1996, s.v. "Abolition"). See entry of 8/14/1860 for an account of this sort of panic.

125. Probably Pleasant McNeel, *1859 Catalogue of the Male Department*, 12.

126. Clarence W. MacGreal, age twenty, listed in the household of Peter MacGreal, forty-five, lawyer (1860 census, Brazoria County).

127. Alex Mims.

128. Sallie's sister, Annie.

129. Captain Joel Spencer (1795–1868) was an early Brazoria County planter.

130. Manly Rowe.

131. Mary T. Whiteside, one of her Baylor classmates.

132. James Boyd Hawkins, a colonel of the militia in Warren County, North Carolina,

settled in neighboring Matagorda County around 1845. According to the 1860 census, Hawkins had 101 slaves and property worth $161,000 (*New Handbook of Texas*, 1996, s.v. "James Boyd Hawkins").

133. Lewis T. Bennet, age twenty-six, planter, and his wife, Josephine, age twenty, lived in the household of his father, Charles H. Bennet, age fifty-three. Charles Bennet settled in Brazoria County very early, at least by 1834. Lewis married Josephine Mary Barnes on April 7, 1858 (1860 census, Brazoria County, Marriage Book I, 1852–1870, p. 68).

134. Promise McNeal was enslaved on the Jordan plantation and continued to live there after emancipation. He is mentioned in the entries of 10/12/1860 and 4/20/1867, in a lawsuit Jordan filed against Evans in 1861, and is listed near the Jordan Plantation in the 1880 census of Brazoria County.

135. Evans was only eighteen when she wrote this novel, her second, and it sold over 22,000 copies the first year of publication. A Southern writer, she was one of the most popular authors of the nineteenth century.

136. Mary Louise McKellar married William Smith Herndon on November 11, 1860.

137. Sarah C. Pier of Travis, parent or guardian, James B. Pier (*1859 Catalogue*, 10). Sallie Pier also wrote a diary, and a transcript of it, as well as her autograph album, is housed in the Texas Collection of Baylor University: *The Diary of Sarah Pier Wiley*, Jan 18, 1863, to May 23, 1870. See mention of her correspondence in the entries of 10/30/1860, 6/13/61, Nov. 1861, and 3/6/1867.

God Help Our Cause

1. The page is damaged here and Sallie's words cannot be determined. South Carolina was rumored to be in arms and by November 10 their legislature had called for a convention to consider secession. South Carolina was the first state to officially secede on December 20, 1860.

2. A few days later, on November 17, a mass meeting was held in Brazoria that supported secession and called for a convention to be held in Galveston on January 8. Two committees of safety were formed to protect the interests of Brazoria County, with a group of minutemen being organized to carry out the orders of the committees. See Anna Irene Sandbo, "The First Session of the Secession Convention of Texas," *Southwestern Historical Quarterly* 18, no. 2 (1914): 162–194.

3. Many slave uprisings were reported across the state, though often founded only upon rumors, with Northern abolitionists being suspected and frequently executed for their supposed involvement. See note on entry of 8/10/1860.

4. Sallie's guess was not far wrong, as Mrs. Louisa J. Banton and Mr. C. C. Millican were married on June 20, 1861, by W. C. Somerville (Brazoria County Marriage Book 1, page 125, license No. 351).

5. Catherine Burkhart, who was married to John Hancock Norris on May 2, 1854 (Matagorda County Marriage Book A, p. 59).

6. Sarah Weekley Mims (1821–1861) and her husband Joseph Mims (1790–1844) were among the original Anglo-American colonists, Stephen F. Austin's Old Three Hundred.

7. Lumbert, Joseph, Alexander, Samuel, Leonard, David, and Josephine were the surviving children of Sarah Mims. Two daughters, Ann Elizabeth (1834–1842) and Julia (1839–1844), preceded her in death (Mims family cemetery).

8. Joseph Mims died Nov. 23, 1844, aged fifty-four years.

9. Mr. Rufus C. Burleson, head of the Male Department of Baylor University.

10. This may refer to a set of Special Laws which are listed in the *1859 Catalogue of the Male Department* (23–24). For example, rule number eight states that "Carrying or keeping of firearms or any other dangerous weapons,—playing cards or any other game of hazard,—using

intoxicating drinks as a beverage,—engaging in "night suppers," or any nocturnal revels or disorders,—lounging about stores or groceries,—entering establishments where intoxicating liquors are retailed, except upon special business, are all positively forbidden; and the student guilty of any one of these offenses shall be deemed worthy of suspension."

11. President Rufus Burleson of Baylor.

12. Possibly to attend Soule University, a Methodist institution, which was well-endowed and had an excellent library and faculty and about 150 students before closing due to the Civil War (*New Handbook of Texas*, 1996, s.v. "Soule University").

13. Alexander or Alex was the oldest of the Mims boys who was still unmarried.

14. Her Newfoundland pup, given by Clarence MacGreal—see entry for 8/26/1860.

15. Possibly Ed Dickson, age eighteen, listed near the Mims and Jordan/McNeill families (1860 census, Brazoria County).

16. On February 1, the Convention of Texas, called to consider federal relations, had adopted an ordinance of secession. An election was held on February 23 for ratifying the ordinance of secession. Following the vote, Gov. Houston issued a proclamation declaring Texas had seceded, as of March 2, the twenty-fifth anniversary of Texas' Declaration of Independence from Mexico. It was the seventh state to leave the union, following in order of secession, South Carolina, Mississippi, Alabama and Florida on the same day, Georgia, and Louisiana.

17. Delegates from the first seven states to secede met in February in Montgomery, Alabama, adopted a provisional constitution on February 7, and elected Jefferson Davis as president on February 9 at the Southern Convention, creating an independent government.

18. The *Galveston Weekly News*, March 5, 1861, reported the results of the secession election, saying that "Judge Jas. H Bell of the Supreme Court, a resident of Travis County voted at the Brazoria precinct against secession. We regret the course of a citizen of his eminent ability and reputation, but are gratified with the spirit that induced him to deposit his vote, as he deemed best, despite the overwhelming majority against him." In Brazoria the vote was 131 for and 1 against. Countywide the vote was 585 for and 2 against. Statewide the vote was about 3 to 1 for secession, with the greatest opposition in Central and North Texas. See Ralph A. Wooster, *Texas and Texans in the Civil War* (Austin, Tex.: Eakin Press, 1995) for more information.

19. Reference to a quotation from a letter from Abraham Lincoln to Thurlow Weed, dated December 17, 1860, "But my opinion is that no State can in any way lawfully get out of the Union without the consent of the others; and that it is the duty of the President and other government functionaries to run the machine as it is." Lincoln is often quoted as having said, "I must run the machine as I find it."

20. Possibly Sue F. Patton, who later married Leonard S. Mims on November 7, 1861 (Brazoria County Marriage Book 1, page 132, license no. 358).

21. Possibly Emma Bassett, age seventeen (1860 census, Matagorda County).

22. Major Asa Stratton (1789–1877) is listed in the Cedar Lake Cemetery along with Mary Chisolm Stratton (1837–1872), who could possibly be his young wife. None of his marriages are listed in either the Brazoria County or Matagorda County Marriage Books, and neither he, nor his wife or children are listed in the 1860 census for either Brazoria County or Matagorda County, nor in the 1850 Brazoria County census. Sarah Emily Stratton, born 1847, later married Samuel Irwin Bryan on August 23, 1866.

23. North Carolina was admitted as the tenth state of the Confederacy. Texas was the seventh state to secede, with secession becoming effective as of March 2, 1861. The postal service in the seceded states was handled by the Federal Post Office Department in Washington through most of May. U.S. postal rates continued with U.S. stamps being used and mail between the North and the South went through with few interruptions.

24. Portion of page missing where date would be.

25. She and her husband were in Burma six years before their first convert was baptized.

26. However, the first Federal warship, the *South Carolina,* appeared off the coast of Galveston some months later in July (Wooster, *Texas and Texans in the Civil War,* 43).

27. Samuel and David Mims, their neighbors, were eventually mustered into Company B of Terry's Texas Rangers in Houston on September 7, 1861.

28. Damage to the diary makes it impossible to read the age of David Mims, but his age is listed as eighteen in the 1860 census. The age of his brother Samuel is listed as twenty-three in 1860, so he was older than Sallie and apparently did not seem so youthful to her.

29. This practice was widespread during the Civil War among Southern women and had a newer connotation of remaining faithful to the soldiers in the military, which may stem from the poem "Adelgitha" by a popular Scottish poet, Thomas Campbell (1777–1844).

30. Oldest child of Mary Rowe Jones and her husband Henry Jones, who lived with the family periodically. The child is also mentioned in the entry of 3/7/1860.

31. John H. Reagan was appointed Postmaster General of the Confederate States of America on March 6, 1861, but did not assume official control of the postal system until June 1. The transfer of mail service was not easily accomplished, and there were no C.S.A. postage stamps until about October of 1861; the small coins needed to pay postage had practically disappeared from circulation.

32. Arkansas withdrew from the Union on May 6, and was admitted as the ninth state on May 18. As mentioned earlier, North Carolina seceded and was admitted as the tenth state on May 21. Tennessee seceded on June 8.

33. John Greenville McNeel, one of Austin's Old Three Hundred colonists, came to Texas in 1822. The marriage mentioned is not recorded in the Brazoria County Marriage Book. Pleasant D. McNeill Jr., one of Calvin's Baylor classmates, was the son of Greenville's brother Leander Harrison McNeel, who died in 1851. Greenville was Pleasant's uncle and guardian. Pleasant, of Company B of Terry's Texas Rangers, died of typhoid fever on March 18, 1863 (*Texas Handbook of Texas Online,* Brazoria County Marriage Book, Online Archive of Terry's Texas Rangers).

34. See http://memory.loc.gov/music/sm2/sm1847/420000/420200/002.gif.

35. This song about an escaped slave and his unsuccessful efforts to win the freedom of his beloved Nellie was written by Hanby, an abolitionist, in attempt to sway popular opinion against slavery. The tragic song apparently nevertheless had appeal to those in the South.

36. American folk hymn, possibly based on "Saw Ye My Father," a folk song of unknown origin.

37. Around 1855, a Mrs. Hughes was reported to have been miraculously healed by the sulfur springs around Lampasas, Texas, a small town in Central Texas, northwest of Austin, prompting many to visit the springs in search of a cure (*New Handbook of Texas*).

38. General Winfield Scott, Commander in Chief of the Union Army until November 1, 1861.

39. Brigadier General Barnard E. Bee and Brigadier Francis S. Bartow were the only two Confederate generals killed at Manassas, but E. Kirby Smith was wounded so severely that he was out of action for two months and may have been reported as receiving mortal wounds. The total estimated casualties were 4,700 with about 2,950 for the Union, and 1,750 for the Confederates.

40. John A. Wharton, lawyer and planter of Brazoria County, was elected captain of Company B, 8th Texas Calvary, known as Terry's Texas Rangers. He later became colonel of the regiment, and is given that rank in the entry of 9/22/1862. He eventually attained the rank of major general.

41. Virginia Cleavland of Independence, Texas, parent or guardian, Wm. H. Cleavland

is listed among the undergraduates in the *Baylor University Female Department Catalogue for 1858–59*, 8.

42. The Burleson-Clark feud caused much controversy. In July 1861, the Independence church called a council of surrounding sister churches to give the case of Abner Lipscomb a hearing and decided that if he withdrew his charges that he would be entitled to restoration into the fellowship of the church. Lipscomb did withdraw his charges in July 1861 and was reinstated (Murray, *Baylor at Independence*, 186).

43. This is the most often quoted biblical verse in Southern women's diaries, according to Anne Firor Scott, *The Southern Lady: From Pedestal to Politics 1830–1930* (Chicago, 1970), 11. She also quotes the verse on 7/25/1867 and makes reference to it on 10/22/1858 and 5/31/1860.

44. On June 28, 1861, the president and faculty of the male department submitted their formal resignations. See Michael A. White, *The History of Baylor University, 1845–1861* (Waco, Tex.: Texian Press, 1968), 52.

45. "Love looks not with the eyes, but with the mind / And therefore is sing'd Cupid painted blind." *A Midsummer-Night's Dream* (1595–1596), act 1, scene 1, line 234, by William Shakespeare (1564–1616).

46. John F. Nuckolls, age eleven, in the household of Fred J. and Mary A. Nuckolls (1860 census, Matagorda County). He may also be the Johny mentioned in the entry of 5/19/1861, and may have attended school on the Jordan plantation. His relative Martha Nuckols, step-sister of Kate Jackson, attended school on the plantation in 1857.

47. Leonard S. Mims and Miss Sue F. Patton were married November 7, 1861, by W. C. Somerville, minister (Brazoria County Marriage Book I, p. 132, License #358).

48. F. M. Snead, age 50, occupation, "negro catcher" (1860 census, Matagorda County).

49. Mose later died during a measles epidemic. See entry of March or April 1863.

50. Sallie McNeel, daughter of Pinckney McNeel of Matagorda County, married Moses Van Dorn. Their marriage is not listed in either Brazoria or Matagorda County Marriage Books.

51. Colonel Joseph Bates was in command of the Fourth Texas Volunteer Regiment, which defended the coast from San Luis Pass to Caney Creek. This state unit became the 13th Texas Infantry of the C.S.A.

52. Captain John W. Veasey, 35th Texas Cavalry, (Brown's Regiment). Veasey, age thirty-five, is listed in the 1860 census of Wharton County, with the occupation of physician. See mention of his wife in entry for 8/14/1860.

53. Sophia M. Sweeny married Edward L. Holmes on June 21, 1838, and then John McGrew on January 1851 (Brazoria County Marriage Book Volume A (1829–1852) p. 75 #21; p. 208, #183).

54. Lumbert Mims, b. 1825 (1860 census, Brazoria County) d. 1869 (Probate 12/30/1869 Brazoria County K356), son of Sarah and Joseph Mims, married Henrietta J. Norris (b. 1831) on 11/16/1846 Brazoria County Marriage Book A/126). She died in 1875 (Probate 8/4/1875 Brazoria County L/55).

55. Rivers Erwin did die in 1861 (family records).

56. Listed in the 1860 census as David Mims, age eighteen, was the youngest son of Sarah and Joseph Mims. He attended Baylor at Independence, listed in the Male Preparatory Department for 1859.

57. Benjamin McNeel, b. about 1837, son of Pinckney McNeel and Harriet Mims Cox. Benjamin was actually a nephew of David, as David was the half brother of Harriet. Both Harriet and David were children of Joseph Mims, but by different mothers.

58. Brigadier General Earl Van Dorn, who had been in command of the Texas district from April to September of 1861, was ordered to report to Richmond. After promotion to major general, he was sent to take command of the combined forces of Ben McCulloch and Sterling Price

in Arkansas. He was moving his forces toward Missouri, where he was defeated at the Battle of Pea Ridge, Arkansas, on March 7–8, 1862. Though he had been very popular in Texas earlier, he received much criticism for his handling of his forces in that engagement (Wooster, *Texas and Texans in the Civil War,* 42–49).

59. Wm. McWillie Williamson and Miss Mary E. Reese were married on April 17, 1862, by W. C. Sommerville, Minister. (Brazoria County Marriage Book A., page 136). She was the orphaned daughter of Sarah Tait Norris and Charles Keller Reese. Although she had many relatives living in the area, her guardian was A. P. McCormick.

60. Her sister, Sarah Emma Reese, was living with one of their aunts, Mary White Norris Davis, in Mobile, Alabama. This sister, Sarah Emma, later married Sallie's brother Calvin in 1875. See mention of Mary Reese in entry of May 20, 1860.

61. Mollie's marriage was apparently not a happy one, as she petitioned for divorce on 5/13/1874 in Refugio County on the grounds that her husband had violated his marriage contract with her by failing to provide for her, abusing her and cruelly treating her, and finally abandoning her. After divorcing Williamson, Mollie married John Richard Martin on May 24, 1874. She died on February 12, 1877. She had eight children, seven during her marriage to Williamson, and one after her marriage to Martin.

62. On May 17, 1862, Captain Henry Eagle of the federal frigate *Santee* called for the surrender of Galveston, but the city did not surrender until October 8. Barr, Alwyn, "Texas Coastal Defense, 1861–1865," in *Lone Star Blue and Gray: Essays on Texas in the Civil War,* edited by Ralph A. Wooster, (Austin: Texas State Historical Association, 1995) 159, 162.

63. James G. Rainey.

64. Emmaline A. Norris was married to Alexander C. Burkhart on May 3, 1862, by John Owen (Brazoria County Marriage Book A, page 143). Her brother, John Hancock Norris, was married to Alex Burkhart's sister, Catherine, who died sometime in January of 1861; see entry of 2/8/1861 for mention of her death. E. Norris is mentioned several times in the diary; see entries of 2/13/1860 and 6/20/1860. The latter entry mentions that she endures a lonely life. After her marriage, she had six children in ten years.

65. Camp Chocolate in Calhoun County was on the road that linked Port Lavaca and Indianola. See Bill Winsor, *Texas in the Confederacy* (Hillsboro, Tex.: Hill Junior College Press, 1978), 13.

66. Napoleon Bonaparte Rowe married Virginia Anne Cleveland on June 29, 1862, in Washington County, Texas (Diary of Lucy Merry Pier 1852–1860, manuscript in Baylor University Texas Collection).

67. May refer to the Second Battle of Manassas, or Bull Run, during the last of August, which was another Confederate victory.

68. This was not the Battle of Murfreesboro, or Stone River, which took place near the end of December of 1862, but an earlier engagement near that location on July 13, 1862, led by Colonel Nathan Bedford Forrest and Colonel John A. Wharton. Sam died of his wounds on July 17.

69. The Union gunboat, *Harriet Lane,* under the command of William B. Renshaw, steamed into Galveston on October 4, 1862, and demanded the surrender of Galveston. He brought in seven more ships and agreed to a four-day truce to allow civilian evacuation of the island, with the Union occupation beginning on October 8 (Wooster, *Texas and Texans in the Civil War,* 62–3).

70. B. F. (Frank) Rowe and S. J. (Josephine) Mims were married November 25, 1862, by J. H. Stribling, M. G. (Brazoria County Marriage Book I, p. 145, License No. 371). Benjamin F. Rowe was in the Preparatory Department of the Male Department of Baylor in 1859, while Sarah J. Mims was listed as an undergraduate in the Female Department for that year. They both were called by their middle names, as he is usually styled Frank and she, Joe or Jose.

71. Alex Mims, the bride's brother, seems to have acted as Jose's guardian. The entry of 2/13/1861 refers to Alex not allowing Jose to return to school following her mother's death, requiring her to become his housekeeper.

72. Federal troopers raided Cedar Lake (Winston's) Salt Works on Nov. 27, 1862. One Union soldier was killed in the attack and five were wounded. The Confederates had no losses (Winsor, *Texas in the Confederacy*, 130). A very similar account of this incident appeared in a Houston newspaper crediting the news of the incident to Henry B. Jones of Brazoria County (*Houston Telegraph*, December 12, 1862).

73. *Galveston Weekly News* on December 10, 1862, reported briefly on this incident, saying that "one of our men was wounded slightly in the foot."

74. Confederate forces under Major General J. B. Magruder made a combined land and sea attack on Galveston on the night of December 31, 1862 (Winsor, *Texas in the Confederacy*, 131, 107).

75. Probably Edmund Weekley.

76. On December 29, 1863, there was heavy skirmishing on Matagorda Peninsula, near Decrow's Point. The next day some of Brown's Regiment attempted to land on Matagorda Peninsula. Twenty men of the landing party froze to death as a severe norther swamped their boats. The survivors were fired on by Union forces (Winsor, *Texas in the Confederacy*, 133–34). Bob's capture may have saved his life by preventing him from participating in the ill-fated invasion party.

77. Her grandparents survived Sallie by quite a few years. Her grandfather died traveling on business to New Orleans in 1873, and her grandmother died in 1882.

78. This was her last entry in the fourth section of the diary. Paper quickly became very expensive and difficult to obtain in the South. The price of certain grades of paper rose from ten cents a pound in 1861 to a dollar a pound in 1863, and those were prices for purchasing in bulk. See L. R. Garrison, "Administrative Problems of the Confederate Post Office Department. I." *Southwestern Historical Quarterly* 19, no. 2 (October 1915): 117.

No Concessions to Make

1. Mary Russell Davis, of Independence, sister-in-law of Horace Clarke and teacher of rhetoric and belles letters at the Female Department of Baylor University, died during the first weeks of November 1865. An entry from the diary of Sarah Pier Wiley dated Tuesday, November 14, says that Miss Mary Davis of Independence "died last week."

2. Although no kinship relationship is known, Kate's older stepsister, Martha Nuckols, did attend school on the Jordan plantation around 1857.

3. Calvin left Baylor at Independence because of a disagreement with President Burleson; see entry of 2/8/1861. He is thought to have attended Soule University at Chappell Hill after the war, but the college was only in existence from 1856 to 1888, and few records have survived.

4. Beginning with this entry, there are four pages that have badly faded ink, but two are slightly more legible than the others. Some legible phrases have been omitted if the context does not allow logical reconstruction.

5. "'Tis strange—but true; for truth is always strange; Stranger than fiction."

6. Eight months ago (11/28/1865) she said she would never want to visit Independence again.

7. The Rowe family mortgaged some of their property, land, and slaves to Levi Jordan in 1858 to secure a loan, and economics after the war forced them to sell out. They moved up to Washington County, and Calvin purchased cattle from them and took over the operation of their plantation.

8. A. E. Stratton Jr. married Louisa H. Waldman on February 7, 1867 (Matagorda County Marriage book A, p. 133).

9. *The Prison Life of Jefferson Davis* (1866) by John J. Craven covered the first seven months

of his imprisonment. The story of the harsh treatment that Davis had received shocked both North and South and created such a public outcry that he was given better treatment. This sensation aided Davis in being released from prison and reunited with his family by 1867.

10. Richard Collins of Brazoria County and Ferrell Vincent formed the Tuxpan Land Company, buying a half a million acres in the area.

11. Caddie was the wife of Joe Mims, and her father was probably Fred J. Nuckols of Matagorda County.

12. Attributed to St. Bernard of Clairvaux.

13. William T. Uzzell would have been about sixty, based on his age given in the 1860 census of Brazoria County.

14. Mary T. Uzzell was married to H. R. Armstrong on 8/1/1867 by S. L. S. Ballowe, J.P.B.C. (Brazoria County Marriage Book, page 328, License No. 517). A subsequent entry indicates that the bride was called by her middle name, Texas.

15. The 1867 yellow fever epidemic was particularly virulent. Thousands became ill with the disease, and at least 725 died in Galveston by early September. The epidemic was widespread. New Orleans lost over 3,000 to the disease, and many inland cities such as Huntsville and La Grange lost 10–20 percent of their population. The role of mosquitoes in the disease was not clearly understood until 1900.

16. Portion of page missing where date would have been entered.

17. Short-lived periodical (1866–69) started by General D. H. Hill in Charlotte, North Carolina, included literature, military history, and agriculture. http://www.worldwideschool.org/library/books/hst/biography/ABiographyofthePoetSidneyLanier/chap11.html.

18. *Frank Leslie's Lady's Magazine* was published from 1863 to 1882 under that title, and from 1857 under different titles. Several popular periodicals were published by Frank Leslie, the professional name of Henry Carter.

19. Possibly the Uzzell's son Samuel, who would have been about sixteen years old according to the 1860 census of Brazoria County.

20. Sallie's handwriting is not clear here; the letters look more like Floy, but she appears to be talking about the Rowe sisters who had moved with their family up to the Independence area.

21. Probably William McGrew, son of John and Sophia McGrew. He would have been about nine years old. This was Mrs. McGrew's second marriage. Her maiden name was Sweeny, and she married Edward L. Holmes on June 21, 1838, and then John McGrew on January 14, 1851.

22. Probably Mrs. Ophelia Armstrong Rutledge. She married William O. Rutledge on June 29, 1854, and in the 1860 census of Matagorda County, she and her husband were still living in the Armstrong household.

23. Her handwriting is difficult to read here, so this name may be incorrect.

24. *St. Elmo* was one of the most popular novels of the nineteenth century, with sales rivaling those of *Uncle Tom's Cabin* and *Ben Hur*.

25. Elizabeth Barrett Browning quotes these lines at the head of her poem, "Romance of the Swan's Nest."

26. This may be a reference to a famous speech by John C. Calhoun delivered during the debate before the Compromise of 1850, in which he wrote, "The South asks for justice, simple justice, and less she ought not to take. She has no compromise to offer but the Constitution, and no concession or surrender to make. She has already surrendered so much that she has little left to surrender."

Epilogue

1. *New Handbook of Texas*, 1996, s. v. "Epidemic Diseases."
2. Ibid., s. v. "Hurricanes."

3. Entry of February 21, 1864.
4. Letter dated February 18, 1880, from Emily McNeill to Kate Jackson.
5. Letter from Emily Jordan McNeill to Kate Jackson dated February 18, 1880.

Appendix A

1. Entry of 2/1/1859
2. The *1859 Catalogue* gives the date of Commencement Exercises as December 23, 1858.
3. Groce's Retreat in *1857 Catalogue*.
4. Washington in *1857 Catalogue*.
5. Kickapoo in *1857 Catalogue*.
6. Waco in *1857 Catalogue*.
7. Rebecca E. in *1857 Catalogue*.
8. Marriage notice in the *Texas Baptist*, 1/27/1859 Vol. 5 No. 4: "Wed. Jan 12 at residence of Mrs. Rebecca Chambers, Austin Co., by Rev. H. Clark. Mr. Charles T. Kavanaugh to Miss. Sarah F. Chambers."
9. Listed as Sarah A. in list of graduates, but as Sarah F. in *1857 Catalogue,* and in appendix of *1859 Catalogue*.
10. Marriage notice in the *Texas Baptist*, 2/15/1859 Vol. 5 No. 5: "On 25th inst. by Rev. H. Clark at the residence of the bride's father. Mr. C. R. Breedlove to Miss Mary Amanda, oldest daughter of W. W. Eddins. All of Washington Co., Tx."

Bibliography

Andreadis, Harriette. "True Womanhood Revisited: Women's Private Writing in Nineteenth Century Texas." *Journal of the Southwest* 31 (1989): 179–204.
Ashkenazi, Elliott, ed. *The Civil War Diary of Clara Solomon: Growing Up in New Orleans, 1861–1862.* Baton Rouge: Louisiana State University Press, 1995.
Barr, Alwyn. "Texas Coastal Defense, 1861–1865." In *Lone Star Blue and Gray: Essays on Texas in the Civil War,* edited by Ralph A. Wooster, 151–174. Austin: Texas State Historical Association, 1995.
Bleser, Carol, ed. *In Joy and in Sorrow: Women, Family, and Marriage in the Victorian South, 1830–1900.* Oxford: Oxford University Press, 1991.
Bloom, Lynn Z. "'I Write for Myself and Strangers': Private Diaries as Public Documents." In *Inscribing the Daily: Critical Essays on Women's Diaries,* edited by Suzanne L. Bunkers and Cynthia Huff, 23–37. Amherst: University of Massachusetts Press, 1996.
Boswell, Angela. *Her Act and Deed: Women's Lives in a Rural Southern County, 1837–1873.* College Station: Texas A&M University Press, 2001.
Brazosport Genealogical Society. *Marriage Records of Brazoria County, Texas, from 1829 to 1870.* Lake Jackson, Tex.: Brazosport Genealogical Society, 1982.
Campbell, Randolph. *An Empire for Slavery: The Peculiar Institution in Texas, 1821–1865.* Baton Rouge. Louisiana State University Press, 1989.
Carroll, Mark M. *Homesteads Ungovernable: Families, Sex, Race and the Law in Frontier Texas, 1823–1860.* Austin: University of Texas Press, 2001.
Cartwright, Gary. *Galveston: A History of the Island.* New York: Atheneum, 1991.
Cashin, Joan E. *A Family Venture: Men and Women on the Southern Frontier.* New York: Oxford University Press, 1991.
Catalogue of the Trustees, Faculty and Students of Baylor University, Female Department, Independence, Texas, for the Year 1857. Galveston, Tex.: Galveston News, 1857.
Catalogue of the Trustees, Faculty and Students of Baylor University, Female Department, Independence, Texas, for the Years 1858–9. Galveston, Tex.: Galveston News, 1859
Clinton, Catherine. *The Plantation Mistress: Woman's World in the Old South.* New York: Pantheon Books, 1982.
———. *Tara Revisited: Women, War, and the Plantation Legend.* New York: Abbeville Press, 1995.
Creighton, James A. *A Narrative History of Brazoria County.* Waco, Tex.: Brazoria County Historical Commission, 1975.
Daughters of the Republic of Texas, Cradle of Texas Chapter, Freeport, Texas. *A List of Old Brazoria County, Texas Cemeteries during or before 1900.* West Columbia, Tex.: Modern Manifold Method, Inc., 1965
Donohoe, Ural Lee, and Jackie Jecmenek. *Matagorda County, Texas Marriage Records, 1837–1899.* Bay City, Tex.: Matagorda County Genealogical Society, 1985.

Downs, Fane. "'Tryels and Trubbles': Women in Early Nineteenth-Century Texas." *Southwestern Historical Quarterly* 90, no. 1 (July 1986): 35–56.

East, Charles, ed. *The Civil War Diary of Sarah Morgan*. Athens: University of Georgia Press, 1991.

Edwards, Laura F. *Scarlett Doesn't Live Here Anymore: Southern Women in the Civil War Era*. Urbana: University of Illinois Press, 2000.

Eighth Annual Catalogue of the Trustees, Professors, and Students of Baylor University Male Department, Independence, Texas, 1859. Galveston, Tex.: Galveston News, 1859.

Farnham, Christie Anne. *The Education of the Southern Belle: Higher Education and Student Socialization in the Antebellum South*. New York: New York University Press, 1994.

Faust, Drew Gilpin. *Mothers of Invention: Women of the Slaveholding South in the American Civil War*. Chapel Hill: University of North Carolina Press, 1996.

Fox-Genovese, Elizabeth. *Within the Plantation Household: Black and White Women of the Old South*. Chapel Hill: University of North Carolina Press, 1988.

Freeman, Martha Doty. *An Overview of the Development of an Historic Landscape on the San Bernard River, Brazoria County, Texas, and a History of the Levi Jordan Plantation*. Austin, Tex.: Report for TBG Partners, 2004.

Friedman, Jean E. *The Enclosed Garden: Women and Community in the Evangelical South, 1830–1900*. Chapel Hill: University of North Carolina, 1985.

Gallaway, B. P., ed. *Texas the Dark Corner of the Confederacy: Contemporary Accounts of the Lone Star State in the Civil War*, 3rd ed. Lincoln: University of Nebraska Press, 1994.

Garrison, L. R. "Administrative Problems of the Confederate Post Office Department I." *Southwestern Historical Quarterly* 19, no. 2 (October 1915): 111–141.

Harrison, Kimberly, ed. *A Maryland Bride in the Deep South: The Civil War Diary of Priscilla Bond*. Baton Rouge: Louisiana State University Press, 2006.

Hedrick, David Layne. "The Investigation of the Caney Creek Shipwreck Archaeological Site 41MG32." Master's thesis, Texas A&M University, 1998.

Henson, Margaret Swett. *Historic Brazoria County: An Illustrated History*. San Antonio: Historical Publishing Network, 1998.

Jewett, Clayton E. *Texas in the Confederacy: An Experiment in Nation Building*. Columbia: University of Missouri Press, 2002.

King, C. Richard. *Victorian Lady on the Texas Frontier: The Journal of Ann Raney Coleman*. Norman: University of Oklahoma Press, 1971.

King, Wilma, ed. *A Northern Woman in the Plantation South: Letters of Tryphena Blanche Holder Fox, 1856–1876*. Columbia: University of South Carolina Press, 1993.

Le Clercq, Anne Sinkler Whaley. *An Antebellum Plantation Household: Including the South Carolina Low Country Receipts and Remedies of Emily Wharton Sinkler*. Columbia: University of South Carolina Press, 1996.

Malone, Ann Patton. *Women on the Texas Frontier: A Cross-Cultural Perspective*. El Paso: Texas Western Press, 1983.

McDavid, Carol. "Descendants, Decisions, and Power: The Public Interpretation of the Levi Jordan Plantation." *Historical Archaeology* 31, no. 3 (1997): 114–131.

Moore, John Hammond. *A Plantation Mistress on the Eve of the Civil War: The Diary of Keziah Goodwyn Hopkins Brevard, 1860–1861*. Columbia: University of South Carolina Press, 1993.

Muir, Andrew Forest. "Railroads Come to Houston, 1857–1861." *Southwestern Historical Quarterly* 64, no. 1 (July 1960): 42–63.

Murr, Erika L., ed. *A Rebel Wife in Texas: The Diary and Letters of Elizabeth Scott Neblett, 1852–1864*. Baton Rouge: Louisiana State University Press, 2001.

Murray, Lois Smith. *Baylor at Independence.* Waco, Tex.: Baylor University Press, 1972.
O'Brien, Michael, ed. *An Evening Alone: Four Journals of Single Women in the South, 1827–1867.* Charlottesville: University Press of Virginia, 1993.
Olmsted, Frederick Law. *A Journey Through Texas; or a Saddle-Trip on the Southwestern Frontier.* New York: Dix, Edwards, & Co., 1857.
Pier, Lucy Merry. *Diary of Lucy Merry Pier 1852–1860.* Manuscript. Baylor University Texas Collection.
Platter, Allen Andrew. "Educational, Social, and Economic Characteristics of the Plantation Culture of Brazoria County, Texas." PhD diss., University of Houston, 1961.
Powers, Betsy J. "'Gone to Texas': The Impact of Southern Migration upon Antebellum Texas." Master's thesis, University of Houston, 1990.
Reed, S. G. *A History of the Texas Railroads and of Transportation Conditions under Spain and Mexico and The Republic and The State.* Houston: St. Clair Publishing Co., 1941.
Robertson, Mary D., ed. *Lucy Breckenridge of Grove Hill: The Journal of a Virginia Girl, 1862–1864.* Kent, Ohio: Kent State University Press, 1979.
Sandbo, Anna Irene. "The First Session of the Secession Convention of Texas." *Southwestern Historical Quarterly* 18.2 (1914): 162–194.
Scott, Anne Firor. *Making the Invisible Woman Visible.* Urbana: University of Illinois Press, 1984.
———. *The Southern Lady: From Pedestal to Politics, 1830 to 1930.* Chicago: University of Chicago Press, 1970.
Seventh Annual Catalogue of the Trustees, Professors, and Students of Baylor University Male Department. Anderson: Texas Baptist, 1858.
Silverthorne, Elizabeth. *Plantation Life in Texas.* College Station: Texas A&M University Press, 1986.
Spencer, Annie Laurie. *Marriage Bonds and Ministers' Returns of Union County, Arkansas, 1829–1870.* El Dorado, Ark.: El Dorado Printing Co., 1962.
Sullivan, Walter, ed. *The War the Women Lived: Female Voices from the Confederate South.* Nashville: J. S. Sanders & Company, 1995.
Tyler, Ron, Douglas E. Barnett, and Roy R. Barkley, eds. *The New Handbook of Texas,* 6 vols. Austin: Texas State Historical Association, 1996.
White, Michael A. *The History of Baylor University, 1845–1861.* Waco, Tex.: Texian Press, 1968.
Wiley, Bell Irvin. *Confederate Women.* New York: Barnes & Noble Books, 1975.
Wiley, Sarah Pier. *The Diary of Sarah Pier Wiley, Jan 18, 1863 to May 23, 1870.* Manuscript. Baylor University Texas Collection.
Winsor, Bill. *Texas in the Confederacy.* Hillsboro, Tex.: Hill Junior College Press, 1978.
Wooster, Ralph A. *Civil War Texas: A History and a Guide.* Austin: Texas State Historical Association, 1999.
———. *Texas and Texans in the Civil War.* Austin, Tex.: Eakin Press, 1995.
———. "Wealthy Texans, 1860." *Southwestern Historical Quarterly* 71, no. 2 (October 1967): 163–180.
———. "Wealthy Texans, 1870." *Southwestern Historical Quarterly* 74, no. 1 (July 1970): 24–35.
Zlatkovich, Charles P. *Texas Railroads: A Record of Construction and Abandonment.* Austin: Bureau of Business Research and Texas State Historical Association, 1981.

Index

Abbott, Jacob, 49
abolitionists, 82, 89, 113
Adams, Eliza A. (Mrs. Adams), 55, 69, 173n 83
Addison, Joseph, 51, 58
African Americans. *See* blacks
agriculture. *See* plantation life
Allen, Elizabeth J. (Bettie), 28
Ambrotype photographs, rituals of taking and sending, 25, 26, 57, 87, 112, 131, 132
archaeological excavation of Jordan plantation, xi, 157
Arnold, J., 49
Arthur's Home Magazine, 45, 51–52, 90–91
Ashford, Mary T. (M. T. W. or Mary W.) (née Whiteside). *See* Whiteside, Mary T. (M. T. W. or Mary W.) (Mrs. Ashford)
Austin, Stephen F., 3

Banton, Mrs. Louisa, 66, 91, 172n 74
Baptist State Convention, 32, 62
Barry, Rachael (Rachel) (Mrs. C. Stewart), 13, 73–74, 76, 91
Bassett, Emma, 98
Bates, Joseph, 111, 178n 51
Baylor University: Annie at, 25, 27, 49; award of valedictory, 31; Burleson-Clark feud, 108, 178n 42; and Calvin, 85, 94, 96; classmates and faculty at, 18–20, 161–62; examinations, 11, 29, 32–34, 53, 65, 72, 76, 106–7, 144; Female Department, *30;* overview of social role, 10–11; post-war visit, 134; requirement to sign pledge, 94; Sallie's commencement, 34; Sallie's diploma, *43;* Sallie's experiences at, 22–39; Sallie's post-graduate trips to, 74–75, 76–80; suspension for letter-writing, 26–27
beach at San Bernard River mouth, 80, 91, 136, 139–54
Bennett, L., 86–87
Bennett, Maggie, 77, 86
Bernardo (dog), 83–84, 96, 106, 139, 176n 14

Beulah (Evans), 88
Big House, 11–12, *12*
blacks: artifacts from Jordan plantation Quarters, 157; Christian preaching to, 146; frustrations with freedmen's labor, 126, 129, 133, 136, 139; Sallie's fear of insurrection, 82, 89; Sallie's prejudices against free, 8, 126–27, 129, 137; as tenant farmers, 6, 157–59. *See also* slaves and slavery
blockade of Southern ports by Union, 5, 101–2, 119
Bloom, Lynn Z., 6
Brazoria County, Texas, 1, 3–4, 6, 21. *See also* plantation life
Breckenridge, Lucy, 9, 15
Brown, Kenneth, xi, xv, 157–58
Brown's regiment, 35th Texas Cavalry: Calvin's complaints about soldiers' treatment, 114; coastal defense mission, 116, 120, 122; disease problem, 117, 118, 119; Galveston defense assignment, 116; at Matagorda Peninsula, 119, 123, 180n 76; McNeill brothers' assignment to, 5
Bull Run, First Battle of, 108
Burkhart, Catherine (Mrs. Norris), 94, 175n 5
Burleson, Rufus (Mr. B.), 18, 26, 65, 94, 96, 108, 178n 42
Byron, Lord (George Noel Gordon), 153

Camp, soldiers at: Calvin's complaints, 114; Camp Chocolate, 117, 179n 65; disease problem, 117, 118, 119
"Campaign" (Addison), 51
Caney (town), 62, 98, 138
Caney Creek, 3, 4
carriage, traveling by, 78, 79
Carter, Bettie B., 26, 44, 79, 98
casualties, Confederate, 15–16, 108
Catholicism, Sallie's horror of, 9, 24–25
Cedar Lake (Winston's) Salt Works, Union raid on, 120, 180n 72

Chance's Prairie, 62, 74
Chase, Oscar, 80–82, 174*n* 123
"Childe Harold's Pilgrimage" (Byron), 153
Chinn, R. H., 70, 71, 105, 122, 147
Christmas celebrations, 92, 113, 135–36
church denominational gatherings: Baptist State Convention, 32, 62; Colorado Baptist Association, 46–47; Quarterly Meetings, 65, 76
Civil War: approaching threat to plantation, 101–2, 122; casualties, 15–16, 108; effect of war risks on marriage rates, 15–16; First Manassas (Bull Run), 108; Galveston battles, 5, 119–20, 121, 179*n* 62, 69, 180*n* 74; on Lincoln's election and fears of war, 89–90; and Lost Cause, 123, 125, 137, 141, 154; mail delivery disruptions, 102, 176*n* 23, 177*n* 31; paper shortage, 123, 180*n* 78; Sallie on progress of, 115; Sallie's despair over, 113; Texas as peripheral to battles, 5; Union blockade of Southern ports, 5, 101–2, 119; Union incursions on Texas coast, 120. *See also* soldiers
Clark, Horace (Mr. C): and Baylor church feud, 108, 178*n* 42; as leader of Female Department at Baylor, 10; post-war visit, 134; religious influence on Sallie, 9; Sallie's affection for, 34; at Sallie's commencement, 34; on women's compositions, 31
Clark, Martha D. (Mrs. C), 19, 24, 135
Cleveland, Virginia (Ginnie) (Mrs. N. B. Rowe), 22, 107, 117
college education, 2, 6, 10–11, 12–13. *See also* Baylor University
"College Life" (McNeill, S.), 37–38
Colorado Baptist Association, 46–47
Columbia, 51, 56, 57, 78, 81, 89
commencement at Baylor, 32–34
"Comus" (Milton), 51
Confederate soldiers. *See* soldiers
corn crop, 44, 55, 68, 133, 153
correspondence. *See* letters and correspondence
Cotton, Dorothy, 158
cotton crop, 4–5, 110, 133
courtship and suitors: advantage of college education for women for, 13; Baylor social dramas, 26; Leo Mims' attempt to woo Sallie, 64–65; and love letters, 26–27; overview, 15; as principle topic of social conversation, 64; Sallie on others' courtships, 49, 128, 131; Sallie's rejection of, 27–28, 47, 63, 67–68, 69, 98–99, 109–10, 131, 132

Cowan's Ferry, 4
crops: corn, 44, 55, 68, 133, 153; cotton, 4–5, 110, 133; field preparation, 53, 58, 93, 100; sugar, 4–5, 46, 48, 58, 120, 126
Cult of Sacrifice among Southerners, 16

daily life, Sallie's diary as window on, 1. *See also* plantation life; reading; sewing
Damon, 40
Dance, Mr., 44, 83
dancing and parties, Sallie's moral disapproval of, 60, 64, 84, 92, 101, 111
Davis, Jefferson, 97, 139, 180–81*n* 9
Davis, Mary Russell (Miss Mary): death of, 127, 180*n* 1; mourning over, 135; religious influence on Sallie, 9; Sallie's close relationship with, 19, 77, 78, 79, 90
deaths and funerals: C. Norris, 94; Davie Mims, 114; Emily Jordan on loss of children, 156; George Weekley, 117–18; hunting dog, 55–56; James McNeill (father), 2; Missie, 104–6, 107–8, 109; Miss Mary Davis, 127, 135, 180*n* 1; Mollie, 112–13; Mrs. Mims, 94
De Lassaulx, Liane, 24–25, 26, 62
diary: historical value of, 1–2; paper shortage, 123, 180*n* 78; private purpose of, 6–10; quill pens for, 73; technical issues of editing, xii–xiii
Dickens, Charles, 114
diseases. *See* illnesses
dog delivery episode, 83–84, 176*n* 14
domestic sphere in Southern planter class, 11, 14, 159
dress code for women at Baylor, 27
Durant, Mrs. (plantation tutor), 12, 54, 57, 171*n* 50

education, 2, 6, 10–11, 12–13. *See also* Baylor University; tutoring on plantation
Eliot, George (Mary Ann Evans), 113
emancipation consequences for Jordan plantation, 6. *See also* freedmen
essays, Sallie's Baylor, 35–39
Evans, Augusta Jane, 88, 147
Evans, John, 45, 60, 87, 92, 114, 169*n* 14

family, name summary, 18
ferries, 4
fire-hunt, 73
fire in slave Quarters, 42
fishing, 53, 70, 100, 101, 118, 141, 142, 151, 152
Fitzball, Edward, 57

Fitzgerald, B. S., 44
Fitzgerald, H. L., 167
Fitzgerald, Mary T., 71
"Flying Dutchman" (Fitzball), 57
"Footprints on the Sands of Time" (McNeill, S.), 35–36
freedmen: frustrations with labor from, 126, 129, 133, 139; Sallie's criticism of, 8, 126–27, 129, 137; as tenant farmers, 6
friendships: cost of isolation to, 49, 76; cost of marriage to, 53, 58, 76; name summary, 18–20; Sallie's losses, 127
Fuller, Tilphia Guthrie (Tippie), 53, 171n 46

Galveston: antebellum trip to, 49, 55, 56–58; Confederate liberation of, 121, 180n 74; defense of, 116; Union capture of, 5, 119–20, 179n 62, 69
Gates, Henry Louis, Jr., 1
gender roles: and college education for women, 10–11, 12–13; condescending attitude of college men, 28–29; and identity loss for women, 14–15, 63; Kate Jackson's rejection of domestic life, 159–60; and need for escort when traveling, 70–71, 77; North vs. South, 11, 14; and planter class status, 1–2, 5, 10–11, 12–13, 14, 159; religious revival's influence on, 8–9; Sallie on women's organizations, 144; Sallie's dependent status, 16, 44, 65, 80, 115–16, 130; Sallie's diary's insight into, 159; and Sallie's rejection of marriage, 13–17; and women's lower social status, 7–8

Harlan, Marion (pseud. for M. V. H. Terhune), 108
Harrisburg, 57, 62, 117
Herndon, Mary Louisa (Puss or Pussie) (née McKellar). *See* McKellar, Mary Louisa (Puss or Pussie) (Mrs. W. S. Herndon)
Herndon, William Smith, 13, 88, 175n 136
The Hidden Path (Terhune/Harland), 108
Hinkle, Ella (Mrs. Charles McNeill), 155–56
Hinkle, Mr., 101, 110, 115
Hinkle's Ferry, 156
Hobby, Edwin E., 13
Holmes, Claiborn (slave), 42, 169n 7
Holmes, Isaac (slave), 44, 169n 10
homesickness at Baylor, 23–24, 25–26
horses, 54, 106, 132
hospital for slaves on Jordan plantation, 8
house, plantation main, 11–12, *12*
Houston, Sam, 29, 50, 170n 26

Houston as stopover on railway trips, 57, 78
hunting, 41, 44, 71, 81, 92, 103, 120

identity: loss of in marriage, 14–15, 63; Sallie's ruminations over, 42–43
illnesses, major: disease problem at Confederate camp, 117, 118, 119; Emily Jordan's, 69, 71, 72, 106–7, 123, 140; measles epidemic, 121, 122, 130; Mollie's, 112–13; Sallie's worries about health, 59, 70, 121, 133, 149; yellow fever epidemic, 141, 147, 154, 155, 181n 15
immigration to Texas, Levi Jordan's role in, 3–4, 43
Independence. *See* Baylor University
"India" (McNeill, S.), 37
Indianola, 102
Inscribing the Daily (Bloom), 6
isolation, Sallie's: and Baylor trip, 77; on beach, 143; and boredom of rural life, 16–17, 44, 45, 46, 47, 49, 58, 60, 69–71, 82, 103, 135–36; and desire to travel, 46, 60, 70–71, 107; and feeling unwanted, 138–39; and lack of easy access to church, 62; loneliness from, 144; and luxuries of city visit, 57; and need for escort, 70–71; and putting up with disapproved people, 93

Jackson, Kate (adopted sister): at beach in 1867, 143, 144, 149, 151; concern for Sallie, 127; rejection of domestic life, 159–60; relationship to family, 2
Jackson, Mary E., 24
Jones, Henry B., 22, 60, 180n 72
Jones, Mary (née Rowe), 20, 44, 56, 60–61, 64, 118
Jordan, Abigail (Mrs. Abner Stone) (great-aunt), 3
Jordan, Emily (Mrs. J. C. McNeill) (mother). *See* McNeill, Emily (née Jordan)
Jordan, Levi (grandfather): and Baylor men's department conflict, 96; birth of, 3, 165n 2; capture of runaway slaves, 91–92; death of, 155; descendants in family tree, 19; illness of, 152; journey to Texas, 2–4; land purchases, 70, 100; loaning money, 5, 54; loss of income after emancipation, 6; photo, *66;* provisions of will, 155; religious experiences, 65; and Sallie, 65, 129–30; slave ownership of, 4; and trials of abolitionists during war, 113
Jordan, Nathan (great-grandfather), 3
Jordan, Rebekkah (née Wallace) (great-grandmother), 3

Jordan, Sarah (née Stone) (grandmother): at beach in 1867, 142–44; control of household by, 122; dealing with freed blacks as servants, 139; death of, 157; disapproval of Sallie's lack of domestic interest, 101; and family structure, 2; illnesses of, 148–49, 152; and Miss Mary's death, 135; origins of, 2–3

Judson, Ann H., 37, 101

Lafitte, Catherine (Mrs. Norris), 72, 78, 173n 103
"Lalla Rook" (Moore), 49
Lampasas, 106
land purchases, 70, 100
"Lay of the Last Minstrel" (Scott), 49
letters and correspondence: courtship-related, 67–68, 69; delivery problems, 49, 102, 176n 28, 177n 36; as emotional life line in isolation, 46; neglect by correspondents, 45, 82; propriety rules for, 26, 68, 109
Letts, Caleb, 4, 64, 70, 172n 70
Levi Jordan plantation: archaeological excavation of, 157; legacy of, 157; main house, 11–12, *12;* as Sallie's home, 1. *See also* plantation life
Levi Jordan Plantation Historical Society (LJPHS), 158
Lincoln, Abraham, 89–90, 97
Lost Cause, Sallie on, 123, 125, 137, 141, 154
Loves of the Angels (Moore), 49

MacGreal, Clarence, 54, 83–84
magazines, popularity of, 41, 45, 51, 59–60, 90–91, 143
Magruder, J. B., 121, 180n 74
mail delivery: disruptions in, 49, 102, 176n 28, 177n 31; and popularity of magazines, 41
Malloy, Barbara Ann (Cousin) (Mrs. Rainey) (cousin), 52, 89, 128, 170n 37
Manassas, Virginia (First Battle of Bull Run), 108
marriage: Annie, 129; education as competitive tool in market, 13; Emma Norris, 95, 116; Fannie Oliphant, 49; Leo Mims, 110, 112; and loss of eligible men to war, 15–16; loss of Sallie's friends to, 53, 58, 76; loss of women's identity in, 14–15, 63; Manly Rowe, 132, 134; Mary Whiteside, 58; Mollie Reese, 116; Puss (M. McKellar), 13, 175n 136; Rachel, 13, 73–74, 76; Sallie's rejection of, 2, 13–17, 63–64, 75–76, 99; in slave community, 50, 100, 110
Martin, Annie Royal (née McNeill) (sister).

See McNeill, Annie Royal (Mc or Sister A) (Mrs. R. F. Martin)
Martin, Robert F., 129, 155
Martin, Royal Furniss (The Col.) (nephew), 137, 141, 145, 148–49
Masterson, Lt., 131, 132
Matagorda, 62, 63, 71, 73, 74, 119, 121
Matagorda Peninsula, Civil War skirmishes at, 122, 123, 180n 76
McDavid, Carol, 158
McGrew, Sophia (née Sweeny), 22, 112, 146–47
McGrew, William (Bill), 145
McKellar, Mary Louisa (Puss or Pussie) (Mrs. W. S. Herndon): at Baylor, 25, 31; on courtship, 68, 81; marriage of, 13, 88, 175n 136; relationship to Sallie, 19
McKinney, Miss, 145
McNeal, Promise (slave), 87, 175n 134
McNeel, Benji, 114
McNeel, John Greenville (G. McNeel), 103, 177n 33
McNeel, Sallie, 111
McNeill, Annie Royal (Mc or Sister A) (Mrs. R. F. Martin) (sister): at Baylor, 25, 27, 49; birth of, 2; on courtship, 69; death of, 156; and diary authorship, xi; disinheritance of, 155; on isolation of beach on rainy days, 149; marriage of, 129; residence with Calvin at Rowe plantation, 137; return home from Baylor, 45; on rumors of Sallie's marrying, 68; at Sallie's commencement, 34; Sallie's concern for, 49, 131–32, 134; Sallie's criticism of, 95–96, 99, 107; sewing, 96; at social gatherings, 64, 111
McNeill, Archibald (grandfather), 3, 171n 44
McNeill, Barbara (cousin), 52–53, 58–59, 87, 89
McNeill, Barbara (née Patterson) (grandmother), 3
McNeill, Calvin (C.) (brother): birth of, 2; at Chappell Hill, 128, 180n 3; departure for Baylor, 85; disinterest in academics, 92, 93, 94, 102, 128, 130, 131, 137; illnesses, 69, 70, 116, 130; kindness to Archie, 121; leaving of Baylor for good, 96; marriage of, 156, 179n 65; response to capture of runaway, 111; Sallie's assessment of, 49, 102, 103–4, 132, 134, 141; Sallie's conflict with, 120; as soldier, 5, 114, 118, 120; takeover of Rowe plantation, 136, 137–38, 156; and trading of photographs, 59; visits home during war, 117, 120; visits to beach in 1867, 141

McNeill, Charles Philip (Charlie or Charley) (brother): birth of, 2; at Chappell Hill, 128, 180*n* 3; at Hampden-Sydney, 136; hunting ritual, 44; illnesses, 72, 77; marriage of, 155–56; and plantation life, 41; Sallie on character of, 59, 82, 130–31; at Sallie's commencement, 34; school experiences of, 54, 62; socializing of, 118; as soldier, 5, 122

McNeill, Ella (née Hinkle), 155–56

McNeill, Emily (née Jordan) (mother): and Baylor trip, 77; birth of, 3; criticism of Sallie, 78; death of, 157; on deaths of children, 156; dedication to children, 72, 77; and family structure, 2; illness of, 69, 71, 72, 106–7, 123, 140; living with sons, 156; marriage of, 3; origins of, 2–3; photo, 24; at Sallie's commencement, 34; Sallie's criticism of, 65, 92, 129–30; Sallie's missing of at Baylor, 23–24, 25–26; as Sallie's one supporter in family, 152; Sallie's worries over health of, 75, 78, 79–80

McNeill, Emily J. (Missie) (sister): birth of, 2; death of, 104–6; and frightening horse ride, 85; illnesses, 61, 72; mourning of, 107–8, 109; reaction to Quarters fire, 42; Sallie on character of, 59; Sallie's disciplining of, 56, 82; school experiences of, 51, 53, 54

McNeill, James C. (father), 2, 3, 4, 24, 43, 66, 78, 85, 130

McNeill, James Calvin, III (grand-nephew), xi

McNeill, Mary Emily (Mollie) (sister), 2, 85, 107, 112–13

McNeill, Sarah Emma (née Reese), 156, 179*n* 60

McNeill, Sarah S. (Sallie): affection for Bob Stanger, 102, 109, 113, 140; Baylor University experiences, 23–39, 43, 74–75, 76–80; on courtship and suitors, 27–28, 47, 63, 67–68, 69, 98–99, 109–10, 131, 132; death of, 155; and diary authorship, xi; on disunion and war, 89–90, 102–3, 113, 115, 118–19; on free blacks, 8, 126–27, 129, 137; and grandfather Jordan, 65, 129–30; identity ruminations, 42–44; illness worries, 59, 70, 121, 133, 149; and Leo Mims, 55, 64–65, 95, 111, 113; life context overview, 2–6; on Lost Cause, 123, 125, 137, 141, 154; on marriage, 2, 13–17, 63, 75–76; on nature, 133; as planter class member, 1–2, 5; private audience of journal, 2, 6–10; restricted gender role for, 16, 44, 65, 80, 115–16, 130; on slaves and slavery, 7–8, 42, 50, 53, 56, 90, 92, 110–11, 113; spiritual expression, 48, 60, 81–82, 94–95; tutoring job at plantation school, 12, 40, 41, 43, 44, 46, 49, 51–52, 53, 81. *See also* daily life; isolation; McNeill, Emily (née Jordan); McNeill, Emily J. (Missie); relatives; religion/religious experience

McNeill, William Archibald Campbell (Archie) (brother): at beach in 1867, 143; birth of, 2; death of, 156; illnesses, 77, 106–7, 121, 122; inheritance of Jordan plantation, 156

The McNeill's SR Ranch: 100 Years in Blanco Canyon (McNeill, J. C. III), xi

measles epidemic, 121, 122, 130

Men's Department at Baylor, women's visit to, 28–29

Mercer, Eli, 50

Metamorphoses (Ovid), 51

Millican, C. C., 72, 91, 173*n* 102

The Mill on the Floss (Eliot), 113

Milton, John, 51

Mims, Alexander, 20, 95–96, 118, 120, 139

Mims, David (Davie), 20, 51, 95–96, 102, 114, 178*n* 56

Mims, Joseph (Joe), 20, 92

Mims, Joseph (patriarch), 20, 175*n* 8, 11

Mims, Leonard (Leo): attempt to woo Sallie, 64–65; and Baylor trip, 78; courtship activities, 98, 99; marriage of, 110, 112; relationship to Sallie, 20; Sallie's critique of, 55, 95, 111, 113

Mims, Lumbert (Mr. Lum), 20, 113

Mims, Samuel, 20, 102, 119, 179*n* 68

Mims, Sarah (née Weekly): background of, 175*n* 6; at church, 66–67; death of, 94; and Galveston trip, 55, 57, 76; inability to board plantation tutor, 54

Mims, Sarah Josephine (Jose) (Mrs. B. F. Rowe), 20, 22, 68, 84, 96, 98, 117–18

Mims, Sarah Tate (Sallie), 72, 73, 174*n* 106

Mims, Susana Caroline (Caddie) (née Nuckols), 20, 55, 139, 148

Mims family, overview, 20

Mims Ferry, 156

Moore, Thomas (poet), 39, 49

moral righteousness, Sallie's: criticism of Mims children, 84, 94; desire to keep Sabbath, 56, 91; disapproval of parties and dancing, 60, 64, 84, 92, 101, 111; distaste for those not respected, 93; evil basis of human nature, 137, 144; opposition to alcoholic beverages, 142; regrets over theater attendance, 61. *See also* relatives

Mose (slave), 110–11, 122

Mosely, Capt., 120

mourning for lost loved ones. *See* deaths and funerals
music, 70, 71–72, 80–81, 118

nature on plantation, 133
Neblett, Lizzie Scott, 15
Neel, Mr. (plantation tutor), 12, 25
Negroes. *See* blacks
neighbors, summary of Sallie's, 20
Norris, Catherine (née Burkhart), 94, 175*n* 5
Norris, Catherine (née Lafitte), 72, 78, 173*n* 103
Norris, Emmaline/Emma, 71, 78, 80, 84, 95, 116, 174*n* 111
Northern vs. Southern attitudes toward women, 11, 14
Nuckols, Charlotte, 11–12, 163–64
Nuckols, John F. (Johnnie), 110
Nuckols, Susana Caroline (Caddie) (Mrs. J. Mims), 20, 139, 148

Oliphant, Fannie, 49
Olmsted, Frederick Law, 8
Ovid, 51

parties, Sallie's disapproval of, 60, 64, 84, 92, 101, 111
patriarchy on plantation, 14
Patton, Sue F. (Fannie), 20, 98, 110, 112
Pettus, Dora, 13, 47–48
photographs, ritual of taking and sending, 25, 26, 57, 87, 112, 131, 132
piano, 70
Pier, Sallie, 88, 106, 112, 137, 175*n* 137
plantation life: Calvin at Rowe plantation, 136, 137–38, 156; cattle driving, 132, 133, 139; Christmas celebrations, 92, 113, 135–36; consequences of emancipation for, 6; construction of buildings, 58, 70; crop cycle, 44, 46, 68, 93, 110; economic overview, 4–5; fire danger to corn cribs, 42; fire-hunt, 73; fishing, 53, 70, 100, 101, 118, 141, 142, 151, 152; horses, 54, 106, 132; hunting, 41, 44, 71, 81, 92, 103, 120; Jordan's use of land, 59; land purchases, 70, 100; main house, 11–12, *12;* mule purchasing, 86, 129; nature description, 55, 133; pets, 102, 107; picking pecans and wild grapes, 103, 110; production during war, 5; Sallie on nature, 133; sick horse episode, 54; Sugar House, 42, 54, 103; swan capture episode, 96, *97;* weather, 53, 62, 77, 82; women's economics in, 41. *See also* blacks; crops; daily life; isolation; tutoring on plantation
planter class and gender roles, 1–2, 5, 10–11, 12–13, 14, 159
politics: Confederacy establishment, 96–97; on Lincoln's election and fears of war, 89–90; and Negro rising rumors, 82; railroad tax abolition petition, 69; rumors of peace prior to war, 99; and Sam Houston, 50; secession, 90, 96
private focus of Sallie's diary, 2, 6–10
puppy, delivery of, 83–84, 176*n* 14

railroad travel, 3–4, 56–58, 74–75, 78–79, 171*n* 57–58
Rainey, Barbara Ann (Cousin) (née Malloy) (cousin), 46, 52, 88, 89, 128, 170*n* 37
Rainey, Emmie, 153
Rainey, James G. (Mr. R), 120, 128, 136
ranch life. *See* plantation life
Raska, Ginny McNeill, 158
reading: on beach in 1867, 143; as escape from tedium of life, 47, 78; magazine popularity, 45, 51, 59–60, 90–91; novels, 73, 143; poetry, 49; Sallie's loss of interest in, 121; Sallie's love of, 41, 47, 51, 56, 65, 80; *Texas Almanac,* 50; travel books, 41
"The Recluse" (McNeill, S.), 38–39
Reese, Mary E. (Mollie), 78, 80, 91, 116, 116, 179*n* 59, 61
Reese, Sarah Emma (Mrs. Calvin McNeill), 156, 179*n* 60
relatives, Sallie's critiques of: Annie, 95–96, 99, 107; Calvin, 49, 92, 93, 102, 103–4, 132, 134, 141; Charley, 59, 82, 130–31; and cousin Barbara McNeill's dilemma, 52–53, 58–59; grandfather Jordan, 65, 129–30; mother Emily, 65, 92, 129–30
religion/religious experience: Catholicism, Sallie's horror of, 9, 24–25; Christianity as source for women's role, 9; church-going experiences, 47, 49, 66–67, 72, 77, 82, 86, 98, 99, 115, 146; conversion experience for Sallie, 9, 31–32, 34–35; denominational gatherings, 32, 46–47, 62, 65, 76; as escape from self-criticism, 76; and lack of easy access to church, 62; Sallie's doubts, 47; Sallie's high expectations for marriage, 15, 63; Sallie's lack of denominational loyalty, 9–10; social context for Sallie's, 8–9. *See also* moral righteousness; Scripture quotations; self-examination

Richmond, 48, 67, 80
roads in Brazoria County, 4
Rogers, Fannie, 31, 34
Romanticism, Sallie's, 8
Rowe, Benjamin Franklin (Frank), 22, 120
Rowe, Fanny A., 22, 144–45
Rowe, Louisa A., 22
Rowe, Mary (Mrs. H. Jones), 22, 44, 56, 60–61, 64, 118
Rowe, Napoleon Bonaparte (Pobe), 22, 117
Rowe, Rosella E. (Emma), 22, 128
Rowe, Sarah, 20
Rowe, Sarah Josephine (Jose) (née Mims), 20, 22, 68, 84, 96, 98, 117–18
Rowe, Shadrack, 20
Rowe, Shadrack M. (Manly): conflict with Baylor faculty, 94; family summary, 22; illness of, 126–27; joining of church, 47; marriage of, 132, 134; naming of daughter after Sallie, 139; Sallie on character of, 93, 131; social pressures on, 131; surprise visit from, 71
Rowe, Stephen Decatur (Dr. R.), 16, 22, 84, 87, 106, 109, 128
Rowe, Virginia (Ginnie) (née Cleveland), 22, 107, 117
Rowe, Virginia (Mrs. Wilson), 44, 46–47, 52
Rowe, William H. (Mr. Billie R.), 22, 47, 64
Rowe family, 20, 22, 80–81, 136, 180n 7
rural vs. city life and Sallie's social isolation, 16–17. *See also* plantation life
Russell, Mr., 98–99

San Bernard River: beach cottage at mouth of, 80, 91, 136, 139–54; as near Jordan plantation, 3; as transportation mode, 4
Sandy Point, 80, 118
San Jacinto, Battle of, controversy over, 50
Sarah Jordan (family schooner), 4
school, plantation. *See* tutoring on plantation
Scott, Anne Firor, 9
Scott, Lizzie, 30, 57
Scott, Sir Walter, 49
Scripture quotations: as moral guidance, 9, 34–35, 44, 60, 93, 95, 127, 132; and mourning loss of war, 125
secession, 89, 90, 96, 97, 175n 2, 176n 21–23, 28
Second Great Awakening, 8–9
self-examination, Sallie's: and discontentment with life, 81, 115–16, 150–51; and feeling unwanted, 152–53; identity and deficiencies, 42–44; initial post-conversion, 32; and lack of energy, 62, 129, 144; and lack of worthiness for marriage, 68; and laziness/idleness, 58, 76, 87, 95, 100, 110, 115, 121, 129, 144–45, 150; on looking "sanctified," 72; need for forgiveness of others, 127; personality analysis, 46–47; on purpose of life, 54; and Romanticism, 8; Sallie's focus on, 2; Scripture quotation as guidance for, 9, 34–35, 44, 60, 93, 95, 127, 132; self-criticism, 44, 45, 51, 59, 60–61, 74, 75–76, 84, 87–88, 92–93, 95, 100–101, 112, 119, 138–39, 141
Separate Spheres ideology, North vs. South, 14
sewing: and Baylor trip preparation, 74, 78; dress making, 50, 51, 55, 56, 70; embroidery, 53, 61, 64, 96, 99; as major focus of Sallie's activities, 138; new machine for sewing, 71; Sallie's dissatisfaction with, 45, 99, 121; shirt mending, 110
slaves and slavery: Christian preaching to, 98; Claiborn, 42, 169n 7; continued work of slaves during war, 5; emancipation's effect on plantation culture, 159; and fear of uprising, 82–83, 89, 174n 124, 175n 3; fire in Quarters, 42; illnesses among slaves, 58, 121–22; Isaac, 44, 169n 10; Jordan plantation's record of, 4, 158, 171n 49; marriages among, 50, 100, 110; Millie, 42, 169n 8; Mose, 110–11, 122; population in Brazoria County, 4; profession of religion, 122; Promise, 87, 175n 134; purchasing of slaves, 45, 54, 59, 87, 100; runaways, 91–92, 100, 110–11; Sallie's doubts about slavery, 113; Sallie's paternalistic prejudices, 7–8, 42, 50, 53, 56, 90, 92, 110–11; Sallie's pity for, 53, 58, 71; Texas' law for treatment of slaves, 7–8; unauthorized trading with, 73
social gatherings: church-going, 47, 49, 66–67, 72, 77, 86, 98, 99, 115, 146; Sallie's disapproval of, 60, 64, 84, 92, 101, 111
social status and gender roles, 1–2, 5, 10–11, 12–13, 14, 159
soldiers, Confederate: Brazoria Rangers, 111; calling up of, 102, 111; Calvin's complaints about treatment of, 114; departure of, 116, 117; disease problem in camps, 117, 118, 119; end of prisoner exchange, 123; Sallie's disapproval of behavior by, 114. *See also* Brown's regiment
Southern vs. Northern attitudes toward women, 11, 14
"Spain" (McNeill, S.), 36–37

Spencer, Joel (Capt. Spencer), 85, 174*n* 129
Spencer, W., 67, 85
spiritual expression, Sallie's, 48, 60, 81–82, 94–95. *See also* religion/religious experience
St. Anthony's Fire, 105
St. Elmo (Evans), 147
Stanger, Robert (Bob): frustrations with freedmen, 129; injury of, 115; and murder of father, 98; as prisoner of war, 123, 180*n* 76; relationship to family, 2; Sallie's affection for, 102, 109, 113, 140; satisfaction at capture of runaway, 111; as soldier, 5, 114, 118; and struggles of plantation operations, 53; visits home during war, 117, 119, 120; visits to beach in 1867, 141
Stewart, Charles, 13, 73
Stewart, Rachael (Rachel) (née Barry), 13, 73–74, 76, 91
Stone, Abigail (née Jordan) (great-aunt), 3
Stone, Abner (great-uncle), 3
Stone, Jesse (great-grandfather), 2–3
Stone, Sarah (Mrs. L. Jordan) (grandmother). *See* Jordan, Sarah (née Stone)
Stone, Susannah (née Lightfoot) (great-grandmother), 2–3
Stribling, James H., 48, 115, 170*n* 20
sugarcane crop, 4–5, 46, 48, 58, 120, 126
suitors. *See* courtship and suitors
supplies/provisions: at beach, 143, 147, 148, 149–50, 152, 153; writing materials, xii, 123, 180*n* 78
Sweeny, Elizabeth Ann (Bettie), 22, 64, 86
Sweeny, Sophia (Mrs. J. McGrew), 22, 146–47
Sweeny, Thomas Jefferson, 22
Sweeny family, 22, 172*n* 71

tenant farmers, former slaves as, 6, 157–59. *See also* freedmen
Terhune, Mary Virginia Hawes (Marion Harland), 108
Texas: ambivalence about slavery in, 7–8; Brazoria County, 1, 3–4, 6, 21; Levi Jordan's settlement in, 3–4; as peripheral to Civil War battles, 5; secession of, 89, 90, 96, 97, 175*n* 2, 176*n* 16–18, 23; slave laws in, 7–8; Union incursions on coast, 120. *See also* Galveston
Texas Almanac, 50
Texas Historical Commission, 158
Texas Parks & Wildlife Department (TPWD), 158
Texas Troubles, 82–83, 174*n* 124

35th Texas Cavalry. *See* Brown's Regiment
Townsend, Virginia Frances, 90–91
TPWD (Texas Parks & Wildlife Department), 158
traders, traveling, 50–51
transportation: by carriage, 47, 57, 60, 64, 78, 79; railroad travel, 3–4, 56–58, 74–75, 78–79, 171*n* 57–58; roads in Brazoria County, 4; steamboat, 57; typical modes for Sallie, 3–4; waterway, 3, 4, 74
travel: to Baylor in Independence, 74–75, 76–80; to Galveston, 49, 55, 56–58; need for escort, 70–71, 77; post-war, 134; Sallie's desire to, 46, 60, 70–71, 107; to Wharton, 47–48, 52
tutoring on plantation: beginnings of, 34; daily lessons, 61–62; Mrs. Durant, 12, 54, 171*n* 50; Mr. Neel, 12, 25; S. D. Rowe, 16, 84, 106, 109; Sallie's job, 12, 40, 41, 43, 44, 46, 49, 51–52, 53, 81
Tuxpan, Mexico, as refuge for Confederate veterans, 139

Union Parish, Louisiana, 2, 3, 43
Uzzel, Mary T. (Texas), 143–44
Uzzel, Mrs., 143–44, 145
Uzzel, William T., 140–41

Vandevere, Mr., 146
Van Dorn, Earl, 116, 178–79*n* 58
Van Dorn, Moses, 111
Veasey, John W., 112, 116, 178*n* 57
Veasey, Mrs., mishap of, 82–83
visiting locally: Bennets, 86–87; and fears of runaway slaves, 100; Mims, 52, 55; and new sewing machine, 71; Sallie's discomfort with Sabbath visiting, 91; Sweenys, 86

Wallace, Rebekkah (Mrs. N. Jordan) (great-grandmother), 3
Walsh, James, 55, 67
waterway transportation, 3, 4, 74
The Way to do Good (Abbott), 49
weather: drought period, 62, 77; rain for crops, 82; snow in January, 135; and supply delays at beach, 148; and workers/slaves exposure to elements, 53
Weekley, George, 117–18
Weekley, Sarah (Mrs. Joseph Mims—senior). *See* Mims, Sarah (née Weekly)
Wharton, John A., 108, 177*n* 40
Wharton trip, 47–48, 52

Whiteside, Mary T. (M. T. W. or Mary W.) (Mrs. Ashford): at Baylor, 20, 24, 26, 30, 31; disappointment as correspondent, 49, 85; finding of composition of, 56; and "Lalla Rook," 49; marriage of, 58
Williams, Hit, 86
Williams, Millie (slave), 42, 169n 8

Williams, Samuel M., 3
Williamson, William McWillie, 116, 179n 59, 61
Wilson, Virginia (née Rowe), 44, 46–47, 52
women in plantation culture. *See* gender roles

yellow fever epidemic, 141, 147, 154, 155, 181n 15